A NEW BLUEPRINT FOR A GREEN ECONOMY

Published in 1989, *Blueprint for a Green Economy* presented, for the first time, practical policy measures for "greening" modern economies and putting them on a path to sustainable development. This new book, written by two of the *Blueprint* authors, revisits and updates its main messages by asking, first, what has been achieved in the past 20 years, and second, what more needs to be done to generate a truly "green economy" in the twenty-first century?

Blueprint had one over-arching theme. Making economies more sustainable requires urgent progress in three key policy areas: valuing the environment, accounting for the environment, and incentives for environmental improvement. Today, with the threat of global warming, the decline in major ecosystems and their services, and fears over energy security, achieving these goals is even more vital.

The current book first summarizes the main messages from *Blueprint* and explains why, given rapid and widespread global environmental degradation, they are still relevant. The book then examines the progress since *Blueprint* in implementing policies and other measures to improve environmental valuation, accounting, and incentives. Although much has been accomplished, additional advances are still required to green economies successfully. The book highlights the new policies and approaches needed for economic management of today's environmental concerns. Over 20 years later, *A New Blueprint for a Green Economy* once again emphasizes practical policies for greening modern economies, and explains why such an economic roadmap to a greener future is essential, if modern economies are to develop successfully and sustainably.

Edward B. Barbier is the John S. Bugas Professor of Economics at the University of Wyoming, USA.

Anil Markandya is Scientific Director at the Basque Centre for Climate Change, Spain.

A NEW BLUEPRINT FOR A GREEN ECONOMY

Edward B. Barbier
and Anil Markandya

Routledge
Taylor & Francis Group

LONDON AND NEW YORK

First published 2013
by Routledge
2 Park Square, Milton Park, Abingdon, Oxon OX14 4RN

Simultaneously published in the USA and Canada
by Routledge
711 Third Avenue, New York, NY 10017

Routledge is an imprint of the Taylor & Francis Group, an informa business

British Library Cataloguing in Publication Data
A catalogue record for this book is available from the British Library

Library of Congress Cataloging in Publication Data
Barbier, Edward B., 1957–
A new blueprint for a green economy / by Edward B. Barbier and Anil Markandya.
  p. cm.
Update to: Blueprint for a green economy / a report by David Pearce, Anil Markandya,
Edward B. Barbier for the UK Department of the Environment. 1989.
Includes bibliographical references and index.
1. Economic development – Environmental aspects. 2. Sustainable development. 3.
Environmental impact charges. 4. Environmental policy. I. Markandya, Anil, 1945–II.
Pearce, David W. (David William) Blueprint for a green economy. III. Title.
Hd75.6.B355 2012
333.7 – dc23   2012009246

ISBN: 978-1-84971-349-8 (hbk)
ISBN: 978-1-84971-353-5 (pbk)
ISBN: 978-0-203-09729-8 (ebk)

Typeset in Bembo
by Cenveo Publisher Services

MIX
Paper from
responsible sources
FSC
www.fsc.org   FSC® C004839

Printed and bound in Great Britain by the MPG Books Group

CONTENTS

BOXES

FIGURES

TABLES

FOREWORD

When I became Britain's Environment Secretary in the late 1980s, there was a prevalent view among politicians, business people and policy makers that the environment was a peripheral issue that excited the interest of an active and rather tiresome minority, to whom an occasional morsel needed to be thrown in order to keep these environmentalists more or less quiet, albeit at some cost to the real economy.

So environmental policy was an expensive add-on to public policy, something to be tolerated when the pressure exerted by opinion became too great to withstand.

David Pearce was one of the first scholars to demonstrate with intellectual rigour that good economics should embrace and enfold environmental factors. This was both morally appropriate and commercially and fiscally smart. Economic policies that failed to price inputs were flawed; commercial policies that ignored environmental impacts were expensive for the community and bad business in the long term for the companies that practised them.

The notion of sustainable growth policies not only faces up to Herb Stein's First Law of Economics that things that can't go on for ever don't. It also has to recognize the damage to the environment of making policies that build up long-term cost and damage health as well as economic prospects. It is interesting that at least in theory, China's leaders appear to recognize this, though there is a considerable distance there between promise and policy. Whether a consensus on the subject in America is an early prospect seems doubtful.

Chairing the corporate social responsibility committee of a major multinational a few years ago, it was encouraging how good environmental policy had become part of the company's DNA. It not only helped to drive down marginal costs but enthused employees who wanted to work for a company that was regarded as a good global citizen.

As this interesting book shows, green economics has rapidly become sensible, mainstream economics. David Pearce would have been happy to see what his own insights helped to produce.

Lord Patten of Barnes CH

PREFACE

Blueprint for a Green Economy (BGE) was never intended to be a book. Rather, it was a report commissioned by the UK Department of Environment, to assist them in formulating a policy response to the 1987 World Commission on Environment and Development – the "Brundtland Commission."[1] Specifically, the terms of reference for the report required us to "review the state of the art on the relationship between the sustainable development concept, national accounting, resource accounting, satellite accounting, and project appraisal procedures."[2]

Within days of submitting our report to the UK government in August 1989, it was apparent that the topics covered had far-reaching appeal, not only to policy makers and our fellow economists but also to the media and even the general public. Requests for copies of the report exceeded our ability to reproduce them.

Fortunately, Neil Middleton of Earthscan Publications, which at that time was a subsidiary of the International Institute for Environment and Development (IIED), agreed to publish the complete report as a book. Richard Sandbrook, the President of IIED, sanctioned the project, and multiple print runs of the book ensued. The 1989 Earthscan publication became internationally renowned, and for some time afterwards was the top-selling book on environmental economics and policy. In 1991, BGE was awarded the Gambrinus Giuseppe Mazzotti Special Jury's Prize. In 2009, BGE was ranked as No. 14 in the top 50 sustainability books of all time.[3]

Often known as the "Pearce Report," BGE also launched its lead author, David Pearce, as a top international and UK economics advisor on environmental policy. Among David's many appointments since BGE were: from 1989 to 1992, Personal Advisor in Environmental Economics to the Secretary of State for the Environment, Chris Patten; from 1993 to 1995, Lead Author, Intergovernmental Panel on Climate Change (IPCC), Working Group III; from 1993 to 1997, Member, Advisory Group to Vice President for Environmentally Sustainable Development, World Bank; from 1995 to 1998, United Nations, High Level Advisory Board on Sustainable Development (Secretary General of the United Nations); and at the time of his death in 2005, Specialist Advisor, Economic Affairs Committee, House of Lords, and Member, Home Office Economics Advisory Panel. For his public service, David Pearce was made an Officer of the Order of the British Empire (OBE) in 2000.

BGE was also instrumental in both our careers as policy advisors and economists. Since its publication, we have acted as advisors in various capacities to several UN agencies and the World Bank, as well as to the governments of China, India, South Korea, the United Kingdom, and the United States.

BGE had one over-arching theme. Making economies more sustainable requires urgent progress in three key policy areas: valuing the environment, accounting for the environment and creating incentives for environmental improvement. This main message has not changed over time, but it has become critical. Today, with the threat of global warming, the decline in major ecosystems and their services, and fears over energy security, achieving these environmental policy goals is even more vital.

Twenty years on, *A New Blueprint for a Green Economy* revisits and updates the main messages of the original BGE by asking two questions: first, what has been achieved in the past two decades, and second, what more needs to be done to generate a truly "green economy" in the twenty-first century?

The book first summarizes the main messages from BGE and explains why, given rapid and widespread global environmental degradation, they are still relevant. We then examine the progress since BGE in implementing policies and other measures to improve environmental valuation, accounting and incentives. Although much has been accomplished, additional advances in policy are still required to green economies successfully. Thus, much of the book highlights the new policies and economic approaches needed for sustainable management of today's environmental concerns.

BGE successfully placed the economics of sustainable development on the policy agenda. Over 20 years later, *A New Blueprint for a Green Economy* emphasizes practical policies for greening modern economies, and argues that such an economic roadmap to a greener future is essential. Modern economies have the opportunity to develop successfully and sustainably, as a means to ensuring the well-being of current and future generations.

EB & AM

1

INTRODUCTION

Published in 1989, *Blueprint for a Green Economy* (henceforth BGE) presented, for the first time, practical policy measures for "greening" modern economies and putting them on a path to sustainable development.

BGE had one over-arching theme. Making economies more sustainable requires urgent progress in three key policy areas: valuing the environment, accounting for the environment, and creating incentives for environmental improvement. Today, with the threat of global warming, the decline in major ecosystems and their services, and fears over energy security, achieving these goals is even more vital. In fact, they are essential to economic welfare and the well-being of current and future generations. Chapter 2 discusses in more detail some of the key global environmental trends and initiatives that have occurred over the past 20 years, and explains why they make the main messages of BGE even more relevant today. Here, in this introductory chapter, we provide a brief summary of the key theme and messages of BGE.

Nature as capital

One of the important contributions of BGE was to argue that the natural environment should be viewed as a form of capital asset, or *natural capital*. Although we were not the first economists to adopt this perspective,[1] BGE sought to demonstrate that efficient management of an economy's natural resource and environmental endowment is essential to achieving the overall goal of sustainable development.

BGE maintained that it is important not to restrict the concept of natural capital just to those natural resources, such as minerals, fossil fuels, forests, agricultural land and fisheries, that supply the raw material and energy inputs to our economies. Nor should we consider the capacity of the natural environment to assimilate waste and pollution the only valuable "service" that it performs. Instead, natural capital is much broader, encompassing the whole range of goods and services that the environment provides. Many have long been considered beneficial to humans, such as nature-based recreation, eco-tourism, fishing and hunting, wildlife viewing, and enjoyment of nature's beauty. However, a wide range of environmental benefits also arise through the natural functioning of *ecosystems*, which are distinct systems of living organisms and communities interacting with their physical environment. Examples of such ecosystem goods and services include water supply and its regulation, climate maintenance, nutrient cycling, enhanced biological productivity and, ultimately, overall life support.

Today, the term "natural capital" is frequently employed to define an economy's environment and natural resource endowment – including ecosystems.[2] Humans depend on and use this natural capital for a whole range of important benefits, including health and sustenance. For all these reasons, our natural wealth is extremely valuable. But unlike skills, education, machines, tools and other types of human and physical capital, we do not have to manufacture and accumulate our endowment of natural assets. Nature has provided this endowment and its benefits to us as part of humankind's common heritage; we have not had to create these assets ourselves.

Yet perhaps because this capital has been endowed to us, we humans have tended to view it as limitless, abundant and always available for our use. The result is that present-day economies have often ended up overexploiting natural capital in the pursuit of economic development, growth and progress. The unfortunate result is that generations today are leaving too little for future generations to use and benefit from. Over the long term, the consequence is to undermine economic growth and human well-being.

Sustainable development

The crucial relationship between the management of natural capital and "sustaining" economic development was an important theme in BGE. By the late 1980s, the concept of *sustainable development* had become popular, and one could pick and choose from many interpretations. As noted at the beginning of BGE:

> Definitions of sustainable development abound. There is some truth in the criticism that it has come to mean whatever suits the particular advocacy of the individual concerned. This is not surprising. It is difficult to be against "sustainable development." It sounds like something we should all approve of, like "motherhood and apple pie."[3]

Yet, by the late 1980s, there was also an emerging consensus definition of sustainable development, which was put forward by the World Commission on Environment and Development (WCED) – often referred to as the "Brundtland Commission" after its chairperson, former Norwegian prime minister Gro Harlem Brundtland. The WCED defined sustainable development as:

> Development that meets the needs of the present without compromising the ability of future generations to meet their own needs.[4]

As explained in Chapter 3, the Brundtland Commission's definition especially appeals to economists as it is consistent with a *capital approach* to sustainable development. That is, it is the *total* stock of capital employed by the economic system, including natural capital, that determines the full range of economic opportunities, and thus well-being, available to both present and future generations. Society must decide how best to use its total capital stock today to increase current economic activities and welfare, and how much it needs to save or even accumulate for tomorrow and, ultimately, for the well-being of future generations.

However, it is not simply the aggregate stock of capital in the economy that may matter but also its composition. In particular, an important issue is whether present generations are running down one type of capital to meet today's needs and accumulate other forms of wealth, and whether this change in the composition of capital will make future generations worse or better off.[5]

In particular, there is concern that current economic development may be leading to rapid accumulation of physical and human capital, but at the expense of excessive depletion and degradation of natural capital. By depleting the world's stock of natural wealth irreversibly, development today could have detrimental implications for the well-being of future generations.

That is, today's pattern of economic development could very well be highly "unsustainable."

The economy–environment tradeoff

Compared to previous approaches to environmental policy, BGE offered a different perspective on the key economy–environment tradeoff underlying development. For example, as the book noted:

> In the 1970s it was familiar for the debate about environmental policy to be couched in terms of economic growth versus the environment. The basic idea was that one could have economic growth – measured by rising real per capita incomes – *or* one could have improved environmental quality. Any mix of the two involved a *tradeoff* – more environmental quality meant less economic growth, and vice versa.[6]

BGE argued instead that, although there must be some "tradeoffs" between narrowly construed economic growth and environmental quality, it is incorrect to suggest that all environmental policy choices amount to a fundamental "economic growth versus the environment" tradeoff. To the contrary, as suggested by BGE:

> There will be situations in which growth involves the sacrifice of environmental quality, and where conservation of the environment means forgoing economic growth. But sustainable development attempts to shift the focus to the opportunities for income and employment opportunities from conservation, and to ensuring that any tradeoff decision reflects the full value of the environment.[7]

The true economy–environment tradeoff, then, is in how one achieves economic development and enhanced human well-being. Natural resource depletion, pollution and ecological degradation arise through a fundamental tradeoff in our use of the environment. This tradeoff can be depicted in a simple diagram (see Box 1.1). Economic development cannot proceed without exploiting natural resources for raw material and energy inputs or using the environment to assimilate pollution and other waste by-products. On the positive side, economic development also leads to the increased production and consumption of human-made goods and services. As these goods and services contribute to overall human welfare, they can be considered the "economic benefits" of development. However, the exploitation and use of

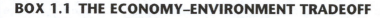

BOX 1.1 THE ECONOMY–ENVIRONMENT TRADEOFF

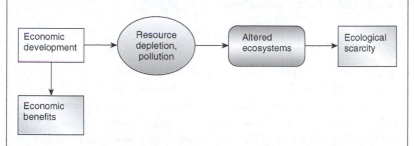

As economic development proceeds, it generates many economic benefits through the production and consumption of commodities. However, development also leads to natural resource depletion, pollution and the alteration of ecosystems. The latter can lead to ecological scarcity, i.e. the relative decline in beneficial ecosystem goods and services. Thus, the fundamental economy–environment tradeoff is between the economic benefits arising from development and any resulting environmental and welfare impacts arising from natural resource depletion, pollution and ecological degradation.

the natural environment by humans for raw materials, energy and waste assimilation also leads to the alteration of ecosystems. The disruption and destruction of ecosystems affect, in turn, their various contributions to human welfare, such as the use of aesthetic landscapes for recreation, the maintenance of beneficial species, the control of erosion, protection against floods or storms, and so forth. The loss of these "ecological benefits," or ecosystem goods and services, as the consequence of economic development can be considered increasing *ecological scarcity*.[8]

The economy–environment tradeoff depicted in Box 1.1 also amounts to a choice between accumulating versus depreciating two different types of capital. The first type is what BGE called "man-made capital," which consists of human and physical capital, or "the stock of all man-made things such as roads and factories, computers, and human intelligence."[9] The second type of asset is an economy's endowment of natural capital. The choice between increased economic benefits and increased pollution, natural resource depletion and ecological scarcity is therefore really about a tradeoff between these two different assets. On the one hand, we are creating economic wealth in the form of human-made capital; on the other, we are sacrificing our available "natural wealth" to do so.[10]

Environmental valuation

Simply because an economy–environment tradeoff exists does not mean that it should be eliminated. In fact, it is technologically infeasible for modern economies to produce and consume commodities without generating some pollution, depleting natural resources and altering ecosystems. Even if we aimed for "zero growth" in today's economies, they would still lead to considerable environmental impacts.

As BGE maintained, not only must we be aware that such a fundamental economy–environment tradeoff exists but also that attaining sustainable economic development requires that we *value* fully any environmental impacts arising from our development choices:

> If there is to be a trade-off, society must choose on the basis of a full understanding of the choice in question. That means the economic value of the environmental cost, if one is to be incurred, must be understood....Rational trade-offs mean valuing the environment properly....There must be informed choice, not choice based on the presumption that the environment is a free good.[11]

BGE placed great importance on correcting the "undervaluation" of the environment, because it lies at the heart of why present-day economic development is inherently unsustainable. As David Pearce suggested in his summary of BGE:

> Valuation is essential if we are to "trade-off" forms of capital....but careful inspection of the values of natural capital (i.e. looking at what environmental assets do for us) will show that the trade-off has been biased in favour of either "consuming" the proceeds (i.e. not reinvesting at all) or investing too readily in man-made assets. Very simply, if the "true" value of the environment were known, we would not degrade it as much.[12]

Thus, a key message of BGE was that: "By at least trying to put money values on some aspects of environmental quality we are underlining the fact that environmental services are *not* free."[13]

Box 1.2 contains an excerpt from BGE that explains why ignoring environmental values undermines both sustainable development and economic policy. As this passage concludes, not only must the various "services" of natural capital be valued correctly, but these correct values must be integrated into economic policy.

Over the past 20 years since BGE, economic methodologies and approaches for environmental valuation have improved substantially, and have become a widely used tool for assisting policy analysis and project planning. In addition, subsequent studies, such as the Millennium Ecosystem Assessment, have emphasized the need to evaluate a wider range of environmental values, the ecosystem goods and services, or "benefits," of natural systems.[14] Valuing ecosystem goods and services has become a major focus for interdisciplinary collaboration between economists, ecologists and natural scientists, which offers hope for progress on valuing many complex but important environmental benefits, such as storm protection and flood mitigation by wetlands, soil and sedimentation control in watersheds, fish diversity in coral reefs and biodiversity of tropical forests.

Chapter 4 reviews the progress on environmental valuation that has occurred since BGE, stressing in particular the general improvements in methodologies, the extension of valuation to include ecosystem goods and services, and the increasing role of valuation in environmental management decisions. However, the chapter also examines the challenges and gaps in our knowledge to conduct environmental valuation correctly, and the need to make continuing progress in this important area of environmental management.

Accounting for the environment

BGE also argued that measuring growth solely in terms of conventionally defined rising real capita incomes is the wrong indicator for judging whether economic development is sustainable. Conventionally defined economic growth does not account for many important environmental values, and is therefore a poor reflection of economy–environment tradeoffs.

A modern market-based economy generates income – wages, profits and rents – through the sale and purchase of all the goods and services produced in the economy. Thus the aggregate income of the economy is usually approximated by the market value of the aggregate commodities produced in that economy – the Gross National Product (GNP). Divided by the total population, and adjusted for inflation, yields real GNP per capita. As this measure of "real income" per capita increases over some period of time, for example a quarter, a year or several years, "economic growth" is said to occur.

BOX 1.2 VALUING THE ENVIRONMENT

BGE offered the following explanation as to why environmental valuation is so essential to both economic policy and sustainable development:

> One of the central themes of environmental economics, and central to sustainable development thinking also, is the need to place proper values on the services provided by natural environments. The central problem is that many of these services are provided "free". They have a zero price simply because no market place exists in which their true values can be revealed through acts of buying and selling. Examples might be a fine view, the water purification and storm protection function of coastal wetlands, or the biological diversity within a tropical forest. The elementary theory of supply and demand tells us that if something is provided at zero price, more of it will be demanded than if there was a positive price. Very simply, the cheaper it is the more will be demanded. The danger is that this greater level of demand will be unrelated to the capacity of the relevant natural environments to meet the demand. For example, by treating the ozone layer as a resource with a zero price there never was any incentive to protect it. Its value to human populations and to the global environment in general did not show up anywhere in a balance sheet of profit or loss, or costs and benefits....The important principle is that resources and environments serve economic functions and have positive economic value. To treat them as if they had zero value is seriously to risk overusing the resource. An "economic function" in this context is any service that contributes to human well-being, to the "standard of living", or "development". This simple logic underlines the importance of valuing the environment correctly and integrating those correct values into economic policy.[15]

However, the problem with conventionally defined real income per capita as the key economic indicator for guiding policy is that GNP is limited in what it measures. Only marketed goods and services produced by the economy contribute to this indicator of growth. Thus, "real income" is not a measure of the overall economic welfare, or benefits, generated by an economy.

Nor does GNP account for all detrimental impacts of economic activity on human well-being. This is especially true for many environmental impacts that affect welfare. As pointed out by BGE, because many goods and services are produced by the environment and benefit humans *without* being supplied through markets, conventionally defined GNP cannot account for changes in the *value* of these goods and services as the environment declines or improves.

For example, changes in environmental quality, whether they are "bads" such as pollution that causes damages to crops, buildings and human health, or "goods," such as biodiversity that enhances ecosystem functioning, tourism and human enjoyment of nature, have no apparent "markets." The result is that these costs and benefits are routinely ignored in GNP estimates. Some marketed natural resource products, such as commercially extracted coal, oil, natural gas and other minerals, do appear in GNP accounts. But measuring only the contribution of such exhaustible resources to current income is misleading, as it does not allow for the depreciation in the value of the stock of these resources as extraction proceeds today. Similarly, GNP records the value of current output of marketed fish, forest and other renewable resource products, but if such production exceeds biological renewal, no account is made for the declining value of the remaining resource stock. Finally, GNP certainly ignores damages to ecosystems and their functioning that result in the decline of a wide range of beneficial ecosystem goods and services, such as water supply and its regulation, climate maintenance, nutrient cycling, enhanced biological productivity and, ultimately, overall life support.

BGE noted that there are many methods by which one can "account" for changes in environmental values, including adding or subtracting changes in natural capital to modify existing GNP accounts. But the objective of any environmental accounting method should be to:

- prepare a "balance sheet" giving a profile of what *stocks* of the resource are available at a given point in time,
- prepare an account of what *uses* are made of these stocks, what *sources* they are derived from and how they are added to or transformed over time, and
- ensure that the *stock accounts* and the *flow accounts* are consistent, so that the balance sheet in any year can be derived from the balance sheet of the previous year plus the flow of accounts of that year.

As pointed out by BGE, "although we naturally think of 'accounts' in money terms, there is in fact no reason why such accounts should not be presented in physical units, as long as they present the stocks and flows in a clear identifiable way and as long as they achieve the reconciliation between the sets of stock and flow accounts as described above."[16] But as in the case of environmental valuation, the need for such accounts to guide economic policy is clear:

> If an effective management of the natural and environmental and resource base is to be achieved, policy makers need to have access to a consistent, reliable and comparable data set, relating to the availability and use of such resources.[17]

Of particular interest since BGE has been the development of measures of adjusted national income to account for the depletion in the stocks or values of key natural and environmental resources. Considerable progress has been made, for example, at the World Bank to develop measures of *adjusted* or *genuine savings* as an indicator of the sustainability of every country in the world.[18] Some national governments and supranational organizations, such as the European Union, have also started to develop systems of environmental accounting along the lines advocated by BGE.

Chapter 5 reviews such progress in accounting for the economic impacts of environmental and natural resource use, and also the limitations to current approaches. For example, certain natural resources, such as fossil fuels, minerals and forest resources, are more amenable to environmental accounting than others, such as pollution, greenhouse gas emissions and ecosystem services. Thus, the chapter also identifies where progress in environmental accounting is urgently required.

Prices and incentives for environmental improvement

BGE maintained that "price is a powerful weapon in the pursuit of the environmental policies needed for sustainable development because it allows resource users to respond in the same way as they do the price signals elsewhere in the market." Moreover, it was argued that current environmental policy relies too much on "the traditional 'standard-setting' approach to environmental policy" rather than "more market-based approaches, using charges and tradable permits."[19]

Today, the use of such market-based instruments and other incentives to promote environmental improvement is much more widespread in developed and even some developing economies. We are also beginning to understand better how to combine prices with other signals that act to change environmentally harmful behavior. However, much of what motivates individual choices is not fully understood, and there is still widespread resistance to the "proper pricing" of pollution and natural resource use, as well as to the removal of harmful subsidies that distort markets and foster environmental degradation. In addition, markets for key global pollutants and environmental threats, such as greenhouse gases, are incomplete.

Chapter 6 surveys recent progress in adjusting prices to reflect environmental costs and creating incentives for environmental improvement, citing case studies of success and failure. This includes the major movement on ecological tax reform and its impacts. Finally, the chapter also identifies the need for global markets, such as for carbon and payment for ecosystem services, if the emerging threats of global warming and ecosystem loss are to be countered.

Policy options for a green economy

Overall, BGE argued that there is a huge sustainability challenge to be overcome, if a truly "green economy" is to be the objective. In a later publication, two of the BGE authors, Pearce and Barbier, summarized this challenge in the following manner:

> efficient and sustainable management of environmental resources, or natural capital, is essential to the long-term development of economies and human welfare. We refer to this as environmentally sustainable development. Unfortunately, we find little evidence that sustainability is actually being achieved. Important environmental values are generally not reflected in markets, and despite much rhetoric to the contrary, are routinely ignored in policy decisions. Institutional failures, such as the lack of property rights, inefficient and corrupt governance, political instability and the absence of public authority or institutions, also compound this problem. The result is economic development that produces excessive environmental degradation and increasing ecological scarcity. As we have demonstrated, the economic and social costs associated with these impacts can be significant. However, possibly the greatest threat posed by unsustainable development may be the long-term, potentially serious impacts on the welfare of future generations.[20]

Box 1.3 highlights the sustainability challenge that the world faces. At the core is the vicious cycle of unsustainable growth whereby the failure of environmental values to be reflected in markets and policy decisions leads to economic development with excessive environmental degradation. If environmental values are not reflected in market and policy actions, then any increasing ecological scarcity will also be ignored in decision making. The result is that the vicious cycle will be reinforced, and the current pattern of economic development will continue on its unsustainable path.

Reversing this process of unsustainable development is possible, but it requires three interrelated steps. First, as emphasized by BGE, environmental valuation and accounting for natural capital depreciation must be fully integrated into economic development policy and strategy. Improvements in environmental valuation and policy analysis are required to ensure that markets and policies incorporate the full costs and benefits of environmental impacts.

Second, the role of policy in controlling excessive environmental degradation requires action based on effective and appropriate information, incentives, institutions, investments and infrastructure (the five *i*'s indicated in Box 1.3). Better information on the state of the environment, including better environmental accounting, is essential for both private and public decision making that determines the allocation of natural capital for economic development. Market-based instruments, the creation of markets and, where appropriate, regulatory measures have a role to play in internalizing this information in everyday allocation decisions in the economy.

Such instruments are also important in correcting the market and policy failures that distort the economic incentives for improved environmental and ecosystems management. However, overcoming institutional distortions and encouraging more effective property rights, good governance and support for local communities are also critical. Reducing government inefficiency, corruption and poor accountability are also important in reversing excessive environmental degradation in many countries. But there is also a positive role for government in providing an appropriate and effective infrastructure through public investment, protecting critical ecosystems and biodiversity conservation, new incentive mechanisms such as payment for ecosystem services, and fostering the technologies and knowledge necessary for improving ecosystem restoration and environmental management.

Third, increasing collaboration between environmental scientists, ecologists and economists will be required to assess and monitor the environmental and welfare impacts of ongoing natural resource depletion, pollution and ecological scarcity. As indicated in Box 1.3, such interdisciplinary ecological and economic analysis is necessary to identify and assess the growing number of complex environmental and ecological problems globally. Further progress in reversing unsustainable development calls for more widespread interdisciplinary

BOX 1.3 REVERSING THE VICIOUS CYCLE OF "UNSUSTAINABLE" DEVELOPMENT

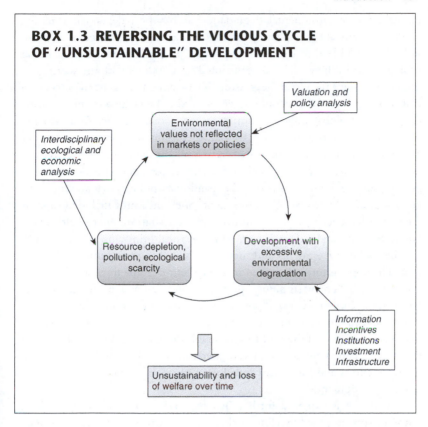

collaboration across the existing fields of economics, ecology and other social and natural sciences in order to analyze complex problems of environmental degradation, biodiversity loss and ecosystem decline.

Chapters 2 to 6 pick up the main messages of BGE outlined in this chapter and explore what further progress has been made and is still required in environmental valuation, accounting and pricing if we are to green today's economies. Chapter 7 stresses the need for global solutions and cooperation as an urgent priority in the twenty-first century if we are to overcome the sustainability challenge highlighted in Box 1.3.

Global policy challenges in the twenty-first century

As we shall discuss in Chapter 2, concerns over ecological scarcity have grown in recent years, and there is now widespread belief that increasing resource use, environmental degradation and carbon dependency in the world economy are precipitating ecological and climatic change on a global scale that could lead to irreversible damages. In addition to this impending ecological crisis, the world was confronted over 2008–9 with the worst economic crisis since the Great Depression. There emerged a general perception that these ecological and economic crises need to be tackled simultaneously: an important global policy response to the economic recession was the acknowledgment that measures to reduce carbon dependency and other environmental improvements could have a role in the economic recovery.

For example, as part of their efforts to boost aggregate demand and growth, some governments adopted expansionary policies that also incorporated a sizable "green fiscal" component. Such measures included support for renewable energy, carbon capture and sequestration, energy efficiency, public transport and rail, and improving electrical grid transmission, as well as other public investments and incentives aimed at environmental protection. The impetus for such "green recovery" efforts came from studies showing that such "green stimulus" policies could foster a more sustainable, low-carbon economic development in the medium term while creating growth and employment in "clean energy" sectors. More recently, the Green Economy Initiative of the UN Environment Programme (UNEP) has called for more sustained public and private investments globally to build on green recovery efforts and turn them into long-term policies for sustainable economic development.[21]

This theme is explored further in Chapter 7, which argues that if the imminent threats posed by climate change, energy insecurity and deteriorating ecosystems are to be reduced significantly, then the green recovery efforts must be broadened into a comprehensive strategy to overcome ecological scarcity in the world economy. To develop such a long-term strategy requires looking further at the role of complementary pricing policies, creating global markets and devising long-term green development strategies.

The need for such a global and long-term strategy, or "blueprint," for a green economy was, after all, a key theme of BGE. It perhaps explains why the main messages of BGE – the overall importance of environmental valuation, accounting and pricing to attaining sustainable economic development – continue to have an impact on policy debates today.

As BGE argued: "Much of the thinking about sustainable development emerged because of the environmental challenges at the end of the twentieth century and the prospective challenges of the twenty-first. Some of these challenges are global – climate change and ozone layer reduction; some are international – transboundary 'acid rain' for example; some are national – coastal waters pollution in many cases, loss of habitat."

Tackling these environmental challenges requires the correct use of environmental valuation, accounting and pricing, a long-term perspective on the policies required for a twenty-first-century green economy, and the political will to implement these policies at the national, international and global level.[22]

Conclusion

The main message from BGE was that to make economies more sustainable requires progress in valuing the environment, accounting for the beneficial services of natural capital and creating incentives for environmental improvement. One aim of this book is to review what has been achieved since BGE in implementing policies and other measures to improve environmental valuation, accounting and incentives. Twenty years on, although much has been accomplished, additional advances in policy are still required to green economies successfully.

In the chapters that follow, we highlight the new policies and economic approaches needed for sustainable management of today's environmental concerns. We emphasize practical policies for greening modern economies, and argue that such an economic roadmap to a greener future is essential to tackle the major environmental threats of the twenty-first century, such as global warming, ecological scarcity and energy insecurity. Overcoming environmental problems does require choices and tradeoffs, and the costs of transitioning to a greener economy will be significant. But the gains in terms of sustaining economic development, improving the environment and enhancing human welfare exceed these costs. Modern economies have the opportunity to develop successfully and sustainably, as a means to ensuring the well-being of current and future generations. In the chapters that follow, we outline the key policies required for achieving this goal.

2

BLUEPRINT FOR A GREEN ECONOMY IN THE TWENTY-FIRST CENTURY

Much has altered over the past two decades or so, especially in terms of what we now know about the pace and scale of global environmental change. Perhaps the most important of these changes has been the growing concern about climate change. When we wrote *Blueprint for a Green Economy* (henceforth BGE), this was an emerging issue and we acknowledged it but did not give it the importance it has rightly received since. In this regard the International Panel for Climate Change (IPCC) has played a crucial role, by assembling the state of knowledge on this topic every five years or so since 1990. Activity in this area is now widespread, with perhaps the most important international effort being the Kyoto Protocol, signed in 1997. However, this treaty is due to expire in 2012 and in any case it has made little impact on the global emissions of greenhouse gases.

Another set of environmental concerns that have risen in the public mind since BGE relate to the important (and neglected) contribution of the systems that constitute our natural environment. These are reflected in the Millennium Ecosystem Assessment (MEA), a process that started in 1998 and led to the publication of a series of reports in 2005. There have subsequently been a number of studies that develop these themes, including the Economics of Ecosystems and Biodiversity (TEEB), which published a series of reports beginning in 2010. Action in this area has been coordinated by the Convention on Biological Diversity, signed in 1992, with subsequent agreements under that umbrella being the Cartagena Protocol on Biosafety in

2000 and the Nagoya Protocol on Access to Genetic Resources and the Fair and Equitable Sharing of Benefits in 2010.

In both of these developments, and others, there is a growing recognition of the links between the economy, society and the environment, something that BGE was at pains to stress. Climate change matters because it affects our well-being, especially for the vulnerable members of society. Action to address it is problematic because it will impose costs on some members as they are required to make changes to their lifestyles. Furthermore action has to be coordinated internationally, something that countries find extremely difficult. Likewise, the causes of the degradation to the ecosystems that support our whole system of production and consumption lie in the fact that we have failed to value them properly; if we can change this and manage their use in a way that recognizes their true value, we may yet succeed in reversing some of the losses experienced in recent years.

Other areas where the economy–environment–society nexus has become more apparent are in the search for stimulus to economies that face falls in output and employment. In 2008–9 we witnessed a major economic crisis, initiated by the fall of the investment bank Lehman Brothers. By 2010 we thought it had been overcome, only to find that, as we write in the summer of 2011, there is another collapse of the stock markets worldwide and employment, already at around 9 percent in the USA and ranging from 7 to 20 percent in Europe, is under risk of going even higher as the world enters another period of recession or at best feeble and intermittent growth. We deal with the question of how to reconcile the goals of sustainable development with those of economic stability in Chapter 7; here we simply note that there is a risk of short-term economic considerations overriding the longer-term goals of sustainable development, with governments, panicking about the economic situation, promoting any measure that will create jobs or sustain output and demand. Yet, as we show later and as BGE had noted, we can address the economic crises through policies that promote green growth. These involve giving a positive weight to policies that have "green" elements and a negative one to policies that do the opposite. This thinking has to infiltrate all areas of government policy and to some extent the process has begun.

This chapter reviews how much progress we have made in addressing the various environmental problems and goals that BGE had identified. It starts by looking at the key global environmental trends and initiatives over the past 20 years, in some respects providing a term report on how we have been performing nationally and globally since 1990. This report is mixed: there has been progress in some areas while there has been deterioration

in others. And there has been a growing divide in environmental performance between the rich and poor countries. We then go on to consider progress
in the policy field. Have we changed our ways of thinking, to reflect the messages from BGE – that we value the different services provided by our natural environment and that we take account of these values when we make
decisions in the public and private spheres? Again the picture is mixed: we
have made some major progress in some areas of environmental valuation
and even in taking account of this valuation when deciding on which technologies to use and which goods and services to regulate. Yet there are others,
notably in the area of food and energy subsidies, where we have continued to
promote practices that are deeply unsustainable. To be sure there remain
major challenges to be addressed.

Environmental trends

What have been the observed environmental trends over the past two to
three decades, when we have undoubtedly seen an increased awareness of
and concern with the quality of the environment? Have these factors had an
influence in physical terms? Of course it is difficult to answer these analyti-
cally, as the counterfactual of what would have happened had we not become
more aware and made changes to policies to reflect this is not available.
Nevertheless it is interesting to track the main areas of interest and compare
them to the recent past.

Climate change

The main measure of climate change is the emissions of greenhouse gases
(GHGs), of which the most important is carbon dioxide. World Bank data
show that emissions of CO_2 increased 36 percent between 1990 and 2007.
The previous 17 years (1973–90) had seen an increase of 31 percent, so in
this respect we cannot claim even to have made a reduction in the rate of
increase.[1] This is perhaps one of the most serious areas where progress has
been very limited. One might argue that developing countries with growing
populations and a low base of emissions needed to increase them to "catch
up" in economic terms with the developed countries, but even the latter
(taken as the Organization for Economic Cooperation and Development
(OECD) member states) have had an increase of 15 percent since 1990. The
Kyoto Protocol had sought to reduce the emissions of the developed countries by on average 5 percent by 2012 relative to 1990 levels. This target may
be achieved by most of the signatories but not all (Canada has decided it will

not meet its target and has withdrawn from the Protocol). Most importantly, the Kyoto Protocol will have made a very small contribution for two reasons. First, because the biggest emitter as of 1990, the United States, did not ratify the agreement reached in Kyoto under which it would reduce its emissions by 7 percent. Instead its emissions have increased 20 percent between 1990 and 2007. Second, emerging economies were not required to make any reductions and have seen emissions growing very rapidly. This is especially the case for China but also India, Brazil and other fast-growing developing countries.

It is generally agreed that we should aim to limit global warming at about 2°C, a target that requires global emissions of GHGs to halve by 2050 relative to 1990 levels, with a peak in emissions being reached in 2020. It is doubtful if this will be achieved, but it is not impossible. If we are to be successful, where will the large cuts in greenhouse gas emissions needed to curb global climate change come from? Today's industrialized countries can perhaps expect to continue to grow at their long-term per capita income rate of around 1 to 2 percent, with no population growth (or possibly even negative growth).[2] So even without any special effort they should manage to hold emissions constant if the long-run trend in the de-carbonization rate holds.[3] With some effort, a modest reduction should be possible and, with a concerted effort in terms of incentives, support for technological development and changes in lifestyles, a more significant reduction can be achieved at a relatively low cost, as Stern and others have noted.[4] But the bulk of the decreases in emissions will have to come from developing countries, especially those that are now catching up with the industrialized world, and that still have population growth to boot. How can these countries contribute to the emissions reductions targets that most observers now consider essential for long-term planetary survival and do it in a way that enhances the attainment of their own sustainable development goals? That challenge remains to be faced and requires a more rapid transition to a low-carbon economy and society than we have ever experienced before.

Biodiversity and ecosystems

The story on biodiversity and ecosystems is also one of continuing loss and degradation, albeit with some notable exceptions. The rate of extinction of species is estimated to be 100 to 1,000 times faster than in geological times, and there is little evidence that this rate has declined in recent years.[5] The WWF Living Planet Index, which tracks population size, density, abundance or a proxy of abundance of over 800 vertebrate species, shows declines between 1970 and 2007 of 28 percent globally and 60 percent in tropical regions. The time series for this change is shown in Figure 2.1. Visually it appears as if the greatest loss in that period was in the 1980s and 1990s. Since 2000, the rate of decline has been somewhat lower.

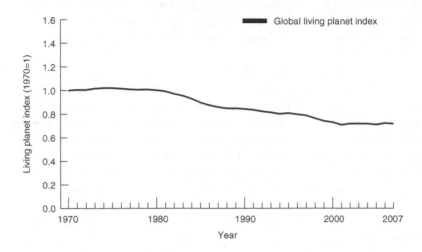

FIGURE 2.1   Living Planet Index, 1970–2007[6]

We are also becoming more aware of the fact that these losses are economically important. For example, between 1981 and 2006, 47 percent of cancer drugs and 34 percent of all "small molecule new chemical entities" (NCE) for all disease categories were natural products or derived directly from them.[7] In some countries in Asia and Africa 80 percent of the population relies on traditional medicine (including herbal medicine) for primary health care.[8] As extinctions continue the availability of some of these medicines may be reduced and new drug developments may well be curtailed. Yet, while we have a number of pieces of anecdotal evidence of these possibilities, and there are several studies that look at the value of biodiversity in specific contexts, no one has estimated the global value of the loss of biodiversity as such.[9] This is because the links between biodiversity and biological systems and the economic and social values that they support are extremely complex. Even the measurement of biodiversity is problematic, with a multidimensional metric being regarded as appropriate, although further work being considered necessary to define the appropriate combination.[10]

For this reason the focus, initiated by the Millennium Ecosystem Assessment (MEA) has been on measuring ecosystem services, which are derived from the complex biophysical systems, rather than on biodiversity.[11] The MEA defines ecosystem services under four headings: provisioning, regulating, cultural and supporting, and under each there are a number of subcategories. Table 2.1 summarizes the main ecosystem services that the MEA has listed.

The first thing to note is that services from ecosystems have also been facing major losses. During the last century the planet has lost 50 percent of its wetlands, 40 percent of its forests and 35 percent of its mangroves. Around 60 percent of global ecosystem services have been degraded in just 50 years.[12] Again, there is little reason to believe that this rate of loss has been attenuated over the last 20 years.

TABLE 2.1 Ecosystem services[13]

Type of ecosystem service	

Provisioning services
Food and fiber
Fuel
Biochemicals, natural medicines
    and pharmaceuticals
Ornamental resources
Fresh water
 	
Cultural services
Cultural diversity, spiritual and
    religious values, educational values,
    inspiration, aesthetic values, social
    relations, sense of place and identity
Cultural heritage values
Recreation and ecotourism
 	
Supporting services
Primary production
Nutrient cycling
Soil formation
	Regulating services
	Air quality maintenance
	Climate regulation (e.g. temperature and
	    precipitation, carbon storage)
	Water regulation (e.g. flood prevention,
	    timing and magnitude of runoff,
	    aquifer recharge)
	Erosion control
	Water purification and waste
	    management
	Regulation of human diseases
	Biological control (e.g. loss of natural
	    predators of pests)
	Pollination
	Storm protection (damage by hurricanes
	    or large waves)
	Fire resistance (change of vegetation
	    cover leading to increased fire
	    susceptibility)
	Avalanche protection
	Other (loss of indicator species)

An interesting measure of the rate of loss of "useful" biodiversity is one developed by the GLOBIO team in the Netherlands, which looks at areas under different ecosystems, adjusted for the mean species abundance (MSA) within them.[14] The MSA area indicator is a pressure-based indicator taking into account the relationship between pressures and species abundance.[15] The GLOBIO team has painstakingly constructed estimates of MSA areas in 1900, 2000 and, under the assumption of continuing trends, for 2050. The figures are given in Tables 2.2 and 2.3.

The last century saw a loss of 21 percent of biomes measured in MSA areas, equal to 2.5 billion hectares, with the biggest losses coming in temperate forests, grasslands, savanna and tropical forests (in that order). These losses were most significant in the OECD, followed by Central and South America (CSAM), Sub-Saharan Africa (SAFR) and South Asia (SASIA). In the next 50 years we can expect a loss of a further 1.2 billion hectares, with the biggest losses coming in savanna, followed by grasslands, boreal forests and tropical forests. The main regions for the losses are Sub-Saharan Africa, followed by Russia and Central Asia (RUS_CASIA) and South Asia. Of course these projections are not determinate – they can be reduced if appropriate policies are introduced.

Air quality

Air quality is an area where we have a mixed picture since 1990. A key variable for air quality is the emissions of particulate matter of diameter less than 10 microns (PM_{10}). These emissions are a key input to determining the concentrations of particulate matter, which are also influenced by other pollutants, such as sulphates and nitrates. A substantial volume of research over the last two decades has indicated that concentrations of PM have a major impact on human health in terms of premature mortality and increased morbidity. As a result technological standards for equipment generating emissions of PM have been tightened and a number of incentives have been introduced to capture emissions that are generated. This has had an effect in reducing the average urban population weighted concentrations in almost all countries over the last 26 years; World Bank data show a global average decrease of 37.5 percent over that period. Moreover decreases have been observed both in developed and developing countries. The main difference between these two groups of nations is that the latter still have quite high absolute concentrations. Table 2.4 summarizes the figures for 2006 (the latest year for which data are available).

TABLE 2.2 Changes in MSA area by biome and world region, period 1900–2000 (1,000ha)[16]

Biome	OECD	CSAM	MEA_ NAFR	SAFR	RUS_ CASIA	SASIA	CHN	Total	% on 1900 levels
Ice and tundra	-18,158	-3,200	0	0	-11,629	-1,627	-19,701	-54,316	-6%
Grassland steppe	-174,658	-34,955	-33,475	-46,282	-58,187	-26,498	-76,689	-450,744	-27%
Scrubland and savanna	-71,234	-135,528	-13,465	-234,860	0	-119,254	-118	-574,459	-26%
Boreal forests	-118,677	-4,062	0	0	-171,040	-3,478	-35,195	-332,452	-16%
Temperate forests	-278,755	-82,342	0	-11,238	-41,840	-33,326	-79,433	-526,934	-45%
Tropical forests	-13,590	-191,819	0	-76,072	0	-133,360	-1,579	-416,421	-25%
Desert	-42,642	-3,905	-49,790	-44,567	-2,793	-22,872	-9,321	-175,890	-8%
Total	**-717,715**	**-455,812**	**-96,729**	**-413,019**	**-285,489**	**-340,414**	**-222,036**	**-2,531,216**	
% on 1900 levels	-23%	-26%	-9%	-19%	-14%	-40%	-24%		-21%

TABLE 2.3 Changes in MSA area by biome and world region, period 2000–2050 (1,000ha)[17]

Biome	OECD	CSAM	MEA_NAFR	SAFR	RUS_CASIA	SASIA	CHN	Total	% on 2000 levels
Ice and tundra	−23,962	−1,942	0	0	−20,946	−1,483	−12,339	−60,672	−7%
Grassland and steppe	−63,278	−14,656	−6,869	−31,315	−37,606	−17,395	−24,171	−195,289	−16%
Scrubland and savanna	−46,646	−42,645	−2,273	−197,689	0	−64,980	−39	−354,272	−22%
Boreal forests	−56,870	−2,302	0	0	−78,001	−2,079	−11,780	−151,033	−9%
Temperate forests	−52,321	−9,476	0	−9,627	−17,456	−12,091	−19,775	−120,744	−18%
Tropical forests	−1,897	−48,078	0	−58,835	0	−35,314	−436	−144,560	−12%
Desert	−38,357	−1,660	−30,055	−31,671	−9,790	−22,385	−5,205	−139,122	−7%
Total	**−283,332**	**−120,759**	**−39,197**	**−329,137**	**−163,798**	**−155,726**	**−73,745**	**−1,165,693**	
% on 2000 levels	−12%	−9%	−4%	−18%	−10%	−30%	−11%		−12%

The data show a major difference between the upper middle income and the middle income groups, and again from the upper middle income and the high income groups.[18] In fact there is even a small increase going from the low income to the lower middle income.

TABLE 2.4 Population weighted urban average PM_{10} concentrations ($\mu G/M^3$), 2006[19]

Region	Concentration ($\mu G/M^3$)
Low income	65.8
Lower middle income	69.7
Middle income	57.5
Upper middle income	32.9
High income	26.3

There has been a considerable debate as to whether there is a "U"-shaped relationship between environmental quality and development, an idea first proposed by Grossman and Krueger in 1995,[20] whose research indicated that pollution levels increase as the economy develops but begin to decrease as rising income passes beyond a turning point. The relationship is referred to as the Environmental Kuznets Curve, after Simon Kuznets, who postulated something similar with respect to development and income inequality. In a very simple way the PM data in Table 2.4 would support such a view, which has now been the subject of many papers. We would note, however, that such a relationship is not deterministic, and that we do observe major differences in environmental quality among countries at a given level of development. For example, among the low income group the concentrations range from around $26\mu G/M^3$ to as much as $165\mu G/M^3$. It makes sense, therefore, to look at ways to improve environmental management at all levels of development and there are significant opportunities for doing this. Hence environmental quality improvements can be expected independently of overall economic growth.

The changes in air quality can also be tracked through what has been happening to SO_2. Here we see a sharper difference between different groups of countries. The data are from the World Resources Institute and only go from 1990 to 2000 but they show that while there was a 2.6 percent global decline in emissions between those dates, a number of developing countries showed a significant increase, and most developed countries showed a much bigger reduction. Indeed the average reduction for the latter was around 30 percent, while the average increase for the former was around 42 percent.

To summarize then, both sets of data indicate that, the environmental Kuznets Curve notwithstanding, we are seeing a divergence in environmental quality between the rich and the poor world.

Water

The concerns about water can be usefully divided into those relating to quantity and those relating to quality. In terms of quantity we see an increasing number of countries where rates of use are unsustainable: the amounts being extracted are greater than the rates of replacement or recharge. An important indicator in this respect is the rate of use of groundwater. Table 2.5 gives the rates of withdrawal as a percent of the rate of recharge over the period 1973–2005 for 13 countries where this figure was over 100 percent. Such rates imply that saline intrusion will become a problem in coastal areas and alternative sources of water will have to be found more generally; for well-off countries this water can come from desalination of sea water or diversion of surface water from other places, but for the poorer countries such options may be unaffordable.

TABLE 2.5 Countries with groundwater extraction at 100 percent or more of recharge (1973–2005)[21]

Country	Rate (%)	Country	Rate (%)
Algeria	195	Pakistan	109
Djibouti	120	Qatar	400
Egypt	542	Saudi Arabia	655
Israel	240	Tunisia	127
Jordan	100	Turkmenistan	111
Libya	854	United Arab Emirates	1,333
Mauritania	300		

Other indicators of problems with quantity relate to prolonged episodes of low rainfall (i.e. droughts) or periods when rainfall is well above average, resulting in floods. In terms of droughts, it is estimated that 400 million people are now living in conditions of "extreme drought."[22] According to the University Corporation for Atmospheric Research the area of the world that could be classified as experiencing very dry conditions was put at 15 percent in 1970; in 2010 it was estimated at 38 percent.[23] One can argue about the reasons for these developments but there is no doubt that water shortages and drought conditions are likely to prevail in more parts of the world now than they did in 1970.

In terms of floods, Figure 2.2, which has been put together by Professor Molina, based on data from the Centre for Research on the Epidemiology of Disasters, summarizes starkly the growing nature of the problem. Ever since the 1950s the number of events classified as floods by this Centre has been increasing in every decade and in every region of the world (the only exception being Australasia, where there was a slight fall between the 1980s and the 1990s). Again the causes of this are being debated (a combination of poor land management, degradation of ecosystems that prevent floods and climate change are probably all responsible) but it is clear that we face a growing challenge in managing the environment to prevent such occurrences and in introducing measures to deal with their consequences.

In terms of quality, the problems are most serious in developing countries, with large numbers not having access to adequate clean water and with agriculture facing problems of salinity because of saltwater intrusion. On clean water and sanitation the global community of 189 nations agreed in 2000 that one of the Millennium Development Goals (MDGs) to be achieved by 2015 was a reduction by half of the proportion of people not having access to safe drinking water and basic sanitation. The base year for the reduction was taken as 1990. Progress on this goal is being tracked by the United Nations Development Programme (UNDP), which reports that on safe drinking water the target will be more than met. If current trends continue, by 2015 an estimated 86 percent of the population in developing countries will have achieved this goal, up from 71 percent in 1990. Four regions – North Africa, Latin America and the Caribbean, Eastern Asia and South-Eastern Asia – have already met the target.[24]

The goal of adequate sanitation is proving more difficult. As UNDP notes:

> With half the population of developing regions lacking basic sanitation, the 2015 target appears to be out of reach. At the current rate of progress, the world will miss the target of halving the proportion of people without access to basic sanitation, such as toilets or latrines. In 2008, an estimated 2.6 billion people around the world lacked access to improved sanitation. If the trend continues, that number will grow to 2.7 billion by 2015. Wide disparities also exist by region, with

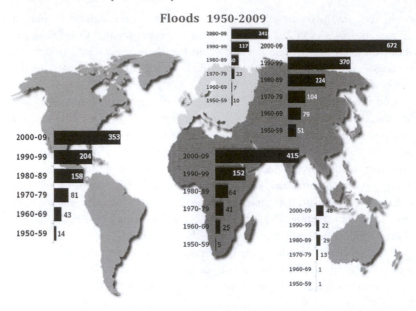

FIGURE 2.2 Floods worldwide, 1950–2009[25]

sub-Saharan Africa and South Asia continuing to lag behind. Recent data show 69 per cent and 64 per cent of their populations still lack access, respectively. And the gap between rural and urban areas remains huge, especially in Southern Asia, sub-Saharan Africa and Oceania.[26]

Water quality is also a growing matter of concern for agriculture, in countries where saltwater intrusion is increasing as a result of over-pumping of groundwater in coastal areas. This is especially the case in Benin, Morocco, Pakistan and Tunisia, among the developing countries, but is also having to be addressed in parts of the United States and in parts of Europe (e.g. Cyprus).

The other quality issue that has been receiving attention in recent years is that of the water in lakes and rivers and the seas. This has been especially the case in developed countries, where recreational and aesthetic demands from the citizens have made clean-up a priority. The result has been an improvement in quality indicators for these water bodies in most cases. Table 2.6 provides some data for a few major rivers in Europe. The improvements are not uniform but they are present in most cases when one compares the decades from the 1970s through the 2000s.

TABLE 2.6 Measures of water quality in selected rivers in Europe[27]

BOD5 Levels mg/L	1970s	1980s	1990s	2000s
Seine – Paris	3.7	4.5	3.2	1.9
Thames – London	n.a.	4.3	n.a.	2.0
Meuse near Namur	n.a.	n.a.	2.3	2.1
Guadalquivir – Cordoba	n.a.	n.a.	11.4	6.3
DO Levels mg/L	1970s	1980s	1990s	2000s
Seine – Paris	9.5	9.8	9.5	10.3
Thames – London	10.7	8.9	9.7	10.1
Meuse near Namur	n.a.	n.a.	10.5	104
Guadalquivir – Cordoba	n.a.	n.a.	8.4	9.3
Rhine close to Bonn	n.a.	8.5	9.6	10.2

Although noteworthy, these advances in quality are not considered enough to meet the demands of the population and most developed countries are seeking to make greater gains. In the European Union the Water Framework Directive is a particularly important piece of legislation that, in combination with other directives, sets a number of requirements for water treatment and management that should result in widespread improvements in water quality.

Water quality is also becoming an issue in developing countries, as the combination of cultural and health benefits of cleaner rivers are being appreciated. In India, for example, the government is giving a high priority to the clean-up of the Ganges, justified largely on these grounds. The focus is particularly on waste water treatment around the major urban areas, which also coincide with the location of places of pilgrimage. Likewise there is a big push to clean up the Mantanza Riachuelo River and basin around Buenos Aires, where there are concerns about the health and other impacts on the 3.5 million inhabitants of the basin. These are just two examples of a growing demand across many developing countries for water bodies not to be used as uncontrolled sewers. Where elected governments are in place they have to respond to these demands.

Natural hazards and disasters

The common perception that we are seeing an increase in the number and magnitude of natural disasters is broadly true. Careful documentation of the events such as the International Disaster Database at the Catholic University of Louvain, Brussels, show an exponential increase in the number of reported disasters going as far back as 1900, with only a small reversal around 2004 (Figure 2.3). The estimated damages associated with these events have also shown continuing growth throughout the period, with a small decline in the

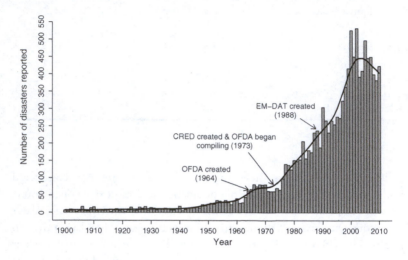

FIGURE 2.3   Number of natural disasters reported, 1900–2010[28]

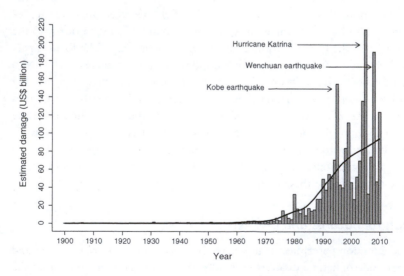

FIGURE 2.4   Estimated damages from natural disasters, 1900–2010[29]

rate of growth in the 1980s and again in the 1990s. While improved reporting and keeping of records over the last 110 years would explain some of the increase, there must be other factors that are responsible for this phenomenon, including both a growing susceptibility of social and economic systems to natural hazards, as well as an increase in the number of such events, caused by unsustainable use of the ecosystems on which the planet is dependent.

As a recent World Bank/United Nations report notes, while the hazards are natural, the disasters they cause depend on the way society is organized and what measures it takes to provide effective protection.[30] The extent of the disaster associated with a natural event depends on many factors and decisions taken over a number of years. These include a neglect of the environment, such as allowing deforestation in places subject to erosion, or ignoring flood risks when deciding where to build new homes. These environmental factors can be addressed and, again as the World Bank/UN report notes, addressing these factors can often be very cost-effective. Unfortunately the necessary measures are not always taken, partly because public and private actions are not coordinated and partly because the nature of the risk is not fully appreciated. This has not changed enough in the last 20 years or so but must change in the near future, as the implications of natural hazards in economic and social terms become ever more severe with urbanization and population growth.

Trends in policies and measures

Since BGE was published there have been a number of changes in the management of the environment. Some of these changes have had a clear benefit; in other cases the evidence is still not so clear. Policies and measures are discussed in other chapters of this book (see in particular Chapters 6 and 7). Here we wish to draw attention to some of the important trends.

We would suggest that there are four areas where important changes have taken place. These are:

1 Increase in access to information, improved public awareness and public participation in decision making.
2 The use of tools and procedures for evaluating investments and regulations that impact on the environment. These include formalization and strengthening of Environmental Impact Analysis, the valuation of environmental resources and pollution within a decision-making framework, the use of regulatory impact analysis and the use of strategic environmental analysis.
3 The adoption of cross-media environmental assessments in setting technological and ambient standards for producers and others that impact on the environment.

4   The increased use of market-based instruments and fiscal incentives as a
    means of encouraging better environmental performance.

Access to information and the role of civil society

An important development has undoubtedly been the increased role for civil
society in influencing environmental policy. In the last 20 years we have
seen a number of movements in this direction, such as the Aarhus Convention
on Access to Information, Public Participation in Decision-making and
Access to Justice in Environmental Matters, which was launched in 1998 and
now has 40 signatories (mainly European and Central Asian). This improves
the information base on which decisions are taken, as well as ensuring that
the demands and interests of a civil society in general are listened to. It makes
it more difficult for governments to hide unpalatable data regarding the environment and establishes public participation as an essential step in the design
of new measures. As the recent United Nations Secretary-General Kofi
Annan (1997–2006) noted:

> Although regional in scope, the significance of the Aarhus Convention
> is global. It is by far the most impressive elaboration of principle 10 of
> the Rio Declaration, which stresses the need for citizens' participation
> in environmental issues and for access to information on the environ-
> ment held by public authorities. As such it is the most ambitious ven-
> ture in the area of environmental democracy so far undertaken under
> the auspices of the United Nations.[31]

An enhanced role for civil society has not only been witnessed in developed
countries. Most developing countries have seen some progress in this area
and some have seen civil groups acting through the courts to enforce standards and regulations that were being violated with impunity. Indeed some
have gone even further to get new regulations enacted and enforced to
address serious environmental challenges. Examples of such actions are to be
found in a number of countries, including Argentina, India and Indonesia.
See Chapter 6 for more discussion of these.

Tools and procedures for making decisions relating to the environment

In the last 20 years governments have strengthened procedures for appraising
investments that may have environmental impacts through advances in

Environmental Impact Analysis (EIAs), in which public consultations are more effective, a result of better civil society involvement generally as noted above. In addition access to more reliable data has strengthened the application of these techniques While some countries still have a lack of adequate data, as well as the capacity to evaluate EIAs that have often been carried out by external agencies and to monitor compliance, it is fair to say that we have made considerable progress in the last two decades.

Increasingly, environmental impacts of investments are also being evaluated in decision tools such as benefit cost analysis, multi-criteria analysis and others. This has been made possible through better measurement of these impacts in physical terms by scientists and engineers, as well as through the valuation of the impacts in monetary terms (see Chapter 4). It is hard to judge the real value of the use of these tools but most experienced analysts and policy makers would agree that the additional information makes for more effective decision making and there has been considerable progress in the collecting of these data.

Another tool that has been developed in the last quarter century and that deserves mention is Strategic Environmental Analysis (SEA). It was developed to provide a wider evaluation of programs and policies, not just those where a single investment is being considered. Strategic decisions such as whether to go for an expansion of the rail system as opposed to the road network, or whether to provide incentives for biofuel production would be examples where a SEA would be undertaken. SEA started to be used in the early 1990s, and received a major impetus when the European Union passed a directive mandating its use in 2001. It is now widely used in member states as well as in other OECD countries and in developing countries with support from the World Bank and other international development institutions.

All these tools have either been introduced in the last 20 years or, where they were available earlier, have become more effective.

The adoption of technological and ambient standards

The regulation of the environment has conventionally been through physical limits imposed on which technologies can be used, or on emissions from plants or on ambient concentrations of pollutants. In recent years their effectiveness has been increased by making decisions on standards and technologies based on an integrated approach to the problem that considers all environmental media (air, water, solid materials) and not on each one separately. The selection of technologies based on a more comprehensive life-cycle review of emissions in all media started to be more widely practised in the 1990s. The uses of the concepts of Best Available Technology (BAT) and Best Available Technology Not Entailing Excessive Costs (BATNEEC), also developed in the 1990s, have been based on an integrated assessment of the impacts of the technologies. Techniques are still improving but even the last 20 years have seen advances in setting of standards based on the adoption of these methods.

The use of market-based instruments

BGE was especially strong in its advocacy of methods of regulation that used fiscal incentives to encourage cleaner production methods. The motivations were several. One was that it provided a more cost-effective way of achieving a given reduction in emissions. A second was that it provided a continual incentive to make improvements, as opposed to fixed standards, which once they are achieved provide no further incentives for improvements. The third set of advantages related to flexibility – industries that could not make reductions at reasonable cost could always opt to pay the environmental charge. Finally there is some evidence that the costs of administration are lower and some of these costs can be defrayed from revenue raised from the use of environmental charges.

Since the 1990s, when there were very few market-based instruments that could be said to apply as part of environmental regulation, there has been a considerable growth in their use.[32] Details are given in Chapter 6 and include emissions trading schemes for SO_2 and CO_2, environmental taxes or charges for a number of pollutants, banking schemes for wetlands and for target reductions in fuel use in vehicles, charges for the disposal of solid waste, charges for specific products and many others. All of these have contributed to the goal of a more effective management of the environment.

Conclusion

Since 1990 we have certainly become more aware of the environmental challenges that face us and we have made progress in addressing some of them more than others.

The good news items include improvements in air quality, especially particulate pollution, across most countries, developed and developing; greater access to safe drinking water in accordance with the Millennium Development Goals; and an upgrading of many of the rivers and lakes in the developed world.

Yet even these positive items need to be qualified – there is a growing gap between the quality indicators in the developed and developing world.

The areas where the news is less positive include climate change, degradation of ecosystems and loss of biodiversity, concerns of water security and increased impacts from natural hazards. In all of these we are witnessing deterioration relative to 1990 and the projections under "business as usual" are not that encouraging. The world needs to act more aggressively in addressing these problems.

On the positive side we have been collecting the necessary data and developing the tools necessary for taking more effective action. Above all, efforts in collecting data on the environment and on developing the links between economic, social and environmental factors are paying dividends. The use of integrated methods of assessment of environmental impacts help us design better standards and make investment and policy decisions that are more likely to be consistent with the overall goals of sustainable development. While there still remain challenges in getting better data and in improving analytical methods, these are not as important as the need to get global commitment to arrest the continuing environmental degradation that we are witnessing.

3

SUSTAINABLE DEVELOPMENT

Since the publication of *Blueprint for a Green Economy* (BGE), much has been written and said about sustainable development. Even by the late 1980s, numerous definitions of the concept had materialized. For example, Annex 1 of BGE listed at least 25 different interpretations of sustainable development. Fortunately, progress has been made in recent years to clarify this concept.

Beginning with BGE, economic interpretations of sustainability usually take as their starting point the consensus reached by the World Commission on Environment and Development (WCED), which as we mentioned in Chapter 1 is often referred to as the "Brundtland Commission" after its chairperson, former Norwegian prime minister Gro Harlem Brundtland. The WCED defined sustainable development as:

> Development that meets the needs of the present without compromising the ability of future generations to meet their own needs.[1]

But despite the universal approval of the WCED definition of sustainability, opinions still diverge on how this goal can be attained. In particular, two approaches have emerged in thinking about the role of the environment in sustainable development. The first adopts a *systems approach* to characterize sustainability as the maximization of goals across ecological, economic and social systems. The second is a *capital approach*, which was favored by BGE and described briefly in Chapter 1.

However, despite their differences, both approaches have in common two perspectives on sustainability. First, both the systems approach and the capital approach consider the environment to have a central role in sustainable development, and second, both also recognize that there are fundamental economy–environment tradeoffs that must be correctly assessed if sustainability is to be achieved.

As explained in Chapter 1, an economy–environment tradeoff underlies all patterns of development because growth and development typically use more raw material and energy inputs, generating waste by-products and altering ecosystems. Thus, there is usually a tradeoff between the economic benefits arising from development and the environmental and welfare impacts arising from natural resource depletion, pollution and ecological degradation.

The sustainability problem, as depicted in Box 1.3, arises when we either ignore this fundamental economy–environment tradeoff or fail to place proper values on the goods and services provided by the environment. The result is a vicious cycle of unsustainability and loss of welfare over time, in which environmental values are not reflected in markets or policies – leading in turn to development with excessive environmental degradation – and thus to increasing resource depletion, pollution and ecological scarcity.

Such a vicious cycle of unsustainable development may be able to generate sufficient goods and services for the economic livelihoods of present generations, but it puts at risk the welfare of future generations. The main reason is that an important source of economic opportunities and welfare – the environmental and resource endowment of an economy – is overused and rapidly depleted.

Consequently, as BGE maintained, "sustainable development has, as its principal aim, the search for a path of economic progress which does not impair the welfare of future generations," which also implies "that the role of maintaining environmental quality in this process of sustainable economic progress must be ranked higher than in the past."[2]

The systems approach to sustainable development

The systems approach can be captured in a Venn diagram (see Box 3.1), which portrays sustainability as a "holistic" concept. The diagram depicts sustainable development as the intersection of the goals attributed to three systems: ecological, economic and social. Attempting to maximize the goals for just one system does not achieve sustainability, because the impacts on the other systems are ignored. For example, achieving greater efficiency, equity and reduced poverty in economic systems may still generate unintended environmental and social impacts that undermine ecological and social systems. Instead, sustainable development can only be achieved by balancing the tradeoffs among the various goals of the three systems. Thus, the economic system should strive for efficiency, equity and poverty reduction, but at the same time account for the impacts on biological productivity, biodiversity and ecological resilience as well as the implications for social justice, good governance and social stability.[3]

The sustainability objective of the systems approach sounds ideal, especially as it takes into account the goals of three important systems: ecological, economic and social. All three systems are important to achieving sustainability, because maximizing the goals for just one system, or even two, does not achieve sustainability as the costs imposed on the other systems are not taken into account. One could argue, for example, that present-day economic development aims to maximize the goals of just the economic system, and possibly considers the social system objectives as well. However, economic development today largely ignores environmental and ecological impacts.

The systems approach does have practical limitations. In particular, there is no guidance as to how the tradeoffs among the goals of the various systems should be made. How should we decide to trade off, for example, more economic efficiency for less biodiversity and ecological resilience?

There is also no explicit indication as to how these tradeoffs among system goals relate to the concept of *intergenerational fairness* that underlies the WCED definition of sustainable development. What do tradeoffs between, say, more economic efficiency and less biodiversity imply for the welfare of current versus future generations? How we depict and assess economy–environment tradeoffs is critical for attaining sustainable development.

As argued in BGE and discussed in Chapter 1, deciding on the fundamental economy–environment tradeoff underlying sustainable development is relatively straightforward, provided that we have a common framework of evaluation. The *capital approach* to sustainable development is one such framework, and has become the dominant economic paradigm for thinking about sustainability.

The capital approach to sustainable development

The capital approach to sustainability is summarized schematically in Box 3.2, and it flows directly from the WCED definition of sustainable development.

BOX 3.1 THE VENN DIAGRAM OF SUSTAINABLE DEVELOPMENT

One popular way of representing sustainable development is to characterize it in a Venn diagram of three interlinked systems: ecological, economic and social. The Venn diagram representation of sustainable development now has many versions, but was first employed by Barbier.[4] The diagram here is adapted from the original.

As explained by Barbier, "each system has its own set of human-ascribed goals"; in contrast, "sustainable development involves a *process of trade-offs* among the various goals of the three systems" as "it is not possible to maximize all these objectives all the time." Attempting to maximize the goals for just one system, or even two, does not achieve sustainability because the costs imposed on the other systems are not taken into account. For example, an economic system may be efficient, and even equitable, in the allocation of resources but still generate environmental degradation that threatens biological productivity, biodiversity and resilience. "The general objective of sustainable economic development, then, is to maximize the goals across all these systems through an adaptive process of trade-offs," which is illustrated by the intersection of the ecological, economic and social systems.[5]

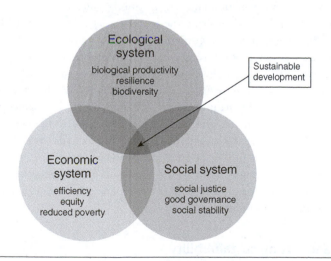

Economists are generally comfortable with the WCED's broad interpretation of sustainability, as it is easily translatable into economic terms: an increase in well-being today should not have as its consequences a reduction in well-being tomorrow.[6] That is, future generations should be entitled to at least the same level of economic opportunities – and thus at least the same level of economic welfare – as currently available to present generations. Consequently, economic development today must ensure that future generations are left no worse off than present generations. Or, as some economists have succinctly put it, per capita welfare should not be declining over time.[7]

As noted in Box 3.2, it is the *total* stock of capital employed by the economic system, including natural capital, that determines the full range of economic opportunities, and thus well-being, available to both present and future generations. Society must decide how best to use its total capital stock today to increase current economic activities and welfare, and how much it needs to save or even accumulate for tomorrow and, ultimately, for the well-being of future generations.

However, it is not simply the aggregate stock of capital in the economy that may matter but also its composition, in particular whether present generations are using up one form of capital to meet the needs of today. For example, much of the interest in sustainable development has risen out of concern that current economic development may be leading to rapid accumulation of physical and human capital, or *human-made capital*, but at the expense of excessive depletion and degradation of *natural capital*. The major concern has been that, by depleting the world's stock of natural wealth irreversibly, the development path chosen today will have detrimental implications for the well-being of future generations. In other words, according to this view, current economic development is essentially unsustainable.

As pointed out by BGE, from an economic standpoint, the critical issue of debate is not whether natural capital is being irreversibly depleted, but what are the costs of these losses and can society today compensate future generations for the current loss of natural capital? For example, as BGE stated, "future generations should be compensated for reductions in the endowments of resources brought about by the actions of present generations."[8]

A key question is what form should this compensation take? On this issue, economists diverge in opinion.

Weak and strong sustainability

Although economists generally endorse the capital approach to sustainability, sometimes divisions emerge over the special role of natural capital in

BOX 3.2 THE CAPITAL APPROACH TO SUSTAINABLE DEVELOPMENT

Sustainable
Development

Development that meets the needs of the present without compromising the ability of future generations to meet their own needs

Welfare does not decline over time

Requires managing and enhancing a portfolio of economic assets

| Natural Capital K_N | Physical Capital K_P | Human Capital K_H |

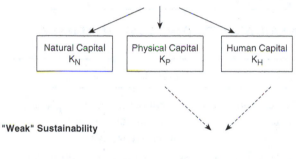

"Weak" Sustainability

All K_N is non-essential ◄---------- *Substitutes for K_N*

"Strong" Sustainability

Some K_N is essential --------► Keep essential K_N "intact" because of:
- Imperfect substitution
- Irreversible losses
- Uncertainty over values

sustainable development. The main disagreement is whether natural capital has a unique or *essential* role in sustaining human welfare, and thus whether special "compensation rules" are required to ensure that future generations are not made worse off by natural capital depletion today. These two contrasting views are now generally referred to as *weak sustainability* and *strong sustainability* (see Box 3.3).[9]

According to the *weak sustainability* view, there is essentially no inherent difference between natural and other forms of capital, and hence the same compensation rules ought to apply to both. As long as the natural capital that is being depleted is replaced with even more valuable physical and human capital, then the value of the aggregate stock – comprising human, physical and the remaining natural capital – is increasing over time.[10] Maintaining and enhancing the total stock of all capital alone is sufficient to attain sustainable development.

BOX 3.3 WEAK AND STRONG SUSTAINABILITY

Weak sustainability	Strong sustainability
• No difference between natural and other capital.	• Cannot view natural, physical and human capital as a homogeneous stock.
• As long as depleted natural capital is replaced with even more valuable physical and human capital, then the value of the aggregate stock will increase.	• Cannot always substitute for natural capital, as uncertainty over current and future values of ecological goods and services, unique environments and biodiversity mean that some natural capital is essential and cannot be replaced.
• Sustainability requires maintaining and enhancing the value of the aggregate capital stock.	• Sustainability requires maintaining and enhancing the value of the aggregate capital stock, and preserving essential natural capital.

In contrast, proponents of the *strong sustainability* view argue that physical or human capital cannot substitute for all the environmental resources comprising the natural capital stock, or all of the ecological services performed by nature. Consequently, the strong sustainability viewpoint questions whether human, physical and natural capital comprise a single homogeneous total capital stock. Instead, proponents of strong sustainability maintain that some forms of natural capital are *essential* to human welfare, particularly key ecological goods and services, unique environments and natural habitats and even irreplaceable natural resource attributes, such as biodiversity. Uncertainty over the true value to human welfare of these important assets, in particular the value that future generations may place on them if they become increasingly scarce, further limits our ability to determine whether we can adequately compensate future generations for irreversible losses in such essential natural capital today. Thus the strong sustainability view suggests that environmental resources and ecological goods and services that are essential for human welfare and cannot be easily *substituted* by human and physical capital should be protected and not depleted. The only satisfactory compensation rule for protecting the welfare of future generations is to keep essential natural capital intact. That is, maintaining or increasing the value of the total capital stock over time in turn requires keeping the non-substitutable and essential components of natural capital constant over time.

The debate between weak and strong sustainability perspectives is not easy to reconcile. Nevertheless, it is clear that the *minimum* criterion for attaining sustainable economic development is ensuring that an economy satisfies *weak sustainability* conditions. That is, as long as the natural capital that is being depleted is replaced with even more valuable physical and human capital, then *the value of the aggregate stock* – comprising human, physical and the remaining natural capital – should be increasing over time. This in turn requires that the development path of an economy is governed by certain principles.[11] First, environmental and natural resources must be managed efficiently so that the welfare losses from environmental damages are minimized and any resource rents earned after "internalizing" environmental externalities are maximized. Second, the rents arising from the depletion of natural capital must be invested into other productive economic assets.

However, the conditions under which depletion of natural capital may or may not lead to more sustainable development clearly depend on what we include as this form of wealth. For example, because they produce goods and services that support economic activity and enhance human welfare, ecosystems should and can be viewed as economic assets. As the economist Partha

Dasgupta reminds us, though, ecosystems are a very unique form of wealth compared to reproducible human-made capital:

> Ecosystems are capital assets. Like reproducible capital assets (roads, buildings, and machinery), ecosystems depreciate if they are misused or are overused. But they differ from reproducible capital assets in three ways: (1) depreciation of natural capital is frequently irreversible (or at best the systems take a long time to recover), (2) except in a very limited sense, it isn't possible to replace a depleted or degraded ecosystem by a new one, and (3) ecosystems can collapse abruptly, without much prior warning.[12]

The provision of goods and services by many ecosystems is poorly understood, and their values are often not marketed and unknown. In addition, the presence of ecological thresholds and the threat of collapse mean that we are often unaware of the full ecological and economic consequences of current levels of ecosystem degradation and conversion. Moreover, once converted, ecosystems may not be irreversibly lost, but reparation and restoration could be prohibitively expensive, if not technically infeasible in some cases. Improving our knowledge in all of these areas is a critical task. Better understanding of the complex workings of ecosystems and the value of the various goods and services they produce may also help to resolve the weak versus strong sustainability debate over what constitutes essential natural capital.

In sum, even if we believe that some natural ecosystems and unique environments might need to be kept "intact," much more work still needs to be done in determining how essential is this natural wealth to the welfare of current and future generations and how costly it may be to protect and conserve this wealth. Resolving the weak versus strong sustainability debate does not mean an end to the contribution of economics to environmental policy debate. To the contrary, choices and tradeoffs over environmental conservation are still required, and that in turn calls for better analysis of the non-market values of natural capital and of the causes and impacts of ongoing environmental degradation.

The sustainability challenge

As we discussed in Chapter 1, the world currently faces a huge task in overcoming current economic development efforts that are inherently unsustainable (see Box 1.3). One persistent difficulty is that the increasing costs associated with many environmental problems – global warming, freshwater scarcity, declining ecological services and increasing energy insecurity – are not routinely reflected in markets. Nor have adequate policies and institutions been developed to handle these costs. All too often, policy distortions and failures compound these problems by encouraging wasteful use of natural resources and environmental degradation.

Stated in such a way, and as shown in Box 1.3, reversing this process of unsustainable development does not appear to be an insurmountable problem. In fact, the main objective of BGE was to offer some concrete steps for overcoming this sustainability challenge and fostering a "greener" economy. Although some progress has been made over recent decades, as the previous chapter indicated, there is still much more that could and needs to be done.

Identifying the ways to achieve more sustainable economic development may be relatively straightforward, but as the last 20 years have shown, implementing the necessary policies for such a transition has proven to be much more difficult. Thus, the fundamental sustainability challenge is to understand why this might be the case. That is, if it is relatively straightforward to articulate the necessary steps for overcoming the various market, policy and institutional failures that are contributing to ecological scarcity, why has it been so difficult to implement these steps?

Institutional inertia and transaction costs

One reason why today's mounting environmental problems seem so intractable is the numerous market, policy and institutional failures that prevent recognition of the economic significance of these problems. However, as BGE made clear, we do have the economic tools to correct many of these failures. The question is: why has it proven so difficult to do so? One possible explanation of this intransigence is what New Institutional Economists (NIE) view as the tendency of many important social institutions to be highly invariant over long periods of time.[13] We can refer to this rigidity as *institutional inertia*.

The NIE define *institutions* as all the mechanisms and structures for ordering the behavior and ensuring the cooperation of individuals within society. They are the formal and informal "rules" that govern and organize social behavior and relationships, including reinforcing the existing social order, which is a stable system of institutions and structure that characterizes society for a considerable period of time.

Consequently, as societies develop, they become more complex, and their institutions are more difficult to change. Institutions help structure the means of production, and how goods and services are produced influence the development of certain institutions. This is a cumulative causative, or mutually reinforcing, process. One reason for this self-reinforcing process is that institutions and the social order become geared toward reducing the *transaction costs* – the costs other than the money price that are incurred in exchanging goods or services – of existing production and market relationships. For example, typical market and production transaction costs include search and information costs, bargaining and decision costs, and policing and enforcement costs (see Box 3.4).

Since the means of production include natural capital, and the way in which an economy uses this endowment, it follows that the existing system of social institutions and structure – the "social order" – becomes fixed around a stable set of economic institutions, including how production is organized and all inputs are combined and used. This includes how natural capital is used in combination with human-made capital, technology and knowledge, in production. Thus, institutional inertia is built up around reducing the transaction costs of the *existing production and exchange relationships* rather than making it easier to introduce new policies and incentives to reduce energy and resource use, pollution and ecological degradation. As a consequence, we may become more aware of the rising resource depletion, pollution and ecological scarcity costs associated with perpetuating the same pattern of resource-based development, including overreliance on fossil fuels and ecological degradation. But the high relative transaction costs involved in making the necessary corrections to the market, policy and institutional failures, compared to perpetuating the same pattern of production and natural resource use, seem prohibitive.

Box 3.4 illustrates how institutional inertia and transaction costs make it difficult to implement new environmental policies, such as pollution taxes, removal of environmentally damaging subsidies, controlling resource harvests and establishing protected areas. Instigating, enforcing and monitoring any new environmental policy to reduce environmental damage involves additional search and information costs, bargaining and decision costs, and policing and enforcement costs (Area A). If the policy calls for market-based instruments, such as taxes, tradable permits or new markets for resources and ecosystem services, then additional transaction costs will be incurred through the need to establish property rights, new administrative procedures and other market-enabling institutions (Area B). Further transaction costs result if additional changes are required in the overall institutional environment and legal system to implement the new environmental policy (Area C).

All three types of transaction cost have proven to be barriers to implementing a wide range of environmental policies. They may be especially relevant for policies to combat global warming and promote the long–run transition to a low-carbon economy. As several studies have shown, transaction costs are attributed to delaying or inhibiting the implementation of carbon taxes or tradable permits, adding to the costs of technological change and greenhouse gas (GHG) abatement, and reducing the effectiveness of the Clean Development Mechanism.[14] Without the successful implementation

BOX 3.4 THE TRANSACTION COSTS OF IMPLEMENTING NEW ENVIRONMENTAL POLICIES

The figure illustrates the magnitude of the problem often confronted with instigating policies to correct market, institutional and policy failures contributing to environmental problems.[15] When a new policy is implemented, such as a tax on pollution or implementing licenses for resource harvest or establishing a new protected area, additional market transaction costs in the form of search and information costs, bargaining and decision costs, and policing and enforcement costs are bound to occur (Area A). However, establishing some market-based instruments and trading mechanisms, such as taxes, tradable permit systems and new resource markets, will also require the establishment or reallocation of property rights to facilitate these instruments, and the setting up of new public agencies and administrative procedures to record, monitor and enforce trades. Thus the full transaction costs of the policies will be areas A and B in the figure. Finally, if additional changes in the institutional environment and legal system are required, the transaction costs will be larger still, including areas A, B and C.

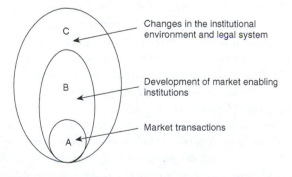

of policies to control GHG emissions, spur research and development into clean energy technologies, and disseminate these technologies globally, economies will remain fundamentally dependent on fossil fuel energy for some time to come.

Transaction costs are also problematic for ameliorating freshwater scarcity. Most policy recommendations for tackling water scarcity emphasize the need for more efficient water allocation and trading to conserve supplies and moderate demand. Although the use of water markets and market-based reforms for a wide range of water sector applications is growing globally, the magnitude and incidence of the transaction costs associated with such allocation mechanisms are often significant. Establishing and enforcing water rights and trading schemes, as well as putting in place mechanisms to resolve conflicts over water rights and use, are some of the more prohibitive costs to effective water markets and trading.[16]

Vested interests

Vested interests and political lobbying reinforce institutional inertia and help delay the transition to sustainable development. Governments can be influenced by powerful interest groups to block policy reforms that redistribute costs and benefits against their interest. In effect, the role of vested interests, political lobbying, and in some cases outright corruption and bribery, is to "expand" each of the transaction cost "bubbles" A, B and C illustrated in Box 3.4. The result is that it becomes even more difficult to implement a new environmental policy, such as removing perverse subsidies that are environmentally damaging or imposing a tax on pollution.

The incentive of vested interests to lobby against policy change is therefore strong. In economics, a growing literature is examining the role of such lobbying in influencing environmental policy outcomes.[17] In all cases, the influence of lobbying, or in certain cases bribery, by powerful vested interests fosters outcomes that work against the greater social interest and perpetuate environmental damages. The greater the political bargaining power of special interests, the more difficult it is to implement reform. Yet there are many examples where such reforms could yield improvements in both environmental outcomes and economic efficiency, as in the case of the removal of fossil fuel subsidies globally (see Box 3.5).

Vested interests are often the main reason for the intractability of many environmental problems. A good example is tropical deforestation. Although it used to be thought that the principle cause of deforestation was conversion by poor farmers, there is increasing evidence that recent forest loss is mainly

BOX 3.5 FOSSIL FUEL SUBSIDIES AND GLOBAL WARMING[18]

The dependence of the world economy on fossil fuels is a major cause of global warming and climate change. The energy sector is responsible for two-thirds of worldwide greenhouse gas (GHG) emissions, and the costs of climate change in terms of adaptation could reach US$50–170 billion by 2030, half of which could be borne by developing countries. The greening of the energy sector requires substituting fossil fuel energy sources with investments in clean energy as well as efficiency improvements, yet vested interests worldwide ensure that we are actually subsidizing our continued dependence on fossil fuels rather than lessening it.

Globally, fossil fuel consumption subsidies amounted to $557 billion in 2008. Production subsidies accounted for an additional $100 billion. Together, these subsidies account for roughly 1 percent of world GDP. Such fossil fuel consumption and production subsidies are an additional market failure preventing improved energy efficiency in economies. By artificially lowering the cost of using fossil fuels, such subsidies deter consumers and firms from adopting energy efficiency measures that would otherwise be cost-effective in the absence of any subsidies. Removal of such perverse incentives would therefore boost energy savings substantially. For example, phasing out all fossil fuel consumption and production subsidies by 2020 could result in a 5.8 percent reduction in global primary energy demand and a 6.9 percent fall in greenhouse gas emissions.

the result of large-scale commercial activities, often supported by government policies (Box 3.6). For example, across the tropics, the principal activity responsible for deforestation appears now to be the direct conversion of forests to permanent agriculture.[19] Although in Africa, deforestation is mainly due to small-scale permanent agriculture, forest conversion to large-scale agriculture, including raising livestock, predominates in Latin America and Asia.

Intragenerational equity

As noted above, the concept of sustainable development is guided by the principle of *intergenerational equity*. The total capital stock – reproducible,

---

BOX 3.6 COMMERCIAL INTERESTS AND TROPICAL DEFORESTATION

Since the 1990s, powerful vested interest in terms of large-scale plantations, farms, ranches, timber and mining operations, and agribusiness enterprises have become the dominant cause of much of the world's deforestation. According to Thomas Rudel, "to facilitate their plans for expansion, large landowners lobbied for the construction of improved and expanded networks of roads. Local politicians and bankers joined the landowners to form 'growth coalitions' that lobbied federal and provincial governments for improved infrastructure." These governments were soon "won over by powerful interest groups of landowners whose agendas involved agricultural expansion at the expense of forests."[20] Investors in these large-scale commercial activities are attracted to frontier forested areas because the lack of government controls and property rights in these remote areas mean that resource rents are easily captured, and thus frontier resource-extractive activities are particularly prone to rent-seeking behavior. Small-scale farmers usually follow because forest and other land is now readily available for conversion, and open access conditions facilitate the conversion. In some regions, large-scale plantation development is initiating the "opening" of forested areas to subsequent smaller-scale cropland expansion; in other regions, it may be timber, mining or energy developments that begin this process.

---

human and natural – should be managed to ensure that future generations have at least the same economic opportunities as the present generation.

However, intergenerational fairness must also be balanced by ensuring *intragenerational equity* as well. That is, economic development is not successful if it creates a widening gap between today's rich and poor. If large segments of the world population are currently languishing in poverty, then demographic trends, lack of economic opportunities and deteriorating environments will make it much more likely that global poverty will worsen rather than improve. Reducing, if not eradicating, poverty must be an important objective of efficient and sustainable environmental management; otherwise, the welfare of many countries and people may decline rather than increase over time.

Most developing countries, and certainly the majority of the populations living within them, depend directly on natural resources. The livelihoods of much of the world's rural poor are also intricately linked with exploiting fragile environments and ecosystems.[21] Well over 600 million of the rural poor currently live on lands prone to degradation and water stress, and in upland areas, forest systems and drylands that are vulnerable to climatic and ecological disruptions.[22] The tendency of rural populations to be clustered on marginal lands and in fragile environments is likely to be a continuing problem for the foreseeable future, given current global rural population and poverty trends. First, despite rapid global urbanization, the rural population of developing regions continues to grow, albeit at a slower rate in recent decades.[23] Second, around three-quarters of the developing world's poor still live in rural areas, which translates into about twice as many poor people live in rural than in urban areas.[24]

The world's poor are especially vulnerable to the climate-driven risks posed by rising sea level, coastal erosion and more frequent storms. Around 14 percent of the population and 21 percent of urban dwellers in developing countries live in low elevation coastal zones that are exposed to these risks.[25] The livelihoods of billions – from poor farmers to urban slum dwellers – are threatened by a wide range of climate-induced risks that affect food security, water availability, natural disasters, ecosystem stability and human health.[26] For example, many of the 150 million urban inhabitants that are likely to be at risk from extreme coastal flooding events and sea-level rise are likely to be the poor living in developing country cities.[27]

As in the case of climate change, the link between ecological scarcity and poverty is well established for some of the most critical environmental and energy problems. For example, for the world's poor, global water scarcity manifests itself as a water poverty problem. One in five people in the developing world lacks access to sufficient clean water, and about half the developing world's population, 2.6 billion people, do not have access to basic sanitation. More than 660 million of the people without sanitation live on less than US$2 a day, and more than 385 million on less than US$1 a day.[28] Billions of people in developing countries have no access to modern energy services, and those consumers who do have access often pay high prices for erratic and unreliable services. Among the energy poor are 2.4 billion people, who rely on traditional biomass fuels for cooking and heating, including 89 percent of the population of Sub-Saharan Africa, and another 1.6 billion people who do not have access to electricity.[29]

Thus, finding ways to protect global ecosystems, reduce the risks of global climate change, improve energy security and simultaneously improve the livelihoods of the poor is an important challenge, but one that could especially benefit poor countries and populations. A transition to a more sustainable economy can contribute to poverty eradication, but it does require incorporating such an objective explicitly among key sustainability goals. For example, the top priority of the UN Millennium Development Goals is the eradication of extreme poverty and hunger, including halving the proportion of people living on less than US$1 a day by 2015. A "greener" economy must not only be consistent with such objectives but also ensure that policies and investments geared towards reducing environmental risks and scarcities are compatible with ameliorating global poverty and social inequity.

Conclusion

Sustainable development has now become widely accepted as an essential economic goal. By advocating the capital approach to sustainability, BGE helped clarify its implications for economic policy. The role of policy is to determine how much of an economy's total capital stock today should be used to increase current economic activities and welfare, and how much should be saved or even accumulated for the benefit of future generations.

However, the total stock of economic assets essential to human welfare should be much broader than conventional reproducible (or fixed) assets, such as roads, buildings, machinery and factories. Investments in human capital, such as education and skills training, are also essential to sustaining development. Similarly, an economy's endowment of natural resources is an important form of "natural wealth."

When the concept of natural capital is further extended to include more complex environmental assets, such as ecosystems, then it can become difficult to determine the most efficient and sustainable tradeoffs between environmental conservation and development. Physical or human capital may simply not be good substitutes for all the environmental resources comprising the natural capital stock, or all of the ecological services performed by nature. But this still means that economists, working with ecologists and other natural scientists, need to determine the extent to which certain ecosystems and their services are essential to the welfare of current and future generations and how costly it may be to protect and conserve this natural wealth. It may mean that assessment of tradeoffs between human-made and natural capital should be extended to include environmental degradation that threatens biological productivity, biodiversity and resilience.

In many cases, however, the transition to more sustainable economic development involves more straightforward improvements in the efficient management of natural resource depletion, pollution and environmental degradation. If the welfare losses from environmental damages are minimized, and the resource rents earned from more efficient depletion of natural capital are invested in other productive economic assets, then much of the current unsustainable economic activity will disappear.

Yet, even though we have become clearer about how to achieve sustainable development, implementing policies to improve the sustainability of economies, and especially the management of natural capital, still remain elusive. Institutional inertia and vested interests are often formidable obstacles to instigating economic policy and technological change, especially with regard to how we use the environment. Powerful vested interests in particular seem to perpetuate policy outcomes that are not only inefficient and environmentally unsustainable but also inequitable.

In addition, present-day patterns of economic development that fail to address persistent problems of global poverty cannot be compatible with sustainability. This suggests that the capital approach to sustainable economic development should not remain narrowly focused on just intergenerational equity concerns but be expanded to include other important goals, such as improving equity and reducing poverty. The capital approach may be necessary for achieving sustainable development, but the wider economic, ecological and social tradeoffs identified by the systems approach are also important to ensuring sustainability.

4

PROGRESS IN VALUING THE ENVIRONMENT

A key message in *Blueprint for a Green Economy* was that, "by at least trying to put money values on some aspects of environmental quality we are underlining the fact that environmental services are *not* free."[1] As explained in previous chapters, one of the major causes of environmental degradation globally is the absence of markets and price signals to reflect the actual value of goods and services produced by the environment. As a consequence, when natural resources and the environment are used by the economy as sources of raw materials, energy and land or as a waste sink for pollution, it is often unclear what valuable environmental goods and services are sacrificed. Too readily we assume that these costs are negligible, which is equivalent to viewing environmental goods and services as "free." The result is the tendency to *overuse* the environment for certain activities, such as extracting raw materials and minerals, producing energy inputs and land conversion.

On the positive side, economic methodologies and approaches for environmental valuation have improved substantially over the past 20 years, and environmental valuation has become an accepted tool for assisting policy analysis and project planning. In addition, the Millennium Ecosystem Assessment has emphasized the need to evaluate a wider range of environmental values, the ecosystem services, or "benefits," of natural systems.[2] Such progress in environmental valuation is helping us understand that proper valuation of the environment is a necessary step if we are to achieve more sustainable economic development. Yet, despite this progress, important challenges and issues still remain.

This chapter reviews recent progress in valuing the environment since BGE, stressing in particular the extension of valuation to include ecosystem services and the increasing role of valuation in environmental management decisions. However, the chapter also examines the challenges and gaps in our knowledge to conduct environmental valuation correctly, and the need to make continuing progress in this important area of environmental management.

Economics and environmental valuation

As we saw in Chapter 3, the idea that the environment provides a range of goods and services that have value to humans is an important step in characterizing the environment as a form of natural capital. That is, just like any other investment asset in the economy, such as roads, buildings, machinery, financial wealth or job skills and education, the environment generates current and future flows of benefits, or *income*. In principle, then, the environment should be valued just like any other asset in an economy. The goods and services provided by the environment are essentially the beneficial flows of current and future "income." And, regardless of whether or not there exists a market for the goods and services from an environmental asset, its social value equals the discounted net present value (NPV) of these flows.

Of course, the environment and its resources can be used for a variety of different purposes. Often, allocating the environment for one set of uses, such as mineral and timber extraction or conversion to agricultural land, may diminish its ability to provide other valuable goods and services, such as wildlife habitat, recreation and clean water. We therefore need to know how changes to the environment affect the values associated with its various goods and services. Ultimately, what we want to find out is whether our choices in using the environment, and any subsequent change to it, make people better or worse off. The main objective of valuation is to assist in this assessment.

In economics, *environmental valuation* is concerned with how to estimate the impacts of changes in the environment on the welfare, or well-being, of individuals. If environmental changes result in individuals being "worse off," then we would like to have some measure of the loss of welfare to these individuals. Alternatively, if the changes make people "better off," then we want to estimate the resulting welfare gain. The basic concepts that economists use to measure such welfare gains and losses are economic values measured as a *monetary payment* or a *monetary compensation*. The essence of this approach is to estimate values as subtractions or additions to income that leaves people equally satisfied in terms of their own sense of well-being with or without the environmental change.

To summarize, the key to environmental valuation is determining how environmental changes, or more specifically changes in the goods and services that the environment provides, affect the well-being of different individuals. This involves establishing how much each individual is either *willing to pay* (WTP) in terms of a monetary payment for changes that have a positive welfare impact, or conversely, how much an individual is *willing to accept* (WTA) as monetary compensation to tolerate a negative effect. Once these valuation estimates are obtained for an individual or an entire household, they can be aggregated to obtain the values that all affected individuals or households place on the changes to the environment.

Box 4.1 provides a summary of the appropriate measures for assessing the gains and losses to welfare associated with an environmental change. As noted above, many changes in the environment involve changes in the quantities and qualities of non-marketed environmental goods and services. Economists use two concepts to measure the gains or losses in welfare that individuals may experience as a result of changes in such non-marketed goods and services. The *compensating surplus* measure is the compensating payment that returns an individual to his or her initial level of well-being after the environmental change occurs. For example, this corresponds either to the individual's willingness to pay (WTP) to get a beneficial environmental change or the payment that the individual is willing to accept (WTA) to tolerate a negative change. Alternatively, *equivalent surplus* is the compensating payment that allows the individual to reach the new level of well-being after the environmental change has occurred. For example, this payment could be the individual's WTA to forgo the beneficial change or the WTP to avoid the negative change.

Although Box 4.1 gives the impression that either WTP or WTA can be employed to value the gains and losses arising from an environmental change, in practice economists have difficulty in measuring WTA. Thus generally, WTP is used to value the benefits of getting a favorable environmental change (compensating surplus), or to value the costs of avoiding a damaging environmental change (equivalent surplus).[3]

Why environmental valuation is important

As discussed above, whereas the services from most assets in an economy are marketed, the benefits arising from natural capital generally are not. If the aggregate willingness to pay for these environmental benefits is not revealed through market outcomes, then efficient management of the environment requires explicit methods to measure this social value. By trying to measure

BOX 4.1 APPROPRIATE WELFARE MEASURES FOR AN ENVIRONMENTAL CHANGE

Welfare measure	Environmental change benefits individuals	Environmental change makes individuals worse off
Compensating surplus	WTP for getting the change	WTA for tolerating the change
Equivalent surplus	WTA to forgo the change	WTP to avoid the change

the WTP for changes in the environment, we are indicating that the value of the benefits or costs of such changes should not be ignored in economic policies and investment decisions.

For example, as discussed in Chapter 1, a major global issue today is the problem of increasing *ecological scarcity*. The economic exploitation and use of the natural environment for raw materials, energy and waste assimilation has led to the alteration and degradation of many important ecosystems world-wide (see Box 4.2). This disruption and destruction in turn affects human welfare, such as the use of aesthetic landscapes for recreation, the maintenance of beneficial species, the control of erosion, protection against floods or storms, and so forth. In fact, the failure to consider the values provided by these increasingly scarce goods and services is a major reason for the widespread disappearance of many ecosystems and habitats. By not measuring explicitly the aggregate willingness to pay for many non-marketed ecological goods and services, their benefits are either ignored or "underpriced." The consequence is excessive land conversion, habitat fragmentation, harvesting, water use and pollution that degrade and destroy ecosystems.

Box 4.3 illustrates why ignoring or "underpricing" the value of changes in an environmental asset, such as a wetland ecosystem, leads to excessive degradation or conversion. Wetlands provide a variety of goods and services, such as recreation, coastal habitat–fishery linkages, raw materials and food production, water purification and flood control.

In the figure of Box 4.3, the marginal social benefits of the wetland goods and services at any time t are represented by the line MB_t for a wetland of given area $\overline{A}$. For the purposes of illustration, this line is assumed to be

BOX 4.2 GLOBAL STATUS OF KEY ECOSYSTEM GOODS AND SERVICES

Condition globally has been enhanced	Condition globally has been degraded	Condition globally is mixed
Crops	Capture fisheries	Timber
Livestock	Wild foods	Cotton, hemp, silk
Aquaculture	Wood fuel	and other fiber crops
	Genetic resources	Water regulation
	Biochemicals, natural	Disease regulation
	medicines and	Recreation and
	pharmaceuticals	ecotourism
	Fresh water	Global climate
	Air quality regulation	regulation
	Regional and local climate	
	regulation	
	Erosion regulation	
	Water purification and waste	
	treatment	
	Pest regulation	
	Pollination	
	Natural hazard regulation	
	Spiritual and religious values	
	Aesthetic values	

Notes

Enhancement is defined as either increased production of or change in the ecosystem good or service that leads to greater benefits for people.

Degradation is defined as if current use exceeds sustainable levels, or a reduction in the benefits obtained from the good or service due to either some human-induced change or use exceeding its limits.

Mixed status implies that the condition of the good or service globally has experienced enhancement in some regions but degradation in others.

The original assessment by the Millennium Ecosystem Assessment of global climate regulation, in terms of net source of carbon sequestration since mid-century, was that this regulatory service has been enhanced. However, recent evidence suggests that progress with this service has been more mixed in recent years.

Source: Adapted from Millennium Ecosystem Assessment. 2005. *Ecosystems and Human Well-being: Synthesis*. Island Press, Washington, DC, table 1.

BOX 4.3 WETLAND CONVERSION TO DEVELOPMENT

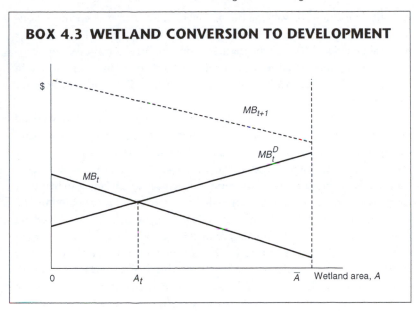

downward-sloping, which implies that for every additional square kilometer of wetland area, A, preserved in its original state, more wetland goods and benefits will be generated, but at a decreasing amount. Note that it is straight-forward to determine the aggregate willingness to pay for the benefits of these services, B_t; it is simply the area under the MB_t line. If there is no other use for the wetland, then the opportunity costs of maintaining it are zero, and B_t is at its maximum size when the entire wetland ecosystem is main-tained at its original land area size $\bar{A}$. The ecosystem management decision is therefore simple; the wetland landscape should be completely preserved and allowed to provide its full flow of services in perpetuity.

However, population and economic development pressures in many areas of the world usually mean that the opportunity cost of maintaining wetlands intact is not zero. The ecosystem management decision needs to consider these alternative development uses of a wetland. For example, suppose that the marginal social benefits of converting the wetland for these development options is now represented by a new line MB_t^D in the figure. The result is that $\bar{A}$-A_t of wetland landscape should be converted for development leav-ing A_t of the original ecosystem undisturbed.

Both of the outcomes discussed so far assume that the willingness to pay for the marginal benefits arising from wetland ecosystem services, MB_t, is explicitly measured, or valued. But if this is not the case, then these non-marketed flows are likely to be ignored in the land-use decision. Only the marginal benefits, MB_t^D, of the marketed outputs arising from wetland economic development activities will be taken into account and, as indicated in the figure, this implies that the entire ecosystem area $\bar{A}$ will be converted for development.

A further problem is the uncertainty over the future values of wetland goods and services. It is possible, for example, that the benefits of a wetland are larger in the future as more scientific information becomes available over time. For example, suppose that in the subsequent period $t+1$ it is discovered that the value of wetland goods and services is actually much larger, so that their marginal benefits, MB_{t+1}, in present value terms are now represented by the dotted line in Box 4.3. If the present value marginal benefits from wetland development in the future are largely unchanged, i.e. $MB_t^D \approx MB_{t+1}^D$, then as the figure indicates, the future benefits of the wetland exceed these costs, and the ecosystem should be restored to its original area $\bar{A}$, assuming of course that it is technically feasible and not excessively expensive to do so. Unfortunately, in making development decisions today we often do not know whether or not in the future the value of a wetland will turn out to exceed development benefits. Our simple example shows that if we have already made the decision today to convert $\bar{A}$-A_t area of the wetland, then in the future we should restore the original wetland ecosystem.

Ecosystem goods and services

As Box 4.3 illustrates, valuing the multiple benefits arising from natural ecosystems, such as wetlands, has become increasingly critical to many conservation and development decisions worldwide. It is increasingly common to refer to these multiple benefits as *ecosystem services*. Or, as the Millennium Ecosystem Assessment defines them, "ecosystem services are the benefits people obtain from ecosystems."[4]

Because of its broad interpretation, the term "ecosystem services" is used frequently to include a wide variety of ecosystem goods and services, which in economics would normally be classified under three different categories: (1) "goods" (e.g. products obtained from ecosystems, such as resource harvests, water and genetic material), (2) "services" (e.g. recreational and tourism benefits or certain ecological regulatory and habitat functions, such as water purification, climate regulation, erosion control and habitat provision), and (3) cultural benefits (e.g. spiritual and religious beliefs, heritage values).[5] Some of these benefits, such as resource harvests, recreation and even non-use bequest values, are well known to economists and have been the focus of environmental valuation efforts for some time. However, other ecosystem services, such as those arising from ecological and regulatory functions, are less well understood and have been rarely valued. As a result, a number of key measurement issues have arisen through recent attempts to value ecosystem goods and services.

The idea that ecosystems provide a range of "services" that have value to humans is an important step in characterizing these systems as *natural capital*. But the way in which these special assets provide their benefits is both complex and unique, and relates to the basic composition of all ecosystems.

Ecosystems comprise the abiotic (non–living) environment and the biotic (living) groupings of plant and animal species called communities. The biotic and abiotic components, and the interactions between them, are often referred to as the *ecosystem structure*. In addition, important *ecosystem functions* are carried out in every ecosystem: biogeochemical cycling and flow of energy. Important processes of biogeochemical cycling include primary production (photosynthesis), nutrient and water cycling, and materials decomposition. The flow, storage and transformation of materials and energy through the system are also influenced by processes that link organisms with each other, such as the food web, which is made up of interlocking food chains. These food chains are often characterized by other important functions, such as pollination, predation and parasitism.

Understanding the basic structure and functions of an ecosystem is often important, as they are the source of the valuable goods and services to humans. For example, some of the living organisms found in an ecosystem might be harvested or hunted for food, collected for raw materials or simply valued because they are aesthetically pleasing. Some of the ecosystem functions, such as nutrient and water cycling, can also benefit humans through purifying water, controlling floods, recharging aquifers, reducing pollution, or simply by providing more pleasing environments for recreation. As summarized in Box 4.4, the ecological production of ecosystem services arises from the structure and functions of these systems, but the latter are not synonymous with its services. Ecosystem structure and functions describe the components of an ecosystem and its biophysical relationship regardless of whether or not humans benefit from them. Only if they contribute to human well-being do these components and relationships generate an "ecosystem service." This distinction is important especially if we want to estimate the value of various ecosystem goods and services.

As we have seen, the majority of ecosystem goods and services are not marketed. These include many services arising from ecosystem processes and functions that benefit human beings largely without any additional input from them, such as coastal protection, nutrient cycling, erosion control, water purification and carbon sequestration. As a US National Research Council report points out: "the fundamental challenge of valuing ecosystem services lies in providing an explicit description and adequate assessment of the links between the structure and functions of natural systems, the benefits (i.e., goods and services) derived by humanity, and their subsequent values."[6] The main reason for this challenge is the "lack of multiproduct, ecological production functions to quantitatively map ecosystem structure and function to a flow of services that can then be valued."[7]

BOX 4.4 ECOSYSTEM FUNCTIONS AND SERVICES[8]

The term "ecosystem" describes a dynamic complex of plant, animal, and microorganism communities and their non-living environment, interacting as a system. Ecosystems encompass all organisms within a prescribed area, including humans. Ecosystem functions or processes are the characteristic physical, chemical, and biological activities that influence the flows, storage, and transformation of materials and energy within and through ecosystems. These activities include processes that link organisms with their physical environment (e.g., primary productivity and the cycling of nutrients and water) and processes that link organisms with each other, indirectly influencing flows of energy, water, and nutrients (e.g., pollination, predation, and parasitism). These processes in total describe the functioning of ecosystems....Ecosystem services are the direct or indirect contributions that ecosystems make to the well-being of human populations. Ecosystem processes and functions contribute to the provision of ecosystem services, but they are not synonymous with ecosystem services. Ecosystem processes and functions describe biophysical relationships that exist whether or not humans benefit from them. These relationships generate ecosystem services only if they contribute to human well-being, defined broadly to include both physical well-being and psychological gratification. Thus, ecosystem services cannot be defined independently of human values.

In recent years substantial progress has been made by economists working with ecologists and other natural scientists on this "fundamental challenge" to improve the application of environmental valuation methodologies to non-market ecosystem services. Nevertheless, a number of important challenges arise in applying these methods.

Box 4.5 provides an overview of the valuation challenge. Human drivers of ecosystem change affect important ecosystem processes and functions and their controlling components. Assessing this change is crucial yet difficult. More importantly, the resulting changes in ecosystem structure and functions need to be linked to their impacts on the production of goods and services that are valuable to humans. Once these impacts are valued properly,

BOX 4.5 ECONOMIC VALUATION OF ECOSYSTEM GOODS AND SERVICES[9]

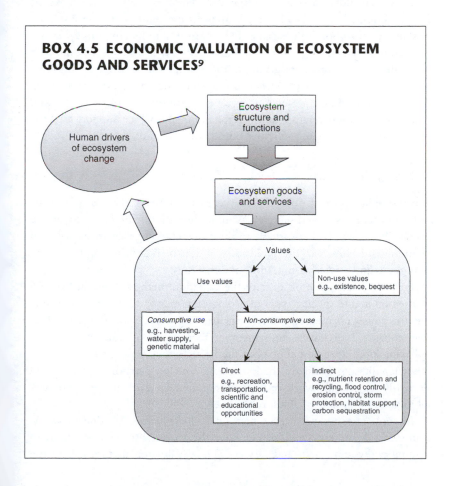

they can be used to inform policy makers about the costs and benefits of the human drivers of ecosystem change, as outlined in the example of wetland conversion discussed previously.

As indicated in Box 4.5, there are a number of different ways in which humans benefit from, or value, ecosystem goods and services. The first distinction is between the *use values* as opposed to *non-use values* arising from these goods and services. Typically, use values involve some human "interaction" with the environment whereas non-use values do not, as they represent an individual valuing the pure "existence" of a natural habitat or ecosystem or wanting to "bequest" it to future generations. Direct use values refer to both consumptive and non-consumptive uses that involve some form of direct physical interaction with environmental goods and services, such as recreational activities, resource harvesting, drinking clean water, breathing unpolluted air and so forth. Indirect use values refer to those ecosystem services whose values can only be measured indirectly, since they are derived from supporting and protecting activities that have directly measurable values. For instance, returning to the example of wetlands, the indirect use values associated with ecosystems services include coastal protection, erosion control, flood protection, water purification, carbon sequestration, maintenance of temperature and precipitation, and habitat support for fishing, hunting and foraging activities outside the wetlands.[10]

Valuation methods

Box 4.6 indicates the various non-market methods that can be used for valuing ecosystem goods and services. As indicated, the methods employed are essentially the standard non-market valuation techniques that are available to economists.[11] However, the application of non-market valuation to ecosystem goods and services is not without difficulties.

First, the application of some of the valuation methods listed in Box 4.6 is often limited to specific types of ecological goods and services. For example, the travel cost method is used principally for those environmental values that enhance individuals' enjoyment of recreation and tourism; averting behavior models are best applied to the health effects arising from environmental pollution. Similarly, hedonic wage and property models are used primarily for assessing work-related environmental hazards and environmental impacts on property values, respectively.

In contrast, stated preference methods, which include contingent valuation methods and choice modeling, have the potential to be used widely in valuing ecosystem goods and services. These valuation methods share the

BOX 4.6 VARIOUS NON-MARKET VALUATION METHODS APPLIED TO ECOSYSTEM GOODS AND SERVICES

Valuation method	Types of value estimated	Common types of applications	Ecosystem services valued
Travel cost	Direct use	Recreation	Maintenance of beneficial species, productive ecosystems and biodiversity
Averting behavior	Direct use	Environmental impacts on human health	Pollution control and detoxification
Hedonic price	Direct and indirect use	Environmental impacts on residential property and human morbidity and mortality	Storm protection; flood mitigation; maintenance of air quality
Production function	Indirect use	Commercial and recreational fishing; agricultural systems; control of invasive species; watershed protection; damage costs avoided	Maintenance of beneficial species; maintenance of arable land and agricultural productivity; prevention of damage from erosion and siltation; groundwater recharge; drainage and natural irrigation; storm protection; flood mitigation

Replacement cost	Indirect use	Damage costs avoided; freshwater supply	Drainage and natural irrigation; storm protection; flood mitigation
Stated preference	Use and non-use	Recreation; environmental impacts on human health and residential property; damage costs avoided; existence and bequest values of preserving ecosystems	All of the above

common approach of surveying individuals who benefit from an ecological service or range of services, in the hope that analysis of these responses will provide an accurate measure of the individuals' willingness to pay for the service or services. In addition, stated preference methods can go beyond estimating the value to individuals of single and even multiple benefits of ecosystems and in some cases elicit non-use values that individuals attach to ensuring that a preserved and well-functioning system will be around for future generations to enjoy. For example, a study of mangrove-dependent coastal communities in Micronesia demonstrated through the use of contingent valuation techniques that the communities "place some value on the existence and ecosystem functions of mangroves over and above the value of mangroves' marketable products."[12] Similarly, choice modeling has the potential to elicit the relative values that individuals place on different ecosystem services. A study of wetland restoration in southern Sweden revealed through choice experiments that individuals' willingness to pay for the restoration increased if the result enhanced overall biodiversity but decreased if the restored wetlands were used mainly for the introduction of Swedish crayfish for recreational fishing.[13]

However, to implement a stated-preference study two key conditions are necessary:

1   the information must be available to describe the change in an ecosystem in terms of the goods and services that people care about, in order to place a value on those goods and services; and
2   the ecosystem change must be explained in the survey instrument in a manner that people will understand so as not to reject the valuation scenario.

For many of the specific ecosystem goods and services listed in Box 4.6, one or both of these conditions may not hold. For instance, it has proven very difficult to describe accurately through the hypothetical scenarios required by stated-preference surveys how changes in ecosystem processes and components affect ecosystem regulatory and habitat functions and thus the specific benefits arising from these functions that individuals value. If there is considerable scientific uncertainty surrounding these linkages, then not only is it difficult to construct such hypothetical scenarios but also any responses elicited from individuals from stated-preference surveys are likely to yield inaccurate measures of their willingness to pay for ecological services.[14] Valuation workshop methods may, however, help in terms of conveying information about complex ecological goods, and investigating the effects on people's values of scientific uncertainty about linkages within the system.[15]

In contrast to stated-preference methods, the advantage of production function (PF) approaches is that they depend on only the first condition, and not both conditions, holding.[16] That is, for those ecological functions where there is sufficient scientific knowledge of how these functions link to specific ecological services that support or protect economic activities, then it may be possible to employ the PF approach to value these services. The basic modeling approach underlying PF methods, also called "valuing the environment as input," is similar to determining the additional value of a change in the supply of any factor input. If changes in the structure and functions of ecosystems affect the marketed production activities of an economy, then the effects of these changes will be transmitted to individuals through the price system via changes in the costs and prices of final goods and services. This means that any resulting "improvements in the resource base or environmental quality" as a result of enhanced ecosystem services, "lower costs and prices and increase the quantities of marketed goods, leading to increases in consumers' and perhaps producers' surpluses."[17]

An adaptation of the PF methodology is required in the case where ecological regulatory and habitat functions have a protective value, through various ecological services such as storm protection, flood mitigation, prevention of erosion and siltation, pollution control and maintenance of beneficial species. In such cases, the environment may be thought of as producing a non-marketed service, such as "protection" of economic activity, property and even human lives, which benefits individuals through limiting damages. Applying PF approaches requires modeling the "production" of this protection service and estimating its value as an environmental input in terms of the expected damages avoided by individuals. However, PF methods have their own measurement issues and limitations when they are employed to value ecosystem goods and services.[18]

For instance, applying the PF method raises questions about how changes in the ecological service should be measured, whether market distortions in the final goods market are significant, and whether current changes in ecological services may affect future productivity through biological "stock effects." A common approach in the literature is to assume that an estimate of ecosystem area may be included in the "production function" of marketed output as a proxy for the ecological service input. For example, this is the standard approach adopted in coastal habitat–fishery PF models, as allowing wetland area to be a determinant of fish catch is thought by economists and ecologists to proxy some element of the productivity contribution of this important habitat function. In addition, market conditions and regulatory policies for the marketed output will influence the values imputed to the environmental input. For instance, in the previous example of coastal wetlands supporting an offshore fishery, the fishery may be subject to open access conditions. Under these conditions, profits in the fishery would be dissipated, and price would be equated to average and not marginal costs. As a consequence, producer values are zero and only consumer preferences determine the value of increased wetland area. Finally, a further measurement issue arises in the case where the ecological service supports a natural resource system, such as a fishery, forestry or a wildlife population, which is then harvested or exploited through economic activity. In such cases, the key issue is whether or not the effects on the natural resource stock or biological population of changes in the ecological service are sufficiently large that these stock effects need to be modeled explicitly. In the production function valuation literature, approaches that ignore stock effects are referred to as "static models" of environmental change on a natural resource production system, whereas approaches that take into account the intertemporal stock effects of the environmental change are referred to as "dynamic models" (see Box 4.7).

BOX 4.7 THE VALUE OF MANGROVES IN SUPPORTING NEAR-SHORE FISHERIES, THAILAND[19]

A comparison was made of the use of a static as opposed to a dynamic model to estimate the value of mangroves in Southern Thailand in supporting near-shore artisanal fisheries. These fisheries are largely open access, and nearly all the fish caught depend on the mangroves as nursery and breeding habitat. The comparative analysis confirms that by incorporating explicitly the multi-period stock effects resulting from mangrove loss, the dynamic model produces much larger estimates for the value of changes in the habitat–fishery linkages. The estimated losses in habitat–fishery support service caused by mangrove deforestation in Thailand over 1996–2004 are around three times greater for the dynamic production function approach ($708 to $987 per ha) compared to the static analysis ($246 to $297 per ha). In addition, the confidence bounds on the welfare estimates produced with the static analysis are significantly larger, suggesting that the static approach yields much more variable estimates of the welfare losses. Given that the multi-period stock effects appear to be considerable, then employing a static analysis that ignores these stock effects may seriously underestimate the habitat–fishery support service of Thailand's mangroves.

There have been some important applications of methods that combine PF with other valuation methods. A particular case is the Impact Pathway Approach to value the impacts of harmful emissions to air and water in monetary terms. This traces the emissions from known sources (such as power generation or transport), through their dispersion in the environmental media, to their impacts on human health, ecosystems and physical property. Finally these impacts are valued in money terms, using the techniques listed in Box 4.6.[20] The numbers have been calculated for several countries, including all member states of the European Union and the USA, as well as parts of China, Russia and India in a series of studies that were initiated after BGE was published. The estimated external costs are important from a policy point of view because they are used to determine air quality standards, as well as the level of charges on emissions (see Chapter 5).[21]

The difficulty of determining how changes in ecosystem structure, functions and processes influence the quantities and qualities of ecosystem service flows can prevent the application of standard non-market valuation methods to many ecosystem services. In circumstances where an ecological service is unique to a specific ecosystem and is difficult to value, economists have sometimes resorted to using the cost of replacing the service or treating the damages arising from the loss of the service as a valuation approach. For example, a number of studies that have attempted to value the storm prevention and flood mitigation services of the "natural" storm barrier function of mangrove and coral ecosystems have employed the replacement cost method by simply estimating the costs of replacing these systems by constructing physical barriers to perform the same services.[22]

The replacement cost method can provide a reliable valuation estimation for an ecological service, but only if the following conditions are met: (1) the alternative considered provides the same services; (2) the alternative compared for cost comparison is the least-cost alternative; and (3) there is substantial evidence that the service would be demanded by society if it were provided by that least-cost alternative.[23] Unfortunately, very few replacement cost studies meet all three conditions. One example that does adhere to these criteria is a study that estimates the value of using wetlands for abatement of agricultural nitrogen load on the Baltic Sea coast of Sweden.[24] The replacement value of the wetlands is defined and estimated as the difference between two cost-effective reductions of agricultural nitrogen pollution: one that uses wetlands for nitrogen abatement, and one that does not. The results show that the use of wetlands as nitrogen sinks can reduce by 30 percent the total costs of abating nitrogen pollution from agriculture in Sweden.

In general economists consider that the replacement cost approach should be used with caution, especially as it has a tendency to overestimate values.[25] A comparison of using an expected damage function approach and replacement cost method of estimating the welfare impacts of a loss of the storm protection service due to mangrove deforestation in Thailand confirms that the latter method tends to produce extremely high estimates – almost four times greater than even the largest upper-bound estimate of the expected damage function approach.[26] But the expected damage function has its own limitations, especially when households are risk-averse, and in such circumstances can be a poor proxy for the *ex ante* willingness to pay to reduce or avoid the risk from storm damages.[27]

Multiple benefits

Many environmental assets, including ecosystems, produce multiple benefits. Box 4.8 outlines the possible range of use and non-use values that may arise from the multiple benefits of an aquatic ecosystem. Although valuing all benefits is rarely necessary to assess whether the environment should be preserved, converted or exploited in some manner, usually more than one benefit needs to be assessed. In addition, there is a risk of "double counting" if you value the indirect use values and add them to the direct or non-use values of an ecosystem. How to estimate the multiple benefits arising from large-scale habitats and ecosystems is therefore becoming an increasingly important valuation issue.

One approach is simply to account for as many of the important ecosystem values necessary for determining conservation versus development tradeoffs, or whether it is worth preserving an existing ecosystem. An example of this approach is a study that estimates the benefits arising from a wide range of ecosystem services provided by the Peconic Estuary in Long Island, New York.[28] The tidal mudflats, salt marshes and seagrass (eelgrass) beds of the estuary support the shellfish and demersal fisheries. In addition, bird watching and waterfowl hunting are popular activities. Incorporating production function methods, the authors simulate the biological and food web interactions of the ecosystems to assess the marginal value per acre in terms of gains in commercial value for fish and shellfish, bird watching and waterfowl hunting. The aggregate annual benefits are estimated to be US$67 per acre for intertidal mudflats, US$338 for salt marsh and US$1,065 for seagrass across the estuary system. Using these estimates, the authors calculate the asset value per acre of protecting existing habits to be US$12,412 per acre for seagrass, US$4,291 for salt marsh and US$786 for mudflats; in comparison, the asset value of restored habitats is US$9,996 per acre for seagrass, US$3,454 for marsh and US$626 for mudflats.

A second approach is to develop integrated ecological–economic modeling to determine the complex "ecological production" underlying multiple ecosystem services.[29] For example, economic studies of large marine ecosystems have extended simple single-species or predator–prey harvesting models to consider multi-species relationships and their impacts on harvesting the commercially valuable species from the ecosystem.[30] These studies find that the non-commercial species in marine ecosystems have value because they support commercial fisheries indirectly via the effect of total diversity on the productivity of the fisheries and overall ecosystem stability. Such a modeling framework has been extended to include a second service, tourism, and show how the food web connections between fish and mammals in the marine system are essential to the provision of both commercial harvest and tourism values.[31]

BOX 4.8 MULTIPLE BENEFITS OF AN AQUATIC ECOSYSTEM

Many large-scale natural habitats and ecosystems may provide a wide range of beneficial goods and services. The following table lists a range of use and non-use values that could be associated with an aquatic ecosystem (e.g. rivers, freshwater wetlands, marine or coastal ecosystems).

USE VALUES		NON-USE VALUES
Direct Use Values	*Indirect Use Values*	*Existence Values* *Bequest Values*
• Commercial and recreational fishing • Aquaculture • Transportation • Wild resources • Potable water • Recreation • Genetic material • Scientific/educational opportunities	• Nutrient retention/ cycling • Flood control • Storm protection • Habitat function • Shoreline/river bank stabilization	• Biodiversity • Cultural heritage • Resources for future generations

Integrated ecological–economic modeling has also been used for terrestrial habitats, ecosystems and landscapes. Box 4.9 describes an example of how such modeling of multiple environmental benefits informs the choice among three different land-use choices for the Willamette River Basin in Central Oregon of the United States.

However, a word of caution: integrated ecological–economic models may lead to better predictions of how changes in an ecosystem can influence the flow of ecosystem services, yet the result may not always matter to environmental policy. A good example is an integrated model of Yellowstone Lake to show how the predictive risks to native cutthroat trout valued by

BOX 4.9 WILLAMETTE BASIN, OREGON, UNITED STATES

An integrated ecological–economic modeling combined with economic valuation was used to analyze land-use options in the Willamette Basin, which covers nearly 30,000 km² in central Oregon.[32] The modeling shows how three different land-use scenarios for the Willamette Basin affect hydrological services (water quality and storm peak mitigation), soil conservation, carbon sequestration, biodiversity conservation and the value of several marketed commodities (agricultural crop products, timber harvest and rural residential housing). Both the baseline and development scenarios generate higher net present value (NPV) over 1990 to 2050 in terms of rural residential housing, timber production and agricultural crops (US$15.26 billion and US$15.27 billion, respectively) than the conservation scenario (US$14.78 billion). However, by 2050 the latter scenario clearly conserves more biodiversity, and thus provides more ecosystem services, than the other two landscape scenarios. The net present value of carbon sequestration from 1990 to 2050 is especially large under the conservation scenario (US$1.6 billion) compared to the baseline and development scenarios (US$0.9 billion and US$0.8 billion, respectively). In fact, if these carbon sequestration values are added to the NPV of marketed commodities, then this scenario generates the most monetary value over 1990 to 2050. This leads the authors to conclude that "if markets for carbon sequestration emerge, payments for sequestered carbon may make it more profitable for landowners to choose [land uses] favoring conservation."

anglers is affected by the introduction of the exotic lake trout invader.[33] Although the integrated model represents ecological changes more accurately, the authors find little difference between the net present value of benefits for the best and worst case scenarios for cutthroat populations. In addition, valuation experiments that elicit preferences for wildlife scenarios reveal that a park visitor cares more about improving road quality than protecting cutthroat trout. Thus, the authors conclude: "Bioeconomic integration matters for species population estimates, but does not matter to the composite visitor, which implies the policy recommendation would be the same regardless of whether one accounts for feedbacks or not: *fix the roads, forget the fish.*"

Utilizing past environmental valuation studies: an example from Europe

As economic valuation methods continue to be applied to a variety of environmental benefits, these studies become important sources for further advancing environmental valuation. One way is in improving the techniques of valuing different benefits, such as ecosystem goods and services that have not been valued previously. A second way is in using the information gained from past studies of environmental benefits to inform and enhance current efforts to value these benefits.

For instance, one of the more important non-market environmental benefits is recreation. In the case of wetlands, forests and coral reefs, enough recreational values have been estimated globally to allow *meta-analysis* of the various studies. Meta-analysis has also been conducted for the many valuation studies of outdoor recreation and recreational fishing.[34]

For example, in Europe there have been more valuation studies of woodland recreation than any other non-market ecosystem service of forests, and as Box 4.10 shows for Great Britain, recreation is usually the highest value of all forest benefits. Thus, estimating the non-market recreation values of the remaining forest landscapes in Europe could therefore prove important for assessing the type of conservation versus development tradeoffs depicted in Box 4.3. However, valuing forest recreation through stated preference and travel cost methods is an expensive undertaking. Thus economists have sought to find ways of avoiding or reducing the costs of estimating non-market recreation values of various forested landscapes by employing previous valuation studies of recreation as potentially useful sources of information for new studies.

One approach is to conduct a meta-analysis of past recreation values and see if they can transfer to the new landscape site. But this approach has its limitations, even in Europe where there are numerous past forest recreation value studies. For example, a meta-analysis of forest recreation in Europe based on studies that have applied the travel cost method covering 26 studies in nine countries since 1979 found large variation in values across these studies.[35] The analysis showed that consumer surplus ranges between €0.66 and €112 per trip, with a median of €4.52 per trip. Including explanatory variables shows that site attributes, GDP per capita and population density play a significant role in the variation in consumer surplus estimates. But how to control for these exogenous influences to make reliable transfers of such varying recreational benefits to very different forest landscapes across Europe seems to be a formidable obstacle.

One possible way of overcoming these difficulties was found by a study that combined meta-analysis of past studies of recreation in the United Kingdom to inform the use of geographical information systems (GIS) techniques within a travel cost model of recreational demand.[36] An important advantage of using GIS techniques in travel cost studies is that it allows standardization and improvement in the accuracy of measuring travel distance and duration variables, which are key determinants in estimating travel time and expenditure by individuals. The study found that the use of GIS-based measures of travel offered substantial improvement in the robustness of benefit estimates compared either to conventional straight-line or road-fitted measures, and were more reliable compared to the highly variable recreational values produced by previous stated preference studies of woodland recreation. In particular, the use of GIS allowed better measurement of journey outset location, modeling journey routing and conducting sensitivity

---

BOX 4.10 FOREST ECOSYSTEM SERVICE VALUES, GREAT BRITAIN[37]

Environmental benefit	Annual value (£million, 2002 prices)	Capitalized value (£million, 2002 prices)
Recreation	392.65	11,218
Biodiversity[a]	386.00	11,029
Landscape[b]	150.22	4,292
Carbon sequestration	93.66	2,676
Air pollution absorption	0.39	11
Total	1,022.92	29,226

Notes
[a] Public preferences and willingness to pay for the non-use biodiversity value of the remaining forest area in Great Britain, which has different biodiversity characteristics from remote coniferous forests.
[b] Public preferences and willingness to pay for forested landscapes, seen either from home or during regular journeys to and from home.

analysis on journey outset locations. In addition, the GIS information could be used effectively to model the predicted number of visitors to a particular woodland site and to test the efficiency of the resultant arrivals function in estimating future visits to other sites in the UK.

There are other ways that past recreation information can be used to improve current valuation estimates. For example, one study evaluated two previous analyses based on 1977 and 1997 national visitor surveys of recreation in 52 forests in Denmark for possible changes in preferences towards forest characteristics and travel over the 20-year period.[38] GIS techniques were also employed to account for site heterogeneity and the spatial pattern of population density and other demographic characteristics. The authors then combine the two past analyses to determine total demand for visits at each forest site, and controlling for changes in trip demand, they conduct a value transfer from 1977 to 1997. Finally, the authors use sensitivity analysis to determine whether the 20-year benefits transfer improves the estimation of the present total demand for recreation. They find that the error margins improve by 282 percent, although the average errors of the best transfer model remain at 25 percent.

Overall, these studies from Europe suggest that careful meta-analysis and transfer of recreational values estimated from past studies is most likely to be successful if confined to transferring these benefit estimates within a specific country (e.g. Denmark) or region (e.g. southern Britain) and where important forest and socioeconomic characteristics are carefully accounted for. Estimating recreational benefits based on past valuation studies, and then attempting to apply the median and average value estimates to different European forest landscapes and countries, is likely to be much less reliable.

Environmental valuation and policy choices: an example from Thailand

As illustrated in Box 4.3, perhaps the most important role of economic valuation of non-market environmental benefits is to inform conservation versus development choices. Such valuation is essential for public policy, because often the *private benefits* arising from such choices are very different from the *public benefits*. An important role for environmental valuation, then, is to show explicitly this difference, thus aiding the correct policy decision with regard to management of environmental resources. An example of economic valuation applied to mangrove land use in Thailand shows the importance of this role.

Since 1961, Thailand has lost from1,500 to 2,000 km² of coastal mangroves, or about 50–60 percent of the original area. Over 1975–96,

50–65 percent of Thailand's mangroves were lost to shrimp farm conversion alone.[39] Although declining in recent years, conversion of mangroves to shrimp farm ponds and other commercial coastal developments continue to be a major threat to Thailand's remaining mangrove areas. Thus, the choice between conserving versus developing mangroves is an important land-use policy decision in Thailand as well as many other tropical countries.

As shown in Box 4.11, when this decision is made on the basis of the private benefits of commercial shrimp farm areas compared to retaining mangroves, it looks as if the aquaculture option should be preferred. For a typical shrimp farm, the present value of commercial profits is around US$9,600 per hectare (ha), whereas the value to local communities of exploiting mangroves directly for a variety of products, such as fuelwood, timber, raw materials, honey and resins, and crabs and shellfish, is only about US$580 per ha. But this comparison of private benefits is misleading. Many of the conventional inputs used in shrimp pond operations are subsidized, below border-equivalent prices, thus increasing artificially the private returns to shrimp farming. A further problem is that intensive shrimp farming usually lasts for only a short period of time, usually five years or even less. After this period, there tends to be problems of drastic yield decline and disease; shrimp farmers then usually abandon their ponds and find a new location. Once the generous subsidies to shrimp farming are accounted for, the actual value of the private benefits of aquaculture, when discounted over the five-year period of normal operation, amount to US$1,220 per ha.

However, during their operation, intensive shrimp farming generates substantial water pollution, as the ponds are often flushed with water that is then discharged into the surrounding environment. The cost of this pollution is estimated to be around US$1,000/ha in present value terms. There is also the problem of the highly degraded state of abandoned shrimp ponds after the five-year period of their productive life. Across Thailand those areas with abandoned shrimp ponds degenerate rapidly into wasteland, since the soil becomes very acidic, compacted and too poor in quality to be used for any other productive use, such as agriculture. To rehabilitate the abandoned shrimp farm site requires treating and detoxifying the soil, replanting mangrove forests and maintaining and protecting mangrove seedlings for several years. These restoration costs are considerable, and are estimated to be US$9,318 per ha. As indicated in Box 4.11, when pollution and restoration costs are included, the *net public costs* of shrimp farming are about US$9,100 per hectare.

But there are also additional *public benefits* from mangroves beyond the direct private benefits to local communities from using the resources. Mangroves serve as nursery and breeding habitats for many species of fish

BOX 4.11 CONSERVATION VERSUS DEVELOPMENT OF MANGROVES, THAILAND[40]

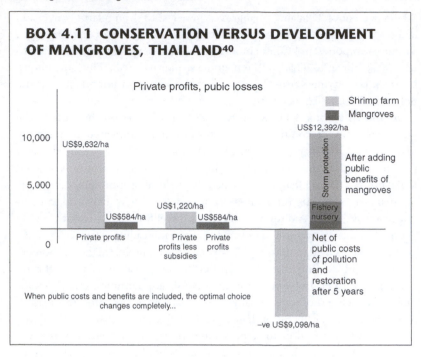

Private profits, pubic losses

When public costs and benefits are included, the optimal choice changes completely...

that are important to offshore fisheries. Mangroves also have an important role as natural "storm barriers" to periodic coastal storm events, such as wind storms, tsunamis, storm surges and typhoons. The present value of mangroves as habitat in support of fisheries is US$987 per ha, and for storm protection is US$10,821 per ha. After adding these two public benefits of mangroves their value increases to nearly US$12,400 per ha.

The Thailand mangrove case study of Box 4.11 illustrates how basing a land-use decision solely on comparing the *private benefits* of conservation versus development options is misleading. The irreversible conversion of mangroves for aquaculture results in the loss of ecological services that generate significantly large economic benefits. This loss of benefits should be taken into account in land-use decisions that lead to the widespread conversion of mangroves, but typically are ignored in private sector calculations. The high restoration costs also reflect the fact that "reversing" mangrove conversion is difficult, and should not always be considered *ex post*. Instead, before the decision to allow shrimp farming to take place, the restoration costs could be treated as one measure of the public costs of converting mangroves irreversibly, and this cost should be deducted from the estimation of the net returns to shrimp aquaculture. Other public costs that occur during the operation of the shrimp farm, such as pollution, should also be included. As the example shows, shrimp farming actually can lead to a large net public cost, whereas conserving the mangroves instead yields a substantial public benefit.

Conclusion

Assessing the non-market value of environmental goods and services is essential to getting the conservation versus development tradeoff right. Valuation is especially important given that many key environmental benefits are not marketed. These include many important services arising from ecosystem processes and functions, such as coastal protection, nutrient cycling, erosion control, water purification and carbon sequestration. In recent years, substantial progress has been made by economists working with ecologists and other natural scientists in applying environmental valuation methodologies to assess the welfare contribution of these and other important environmental benefits.

As we gain familiarity with different valuation approaches and the difficulties in applying them to value various environmental benefits, further progress will be made. It is also encouraging that, over the past 20 years since BGE was first published, environmental valuation has become more accepted as having an important role in informing policy decisions.

Most importantly, two conclusions stated in BGE concerning environmental valuation are still valid today:

1 By placing monetary values on non-marketed environmental goods and services we are at least recognizing that these benefits are *not free*. Their values should be considered alongside marketed goods and services when considering environmental management decisions. The absence of markets for environmental benefits must not be allowed to disguise this important fact.

2 By valuing environmental goods and services we are forced into a rational decision-making frame of mind. Quite simply, we are forced to think about the gains and losses, the benefits and costs of what we do with respect to the environment. If nothing else, environmental valuation over the past 20 years has made a great advance in this respect.

5

ACCOUNTING FOR THE ENVIRONMENT AND SUSTAINABILITY

In *Blueprint for a Green Economy* (BGE) we noted that standard national accounts, which produce estimates of Gross Domestic Product (GDP) and the like, are flawed to the extent that they do not allow for the relationship between economic activities and the environment. Higher levels of GDP imply more emissions and more pollution but the consequences of that pollution on well-being are not subtracted from GDP. Indeed when the higher levels of pollution make us spend more to overcome its effects, such as by double glazing our homes against noise and using eye drops to stop the irritation caused by particles in the air, any outlays associated with these "defensive" expenditures make a *positive* contribution to GDP when, arguably, they should be deducted from that aggregate measure if it is to be seen as a guide to overall well-being.

The early attempts at accounting for the environment were divided in BGE into two camps: the physical and the monetary accounts. Physical accounts provide information on flows of environmental goods and resources and pollution, as well as changes in stocks of renewable and non-renewable resources between time periods. Monetary accounts place values on the defensive expenditures and damages from pollution on the flow side and account for changes in the stocks of natural assets on the stock side, making the point that a correct measure of net national output should allow for changes in the stocks of all the resources that have some value.

Since the publication of BGE a lot has been done to improve our knowledge about the uses of the environment and how it is linked to the production of goods and services of value (see Chapter 4). What has not changed, however, is the view that environmental accounts should not be merged with the national economic accounts. If we recognize that the latter serve a different purpose from that of acting as a guide to social welfare then this separation should not matter much. Yet it remains a matter of concern to many that GDP is seen as a measure of national well-being and some policies that are enacted to increase it would not be taken if we tracked their consequences through a better measure or measures of social welfare.

One of the more recent expressions of the disillusionment of GDP as an indicator of national success came from the former President of France, Nicolas Sarkozy, who set up a high-level Commission under the chairmanship of the Noble-Prize economist, Joseph Stiglitz, to look into the adequacy of this measure. The terms of the Commission were: "to identify the limits of GDP as an indicator of economic performance and social progress, to consider additional information required for the production of a more relevant picture, to discuss how to present this information in the most appropriate way, and to check the feasibility of measurement tools proposed by the Commission."[1] The Commission started out by noting that GDP was not even a good measure of the value of production, with the quality changes of goods not being properly measured and the outputs of publically supplied goods and services being undervalued.[2] It also made an important distinction between how best to measure current well-being and how to assess sustainability. While some modifications to the way GDP is measured are justified for the reasons given above, well-being requires a different metric or set of metrics. No one indicator can pick up the complex nature of this concept. At the same time some simple changes can help design a set of indicators that provide the necessary information to guide us on how well-being is changing. These are:

a. Focus on consumption rather than income.
b. Track household consumption rather than GDP (per capita).
c. Consider both income and wealth when assessing changes in well-being.
d. Give more prominence to the distribution of income and consumption.
e. Broaden income (and consumption) measures to include non-market activities, including leisure and unpaid activities performed in the home but also track measures that look at health, education, the environment, security and social and political aspects of peoples' lives.
f. Use quality of life indicators to pick up the factors mentioned above as well as the state of inequalities in societies in a comprehensive way.

The Commission also recommends using a multiplicity of indicators for sustainability that measure changes in key economic assets that contribute to present and future well-being. A monetary indicator of sustainability such as genuine savings (see Box 5.1[3]) could be one of these indicators but it should not be the only one. Finally it recommends that environmental aspects of sustainability be tracked through a well-chosen set of physical indicators.

In some respects these recommendations reflect a lot of what has been happening in environmental and sustainability accounting. Both governments and private sector institutions are developing a range of indicators of sustainability that are widely available. Some of them have targets set, so that those responsible for the related sectors can be held to account. Nevertheless, in spite of this, and a lot of other good work in this area, there is a sense that economic policy is dominated by indicators such as GDP and a lot still needs to be done to bring these new indicators to the heart of the policy-making arena.

We view the main lines of development of environmental accounting during the last 20 years or so as coming under three headings. First, there is the work on extending the National System of Accounts (NSA) to incorporate environmental considerations. This is led by the United Nations (UN)

BOX 5.1 GENUINE SAVINGS AND ADJUSTED NET SAVINGS

Sustainability requires that the welfare of future generations is not compromised by our actions. A necessary (but possibly not sufficient) condition for ensuring this is to pass on an amount of wealth at least as large as the one we inherited. Wealth in the form of physical capital will decline only if the additions to the stock are non-negative and that in turn requires that net savings (gross savings less depreciation) not be negative. This is well known of course but the idea was extended to include natural capital by David Pearce and Giles Atkinson who started with the standard measure of net savings and then subtracted any net loss of natural assets and called this genuine savings (GS). If GS are negative one should be worried about sustainability. In its World Development Indicators, the World Bank now reports for nearly all the world economies their annual genuine savings since 1970, although this indicator is now called "adjusted net savings" (ANS).

under its program for the System of Environmental Economic Accounts (SEEA), which has been ongoing since the early 1990s and has led to a series of statistics that are useful to policy makers. Second, we have the work on monetary income and wealth accounting that tries to combine economic and environmental factors into monetary measures of sustainability. One important component of that is the World Bank's program on wealth accounting, which seeks to track changes in all forms of wealth, including that embodied in a country's natural resources. Third, there is the development of a range of sustainability indicators (mostly physical but some that include monetary elements) that pick up on different dimensions of the sustainability of current use of resources.[4]

National accounting systems and the environment

The UN has been making a major effort to provide guidance on how to construct "satellite" environmental accounts that supplement the system of national accounts.[5] On the physical side it defines the different categories of items to be included (mineral and energy resources, water, soil, timber and natural aquatic resources and inputs from renewable energy resources such as solar, wind, etc.). Asset accounts record (where appropriate) the stocks of the different resources and changes in the stock of environmental assets, while relationships between the changes in stocks and allocations of those changes to different economic activities through the physical supply and use tables (PSUT) define the physical flow accounts. The latest SEEA document carefully explains how each item is defined, and how the different "uses" are to be recorded (to whom they should be attributed), including that part of a resource that is not used in production but returned to the environment as a "residual." This residual may not take the same form as the original substance from which it was derived (e.g. the overburden from mining is the residual from mineral extraction, while emissions of particles and other air pollutants are residuals from the air and other natural resources in the production process).

These details are not exciting but it is important to get them right so we ensure the correct classifications and consistency in application across countries and over time. The result of the whole exercise is a set of "supply and use tables," which detail the quantity of each natural resource used in a given period, which sectors have used it, and where the residuals created from its use have gone. These tables can be the basis of an environmentally extended input–output (EEIO) matrix, which then also includes the flows of goods and services between sectors. Together the two can provide a powerful basis for the analysis of different policy options (see Box 5.2 where we describe the results from a recent program called EXIOPOL, for which one of the authors was a coordinator).

For the monetary accounts the guidelines explain how to value natural resources but they do not value the different polluting emissions. They also provide the basis for calculating environmental protection expenditures, both current and capital and both by the private and public sectors. Indeed some data are available for most developed countries for the last decade or so. Although incomplete, they provide useful information on which sectors are making the outlays to protect against the environmental burdens that are created, the amounts being spent and how they compare across countries. Unfortunately, to date, there are no data collected on environmental protection expenditures by households (also referred to in the literature as defensive expenditures).

Some issues arise in defining environmental expenditure. For example, how do you allocate investment in clean technology that is only partly undertaken to reduce emissions? One approach is to ask the investor how much additional cost was incurred specifically for abatement, but this is not easy to answer.[6] The Organization for Economic Cooperation and Development (OECD) and the UN have set out guidelines on how to treat such cases and some preliminary data have been reported by the OECD and Eurostat.[7] Both data sets are patchy and a lot of the information is out of date but Eurostat has assembled consistent information for most European countries. The OECD data are shown in Table 5.1; of all OECD countries only those included in the table had provided data for all categories of spending at the time the report was prepared. It is clear that a lot of countries are missing; we do not have consistent information for every year and the data are not up to date. So while it is a start, more needs to be done to provide reliable and consistent statistics. What data are available show that total expenditures are generally between 1 and 2 percent of GDP, with the public sector accounting for more than the private sector.[8] Compared to the estimated damages from environmental pollution, which we show later to be between 2 and 10 percent of GDP, these expenditures on environmental protection are notably less.

Another development in environmental accounting has been to document how much is collected in "environmental taxes."[9] Again most data are available for the EU and selected other European countries from Eurostat. Table 5.2 provides the latest figures, which show that such taxes have been more or less constant across the EU over the last decade and amounted to a little under 2 percent at the bottom end (Spain) to close to 5 cent at the top

TABLE 5.1 Pollution abatement expenditure by sector as a percentage of GDP: selected countries: latest available year

	Year of data	Total	Public sector	Business sector
Canada	2002	1.2	0.6	0.6
Korea	2003	1.4	0.6	0.8
New Zealand	2003	0.9	0.7	0.2
Belgium	2002	1.1	0.5	0.6
Czech Republic	2002	0.6	0.3	0.3
France	2002	1.3	1.1	0.2
Germany	2003	1.6	1.3	0.3
Hungary	2002	1.5	1.1	0.4
The Netherlands	2003	2.1	1.1	0.5
Poland	2004	1.5	1.0	0.5
Slovak Republic	2003	0.8	0.1	0.7
Switzerland	2003	1.1	0.7	0.4
United Kingdom	2003	0.6	0.4	0.2

Note: Only countries for which the latest data were 2002 or later have been included.

(the Netherlands). Such differences could have an effect on the quality of the environment, although the links have not been established. As a share of all taxes they accounted for between 5 and 10 percent, with the lowest being in Belgium, Iceland and France (around 5 percent) and the highest being in the Netherlands and Bulgaria (around 10 percent). As we discuss in Chapter 6, higher taxes on environmentally harmful inputs and outputs can have a major benefit in reducing the levels of pollution and damage to human health and the environment.

Monetary wealth and income accounting

Wealth accounting

An important development post-BGE has been to create wealth accounts that allow us to track how sustainable is the development of any country (see Box 5.1). In order to do this we need to construct wealth accounts that include all types of capital: physical, human, social and natural. Of course we have long had data on physical capital but there have been less available on the other forms. The World Bank has made a major effort to collect these data and constructed a measure in which human and social forms of capital are aggregated as "intangible capital." The method consists of starting with

BOX 5.2 EXIOPOL

EXIOPOL (an acronym for *Externalities, Input–Output* and *Policies*) was a project financed by the European Commission, which constructed an environmentally extended input–output database covering 43 countries individually (95 percent of the global economy) and the rest of the world (combining 150+ countries). This was derived from the supply and use tables for individual countries as explained in the text. It distinguished 129 industrial sectors and recorded 30 emitted substances as well as 80 natural resources. The structure included full trade matrices showing what goods and services as well as emissions and natural resources were transferred from one country to another. The whole database (called EXIOBASE) has been used to track imports and exports of natural resources and pollutions from Europe to the result of the world. It turns out that in general Europe is a net importer for land and water services (its imports contain more natural resources and emissions than its exports), while its imports and exports of energy and greenhouse gases are relatively close to balance.

EXIOBASE has been used to analyze specific policies. One was the impacts of changes in diets in the EU, taking account of all the trade flows and cross-sectoral impacts. Different scenarios were considered but, as an example, suppose all member states shifted to a Mediterranean diet, with the same Kcal level as the Mediterranean states. This would reduce GHG emissions by 0.9 percent, water by 3 percent and energy by 0.8 percent within the EU. At the same time employment would decline by 2.6 percent and GDP would fall by 0.3 percent. The rest of the world would be little affected, but there would be very small increases in all the emissions and natural resources. Health improvements are not recorded.

Other examples of the application of EXIOBASE include: scrappage subsidies for old cars, a directive to improve energy performance of buildings and tracking the impacts of different growth paths in terms of key aggregate indicators.

Source: <http://www.feem-project.net/exiopol/>

TABLE 5.2 Environmental taxes as a percentage of GDP and as a percentage of all taxes

Country	1998	2009	2009 as % of all taxes	Country	1998	2009	2009 as % of all taxes
Belgium	2.44	2.03	4.66	Hungary	3.31	2.62	6.64
Bulgaria	2.27	3.03	10.48	Malta	3.93	3.34	9.77
Czech Rep.	2.42	2.49	7.23	Netherlands	3.83	3.98	10.42
Denmark	5.27	4.79	9.97	Austria	2.31	2.43	5.69
Germany	2.12	2.26	5.69	Poland	1.85	2.56	8.05
Estonia	1.95	2.98	8.31	Portugal	3.38	2.5	8.07
Ireland	2.99	2.37	8.39	Romania	3.07	1.88	6.99
Greece	2.9	1.98	6.52	Slovenia	5.08	3.56	9.47
Spain	2.28	1.63	5.35	Slovakia	1.92	1.94	6.76
France	2.69	2.09	5.04	Finland	3.32	2.66	6.17
Italy	3.29	2.62	6.08	Sweden	2.98	2.82	6.02
Cyprus	2.52	2.89	8.23	UK	3.08	2.59	7.44
Latvia	3.03	2.32	8.69	Iceland	3.33	1.55	4.60
Lithuania	2.54	2.05	6.98	Norway	4.09	2.7	6.53
Luxembourg	2.93	2.45	6.61				

Source: Eurostat: <http://epp.eurostat.ec.europa.eu/portal/page/portal/environment/data/main_tables>

estimates of physical capital, adding to them the value of urban land (based on the value of assets located on that land) and subtracting any net foreign debts. To this is added the value of natural capital, which consists of agricultural land, sub-soil assets, forest resources and protected areas. The whole exercise is now done regularly for more than 150 countries.

The valuation of the different components is complicated and requires a number of assumptions. Agricultural land and sub-soil assets are valued as the discounted present value of expected rents from the land. This of course requires some assumptions about the future prices and productivity of these assets, which in turn is based on their productive potential (on the remaining stocks of sub-soil resources such as oil and on estimated yields from crop and pasture land). Forest areas are valued similarly: taking account of their current outputs as well as how sustainably they are being used, which will determine what their future outputs will be. Protected areas are valued minimally as worth at least what they would yield if they were converted to agricultural use. Finally total wealth is estimated as the present value of future sustainable consumption, given past trends and expected future growth. The remaining component (intangible wealth) is then estimated as the residual – i.e. the difference between total wealth and physical and natural capital. The results are available in the World Bank databases with supporting documents.[10]

There are gaps in this measure (e.g. biodiversity and several ecosystem services are undervalued and some resources such as fisheries are not covered). Nevertheless it represents a starting point to being able to track a nation's true wealth and sustainability, and considerable work is going on to upgrade the estimates. Even with what we have we can get a good idea whether a country is proceeding sustainably by looking at whether total wealth has been declining or not.

Figure 5.1 shows the progress of developing countries in three regions with respect to adjusted net savings from 1977 to 2009. Whereas East Asia has consistently high values, and ones that increase from 1982 onwards, the Middle East and North Africa region has a number of years with negative GS and Sub-Saharan Africa is teetering on the edge till 1997 after which it has

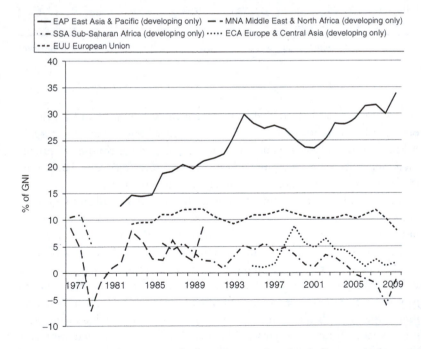

FIGURE 5.1 Regional measures of adjusted net savings (excluding particulate emission damage)
Source: World Bank, World Development Indictors (2012).

gone significantly negative. It is important to know why a particular country is suffering from negative ANS and that means going more deeply into the calculations. In the case of the Middle East it is a case of running down of assets like oil stocks and not replacing them with other forms of physical capital. In the case of Sub-Saharan Africa it is often the result of declining agricultural yields and loss of forest resources.

Some other findings from the wealth accounting work are worth mentioning. First, the largest component of wealth is not physical or natural capital but intangible capital. In low income countries it accounts for around 60 percent of the total and in high income ones it makes up 80 percent. Second, natural capital is most important in poor countries, where it has more than a quarter of the share; in rich countries natural capital has a very small share (around 2 percent) but in value terms natural capital is often worth more than that of poor countries. Third, genuine savings are often a problem in countries where minerals account for a large share of total income: they find it hard to invest enough of that income to ensure sustainability.

Income accounting

At the same time as preparing wealth accounts a number of exercises have been conducted that relate to current income and how it ought to be altered to account for the environmental and social impacts that are not picked up by the national accounts. In Europe studies of national damages from environmental pollution have been carried out in several research projects; in addition the World Bank has recently led the way with a series of studies on the Costs of Environmental Degradation.[11]

Before discussing these, two developments are worth examining. First, as a bridge between wealth accounting and income accounting there has been an estimate of adjusted net domestic product (ANDP). Box 5.3[12] provides a brief introduction to this concept and its application for the USA. It shows that ANDP has tracked NDP but at a lower level and the gap between the two has been widening.

The second set of ideas that are relevant in this context are those relating to strong and weak sustainability. These were introduced and explained in some detail in BGE and have been revisited now in Chapter 3. The interpretation of sustainability that has been taken in the wealth accounts is one of weak sustainability – total wealth is an indicator of sustainability only if there is substitutability between different kinds of capital. Indeed the accounts show a decline in the *share* of natural capital over time for most countries, although this does not generally mean a decline in the *value* of capital.

BOX 5.3 ADJUSTED NET DOMESTIC PRODUCT

For most economies, the standard measure of economic progress is real per capita gross domestic product (GDP), the market value of all final goods and services produced within the economy. The problem with GDP as an economic indicator, however, is that it does not reflect changes in the capital stock underlying the production of goods and services. Since the purpose of new investment is to increase the net quantity and quality of the economy's total capital stock, or wealth, adjusting GDP for net new investment (after depreciation) would measure more accurately whether net additions to capital are occurring. In national accounts, the conventional indicator for this purpose is net domestic product (NDP), which is the GDP of the economy less any depreciation (in value terms) of previously accumulated reproducible capital stocks.

However, the total stock of economic assets should be much broader than conventional reproducible (or fixed) assets, such as roads, buildings, machinery and factories. Investments in human capital, such as education and skills training, are also essential to sustaining development. Similarly, an economy's endowment of natural resources is an important form of "natural wealth." Thus, a better indicator of an economy's progress would be an expanded measure of NDP that is "adjusted" for real depreciation in reproducible and natural capital, as well as any net additions to human capital, such as through real education expenditures in the economy.

An approximate estimate of adjusted net domestic product (ANDP) per capita can easily be constructed for many world economies from the World Bank's *World Development Indicators*, which includes consumption of fixed capital, total education expenditures, and depreciation of some natural resources, such as fossil fuels, minerals and timber. Figure 5.2 compares trends in real GDP and ANDP per capita for the United States from 1970 to 2008. Although the two measures generally follow the same long-run trend, ANDP per capita is consistently lower than GDP per capita. In addition, the gap between the two indicators has been widening. These comparisons of GDP and ANDP per capita for the United States are revealing in several respects. First, ANDP is a better indicator of whether or not current increases in an economy's real income from domestic production is leading to net additions to capital. Second, the US economy remains dependent on depreciating its mineral and energy assets. Finally, the widening gap is also caused by the failure of investments in human capital to keep up with the long-term depreciation in natural and reproducible capital in the USA.

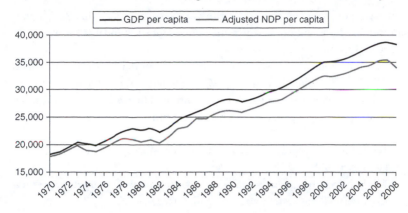

FIGURE 5.2 GDP and Adjusted NDP (constant 2000 US$) per capita, United States

Source: Barbier, E.B. 2011. "Tracking the Sputnik Economy," The Economists' Voice 8(1): art. 9. <http://www.bepress.com/ev/vol8/iss1/art9>

Nevertheless even if there was a decline in the latter, but it was accompanied by an increase in the total value of capital, some would say that the economy was following a sustainable path. This conclusion is contested by those who believe that substitutability between capital types is limited and what we need is for each type of capital (especially natural capital) to be non-declining. Moreover this is to be measured not in monetary terms but in physical units. Of course no one could expect that all forms of natural capital should remain intact for all time; hence the way in which strong sustainability is usually made operational is to set physical thresholds for different natural resources and require that these not be breached. An example of such a strong sustainability limit would be to set concentrations of greenhouse gases such that future temperature increases do not exceed 2°C.

If such limits to the loss of resources make sense, and one could argue that they do, then how do we measure the performance of an economy relative to them? One approach that has been developed is to impose a number of sustainability constraints and then use a model of the economy to see what maximum level of output would be consistent with them. This is essentially what the GREENSTAMP approach did, pioneered by a group of Dutch economists,[13] who then went on to measure this level of income, which was considered to be the sustainable level. This approach has something to commend it but the problem in practice is to determine what the constraints should be. While there may be a fair degree of agreement on some (e.g. the stabilization of global mean temperatures at a level no more that 2°C higher than today), there will not be the same agreement on standards for water, air quality and so on.

In some follow-on work carried out under a project called GREENSENSE,[14] the GREENSTAMP approach was extended to compare different approaches to sustainability accounting. The project looked at three countries: Germany, Spain and the UK and estimated:

a.   The value of the damages from air, water and solid waste pollution in 1990 and 1998.
b.   The value of the damages in 2006 if two sustainability targets were met: an "intermediate" target and a "strong" target.
c.   The costs of meeting these two sets of targets.

The different targets are described in Table 5.3.

The estimates for the three sets of costs and damages are given in Table 5.4. They show that environmental damages for the four categories included fell sharply between 1990 and 1998. This is mainly the result of improvements in air quality. By the end of the last century they amounted to between 1.6 (UK) and 4 percent (Spain) of consumption. The costs of moving to the sustainability standards are around 0.5 to 0.8 percent of consumption for the intermediate target and around 0.6 to 0.9 percent for the stronger and stricter standard. The additional benefits, on the other hand, are the difference

TABLE 5.3 Different sustainability targets

Environmental impact	Intermediate sustainability target	Strong sustainability target
Air pollution	Meet current (2000) legislation regarding emissions ceilings	Aim for the maximum technical feasible solution in terms of emissions reductions
Toxic substances	Meet concentrations standards for lead and cadmium as given in EC directives	Aim for maximum technical feasible reductions in concentrations
Waste	Attain a maximum landfill of 35% of household waste Recycle at least 25% of waste	Attain a maximum landfill of 35% of household waste Recycle at least 25% of waste
Water pollution	Meet the EC Water Framework Directive	Meet the EC Water Framework Directive

TABLE 5.4 Damages and costs of different sustainability standards

					Intermed.	Strong
			1990	1998	2006	2006
	Per capita consumption expenditure	€2000	10,910	18,563	25,313	25,313
UK	Env. damages as % of consumption	%	3.91	1.58	0.64	0.56
	Avoidance cost as % of consumption	%			0.58	0.85
	Per capita consumption expenditure	€2000	17,025	23,791	28,198	28,198
DE	Env. damages as % of consumption	%	6.62	2.50	1.31	1.25
	Avoidance cost as % of consumption	%			0.76	0.85
	Per capita consumption expenditure	€2000	10,910	18,563	25,313	25,313
ESP	Env. damages as % of consumption	%	3.91	1.58	0.64	0.56
	Avoidance cost as % of consumption	%			0.52	0.62

between damages in 1998 and the estimated damages with the standard in 2006, which turn out to be greater than the costs for all three countries and for both the standards. This would suggest that the stricter sustainability standards are justified.

The analysis just presented tries to reconcile the two approaches of weak and strong sustainability. Where we go for strict standards some people are bound to ask: what are the costs involved and are they justified? We should always be able to answer the first part of that question and sometimes we can also answer the second. When we can it makes pursuit of these standards more widely acceptable.

The other core work on income accounting related to the environment has been on measuring the costs of environmental degradation in terms that can be compared with GDP. The World Bank in particular has made a major effort to calculate these costs for a number of countries, covering impacts of poor air and water quality on health, and loss of services from forests and other ecosystems.

Figure 5.3 shows the costs for a few developing countries. We find significant differences between countries: Ghana has damages close to 10 percent whereas Peru is closer to 4 percent. In general the largest share of these damages is from health, followed by agricultural degradation. Similar results were found in studies for countries in the Middle East and North Africa, with damages ranging from a low of 2 percent in Tunisia to a high of nearly 5 percent in Egypt.[15]

These losses are significant but they are even more important when one realizes that some of these costs are often borne by the less well off in society. Another way of looking at the role of environmental resources is in terms of the "GDP of the poor," which can be taken as the part of GDP coming from agriculture, forestry and fisheries.[16] Based on this notion the degradation losses on the GDP of the poor can amount to about 16 percent GDP of the poor in India.

Environmental and sustainability indicators

This last section looks at the voluminous and growing literature on sustainability indicators, almost all of it having emerged after BGE was published.

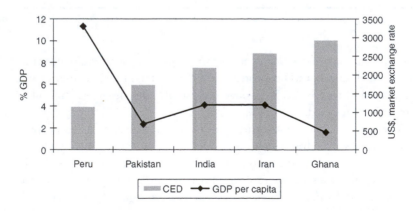

FIGURE 5.3 Costs of environmental degradation in selected developing countries

Source: Peru: Cost of Environmental Degradation, World Bank, 2006; Islamic Republic of Iran: Cost Assessment of Environmental Degradation, World Bank, 2005; Ghana: Country Environmental Analysis, World Bank, 2006; Pakistan: Country Strategic Environmental Assessment, World Bank, Volume II, 2007. India: Costs of Environmental Degradation, World Bank, 2011.

There is certainly no shortage of ideas on what we should measure when tracking sustainability of broad economic performance and almost all major institutes working in this area seem to have either a set of indicators or an aggregate measure of sustainability that they contend is better than GDP per capita. Indeed this is partly a problem: there is no set of indicators that command agreement in the way that GDP does, so comparisons across countries remain difficult and a single alternative measure has not emerged. Table 5.5 summarizes some of the key areas of research on such indicators and the resulting measures that have been derived.[17] Out of a larger set of indicators in this area we have restricted ourselves to those which specifically include something on the environment.

A few key messages emerge from this survey. First, there are now a number of sets of indicators that allow one to track progress with respect to what are clearly important constituents of a sustainability strategy. These do not offer a direct alternative to or a comparator for GDP-based measures but they provide a lot of useful information. On the environment side we have the Core Indicators collected by the European Environment Agency (EEA) and the European Benchmark Indicators, and with wider coverage we have the EU and UN Sustainable Development Indicators. None of these attempt any kind of aggregation but provide information of the kind that the Commission set up by former President Sarkozy and led by Professor Stiglitz recommended.

Second, we also have a multiplicity of aggregate indicators, some covering only the environment and some covering all aspects of sustainability. On the environment side there is the Ecological Footprint and the Natural Capital Index. As far as indicators with wider coverage are concerned we have identified eight: the Canadian Index of Wellbeing, the Human Development Index, the Index of Individual Living Conditions, the Genuine Progress Indicator, the Happy Planet Index, the Japan for Sustainability Indicator, the Index of Sustainable Economic Welfare and the FEEM Sustainability Index.

The environmental aggregates provide valuable information on the sustainability of different policies. As far as the wider indicators are concerned we can divide them into those that basically modify the GDP measure and those that construct a score based on a weighted value for the individual components that cover economic, social and environmental factors.

There are two very similar GDP-based indicators: the Genuine Progress Indicator (GPI) and the Index of Sustainable Economic Welfare (ISEW). Both come up with the same message: a wider measure of sustainability income shows that there has been much less progress in the developed world

TABLE 5.5 Indicators of environmental performance and sustainability

Indicator	Main features	Comments
Canadian Index of Wellbeing (CIW)[1]	Made up of 8 quality of life domains: living standards, health of the population, its literacy and skill levels, community vitality, ecosystem health, civic engagement, how people use their time and activity in the arts and culture. These are blended into a composite index.	Between 1994 and 2008 GDP in Canada went up 34%, while the CIW only rose 11%. The main reason for the differences is that ecosystem health, use of time and activity in arts and culture all declined over this period. Also the increase in health was much smaller than that of GDP. Questions remain about how the weights are drawn up and link to sustainability is unclear.
Core Set of Indicators of the EEA[2]	Comprises 37 indicators covering 6 environmental themes: air pollution, ozone depletion, climate change, waste, water, biodiversity and terrestrial environment. Selection was based on frequency of use. Information is tracked and reported regularly.	The data on contaminated sites gives an idea of what is there: there are 250,000 sites in Europe that require clean-up, 3 million that are potentially polluting (and the number is growing) and 80,000 that have been cleaned up in the last 30 years. This is key information for planning and setting targets but does not of course make any judgment of sustainability.
European Benchmark Indicators (EBI)[3]	The EBI has been divided into two parts: (1) a socio-economic profile tracks environmental performance, and (2) an environmental profile based on the OECD Pressure–State–Response (PSR) framework is recorded. Within such themes as Air Quality and Climate Change performance is measured on the basis of environmental pressures, technology, quality and progress towards international commitments.	The individual indicator scores are not aggregated to a composite index. Components are mainly environmental and can include other indicators (e.g. the ecological footprint) and other areas (e.g. Growth and Competitiveness Index). It allows e.g. to see how a country's air quality compares with that of others and what and why a particular value of the quality index is observed (source of emissions, population density, etc.). The database is not accessible from the website so it is hard to evaluate it further or to see how the non-environmental indicators fit into the picture.

Indicator	Main features	Comments
Ecological Footprint[4]	Measures the resources we consume in production as well as the waste we generate. It does so by adding the land areas used to provide these services, giving us the footprint for any given set of production activities.	By comparing the footprint with the biocapacity of the plant (also measured in land area) and sharing that between countries it calculates the extent of ecological unsustainability as the excess of the footprint over the biocapacity. It is a useful guide to the possible overuse of resources although biocapacity may be more flexible than is assumed in some calculations.
EU Sustainable Development Indicators (SDIs)[5]	Consists of about 98 indicators grouped into 10 themes: socio-economic development, sustainable consumption, social inclusion, demographic changes, public health, climate change, sustainable transport, natural resources, global partnership and good governance.	The information is not aggregated into a single indicator. For each theme there is a headline indicator and sub-themes with more detailed indicators and the monitoring report is a detailed factual document, which serves to inform policy makers on key environmental trends.
Human[6] Development Index (HDI)	Consists of 3 dimensions: life expectancy, adult literacy and GDP per capita in purchasing power terms, on the basis that all three are key to human development.	Gives weight to important other factors, but varies little between developed countries other than because of GDP per capita (although e.g. the gap between Italy and the USA is smaller on HDI than on GDP per capita).
Index of Individual Living Conditions[7]	Based on micro data at household level it combines 7 sub-indices: income, housing, housing area, education, health, social relations and work. Each is scored from 1 to 5.	Provides useful information for different groups within society and how they compare across groups and between countries for a given group. Problems of weighting are there but one can use sub-scores to track individual components. No notion of sustainability in the scoring or targeting.

TABLE 5.5 (Continued)

Indicator	Main features	Comments
Genuine Progress Indicator (GPI)[8]	Starts with personal consumption and adjusts it for inequality. Adds in the value of non-waged work and subtracts the costs of crime, unemployment, environmental pollution, depletion of natural resources and net foreign borrowing.	While per capita GDP in the USA has risen from US$11,672 in 1950 to US$36,595 on 2004 per capita GPI has stagnated in the US$14,000 to US$15,000 range since the later 1970s. Value judgments about the inequality adjustment make the indicator inherently subjective but the results are striking and the reasons for the divergences useful for policy makers.
Happy Planet Index (HPI)[9]	HPI uses the concept of Happy Life Expectancy, which combines a measure of life satisfaction (scored 1–10) multiplied by statistical life expectancy. This is divided by land area needed to sequester the GHG emissions generated by a country in any year.	Europe comparisons show the Scandinavian countries doing best and East European countries worst. Using only the carbon footprint as indicator of input is limiting and arbitrary but the data are interesting and revealing when compared to others such as GDP per capita. Not a sustainability indicator.
Japan for Sustainability Indicator (JFS)[10]	Based on 20 headline indicators drawn from over 200 data sets covering the environment, economy, society and well-being. Each of the 4 subsets is scored separately and a single aggregate is also calculated.	Reports a decline for Japan of 19% from 41.3 in 1990 to 33.5 for 2005, a different story from per capita GDP, which has risen 21%. The details of how the different components are scored and weighted is important and while the coverage is thorough there are strong value judgments involved.
Dashboard for Sustainability[11]	The basic notion is that policy makers need a "dashboard" of indicators to steer the economy in the right direction. This information is available for the 60 indicators in the UN Council for Sustainable Development set and an	The data presented recently using the approach show countries coming out on the sustainability score pretty much as they would on a GDP per capita score (with some exceptions). The value of the data set is probably in the detailed information available for

Indicator	Main features	Comments
	aggregate is constructed based on how far a country is on a scale from the best to the worst. Covers the 4 pillars of social, environment, economic and institutional.	the 4 pillars and the individual indicators within each pillar.
Natural Capital Index (NCI)[12]	Focuses on the loss of ecosystem and the product of "quantity" and "quality." Quantity is measured in area of a given biome and quality in terms of its mean species abundance. Each is normalized relative to pristine conditions.	The calculations are made for all the biomes and for the whole planet. Globally we have seen declines over a long period and under current trends the NCI will go from a score of 95% in 1700 to 63% in 2050. The indicator covers neglected areas but addresses only one environmental issue.
Index of Sustainable Economic Welfare (ISEW)[13]	Starts with personal consumption and makes the same adjustments as GPI but also re-values public expenditures which are considered undervalued in the national accounts. Now also calculated at the regional level within a country.	The calculations show that from 1950 onwards the growth in ISEW is much less than that of GDP. In the case of e.g. Germany, GDP went up more than fourfold between 1950 and 1995, while ISEW increased only about 2.8 times. The results send a clear message but as with GPI there is a strong subjective element in the inequality adjustment.
FEEM Sustainability Index[14]	Made up of 18 indicators drawn from the economic, social and environmental themes. Each of the different components is classified at 4 levels, with a score that ranges from 0 to 1. An innovation compared to previous work is that the index is calculated for future years based on an economic world model that links the components of the index to the levels of economic activity and	The results show similar rankings of sustainability to some previous indicators, with the developed, rich countries at the top and the poorer countries, especially in Africa, at the bottom. The value added from the FEEM index is to be able to estimate values in 2020 and to see how the index will change in response to policy measures. The application by the FEEM team finds, e.g., that under a business as usual scenario

TABLE 5.5 (Continued)

Indicator	Main features	Comments
	their environmental and social impacts. This has the advantage of allowing researchers to evaluate the impacts of policies that alter the nature of economic activity, but it has the limitation of only allowing those indicators that can be modeled in a restricted economic framework. Moreover social aspects are difficult to capture in the framework.	rankings to 2020 do not change much, except for a few countries such as Spain (which declines 5 places) and Brazil (which goes up 4 places). Policies that serve to improve sustainability include reductions in GHGs, education subsidies and health subsidies. Like all such indicators one can question the weights used to construct the composite index.

1. CIW: http://ciw. ca/en/TheCanadianIndexof Wellbeing.html.
2. Core Indicators of the EEA: http://themes.eea.europa.eu/IMS/CSI
3. European Benchmark Indicators: http://www.pbl.nl/en/publications/2006/European BenchmarkIndicators
4. Ecological footprint: http://www.footprintnetwork.org/en/index.php/GFN/
5. European SDI: http://epp.eurostat.ec.europa.eu/portal/page/portal/sdi/indicators
6. HDI: http://hdr.undp.org/en/statistics/hdi/
7. Index of Individual Living Conditions: http://www.gesis.org/eusi
8. GPI: http://www.rprogress.org/sustainability_indicators/genuine_progress_indicator.htm
9. HPI: http://www.happyplanetindex.org
10. JFS: http://www.japanfs.org/en/
11. MDG Dashboard: http://esl.jrc.it/dc/dbgal_en.htm
12. NCI: http://www.globio.info/publications/128-the-natural-capital-index-framework
13. ISEW: Jackson, T. and N. McBride 2005. "Measuring Progress? A review of adjusted measures of economic welfare in Europe." Report to the European Environment Agency. Guildford: University of Surrey.
14. http://www.feem.it/getpage.aspx?id=1935&sez=Research&padre=18&sub=70&idsub=86

than GDP per capita shows. We find their evidence that GDP growth systematically overvalues the growth in sustainable income convincing. Unfortunately both the indicators have a major subjective element in how they treat inequality and not everyone would agree with the measure. Perhaps they would be more useful for policy purposes if we separated out the impacts of the different components on GDP.

The other seven indicators score different components on a non-monetary scale and clearly the question of how they weight these components is critical. We would need to have at least national (and preferably international) agreement on these weights if the indicators are to be used for official purposes; there is no such agreement and the fact that we have so many indicators shows that agreement is likely to remain elusive. As with GPI and ISEW a number of these indicators point to a markedly different performance of countries compared to GDP per capita and draw attention to important other aspects of well-being or sustainability. We also note that the link of some of them to sustainability is unclear or absent (e.g. the Happy Planet Index or the Index of Individual Living Conditions).

Conclusions

We started out by noting there was delusion in several quarters with GDP as a measure of well-being or of sustainability. On this we think everyone who knows anything about the area would agree: since GDP was never intended to serve as a measure of these goals it is not surprising that it does not do the job. At the same time as a guide to economic output it is still important and although it could be improved even in that regard, we see such changes are a separate matter. A broad consensus has emerged that environmental accounts and sustainability indicators will be presented as additional information to policy makers.

A lot has been done to make such satellite information available. The SEEA has laid out the basis for physical accounts that have now been developed to a considerable extent and the supply and use tables have fed into environmentally extended input–output tables that allow us to analyze a range of policies from a wider perspective. We also have a better idea of what is being spent on environmental protection and what is being collected from taxes on environmentally damaging activities (although these data are still incomplete). Measures have been made of the environmental losses resulting from economic activities and accounts for sustainability have been advanced through wealth accounting as well as accounting for sustainability through the costs (and benefits) of strong sustainability targets. Finally we have made a lot of progress on non-monetary environmental and sustainability indicators.

Broadly we would agree with the conclusions of the Sarkozy Commission and see the future as one in which a wide range of information of the kind being collected will allow better decisions to be made regarding the use of resources. Some of this will take the form of data sets (the dashboard analogy is prescient). But there is also room (and a need) for aggregate indicators. The problem with these is the getting agreement on what criteria should be included and weights should be used. Perhaps there is room for an international consensus-building exercise in this area.

6

PROGRESS IN PRICES AND INCENTIVES FOR ENVIRONMENTAL IMPROVEMENT

In *Blueprint for a Green Economy* (BGE) we noted the importance of using market-based instruments to prevent the overuse of environmental resources. Such resources are not infinite in supply but they tend, for various reasons, not to have a price. This results in a worse environmental quality than is desirable. As BGE explained, the mechanism by which this comes about is through a divergence between the market price of goods and services and the social costs of producing those goods and services. One cost that is not fully reflected in the market price arises through environmental damages, such as those caused by pollution or over-exploitation of natural resources. This can be rectified through the creation of markets for environmental resources or through the introduction of taxes or other charges on producers that use the resources or pollute the environment. Alternatively the public authorities can issue administrative orders requiring changes in the way that production processes impact on the environment such that the desired level of environmental quality is attained. This last approach is also referred to as "command and control."

All these approaches are said to "internalize" the environmental costs into the final prices paid. They are also consistent with the "Polluter Pays Principle," which stipulates that the costs of achieving the desired environmental standards should be borne by those responsible for creating the environmental burdens, as long as no subsidies are given to the producers in implementing the command and control regulations or in the way that market rights are allocated.[1]

BGE provided some examples of the use of charging mechanisms in countries from the Organization of Economic Cooperation and Development (OECD) as well as the application of market permits in the United States that simulated market conditions for the relevant air emissions. Since then there has been an explosion of interest in the use of such instruments and their application has expanded enormously. In this chapter we look at these developments in some detail.[2] There are five approaches to market-based instruments that are worth exploring. First is the use of taxes and charges on emissions of pollutants and on polluting activities. This includes progress in reducing subsidies to environmentally damaging activities. Second is the role of subsidies to meet certain environmental goals. Third is the use of mechanisms such as tradable permits to meet the same objectives. Fourth is the "Payment of Environmental Services" (PES), in which the beneficiary pays the polluter rather than the other way round. Finally there is the considerable growth in voluntary mechanisms such as environmental labeling that have helped promote better environmental standards. In each case there has been progress in both developed and developing countries. The latter are especially interesting as at the time of BGE there was very little use of fiscal incentives in those countries.

Taxes and charges for environmental services

Examples from developed countries

The application of charges for environmental services has been a major area of growth in the last quarter of a century. A range of pollution charges and some charges on the use of natural resources have been implemented in the more developed countries, as a national response to addressing environmental problems in an effective way. Table 6.1 summarizes the situation as of 2011 across a selection of the 34 OECD countries.[3]

Whereas when we wrote BGE only a handful of examples could be found, a wide range of tax instruments are now in use – we have identified 388 in total based on the classification used in Table 6.1. The most common applications are energy taxes and taxes on petroleum products (all 34 countries have them), followed by waste disposal levies and charges for water abstraction The motivations behind the instruments are essentially three: (1) raising revenue for public environment and related activities, (2) providing an incentive to reduce emissions and/or save on the use of natural resources, and (3) covering the costs of delivery of environment-related services (e.g. waste water collection and treatment). The most notable features of the system of charges are the following.

TABLE 6.1 Taxes and user charges related to the environment in selected OECD countries

Country	Australia	Austria	Belgium	Canada	Czech R.	Denmark	Finland	France	Germany
Emissions Charges	1	1	1	1	1	1	1	1	1
Aircraft Noise and Emissions Charge	√						√	√	√
Emissions to Water – BOD	√		√	√	√	√			
Emissions to Water – Pesticides	√		√					√	
Emissions to Water – Other	√		√		√	√			
Emissions to Air – NOx	√		√	√	√	√		√	
Emissions to Air – Particles/ Dust	√			√	√			√	
Emissions to Air – SOx, Sulfur	√			√	√	√		√	
Emissions to Air – Other	√			√	√			√	
Carbon Tax	√			√		√	√		
Energy Tax for Fossil Energy/ Electricity		√	√			√	√	√	√
Solid Waste Disposal to Landfill Fee	√	√	√	√	√	√	√	√	√
Ozone Depleting Susbtances Levy	√				√	√			
Manure Tax			√						
Product Charges									
Green Vehicle Tax Differentiation	√		√	√	√	√	√	√	√
Excise Taxes on Petroleum Products	√	√	√	√	√	√	√	√	√
Oil Recycling/Treatment Levy	√			√			√		
Levies on Pesticides				√		√	√		
Levies on Fertilizers						√			
Collection/Disposal of Batteries		√	√	√		√			
Collection/Disposal of Electric/ Electronic Products				√					
Levies on Plastic Products			√				√		√
Levies on Aluminum Sheets & Strips			√						√
Levies on Disposal Cameras			√						
Levies on Paints, Inks & Solvents			√	√		√			
Levies on Tires				√			√	√	
Levies on Collection & Disposal of Vehicles							√	√	

Italy	Japan	Korea	Mexico	N'lands	Norway	Poland	Portugal	Slovak R.	Slovenia	Spain	Sweden	Switzerland	UK	USA
1	1	1	1	1	1	1	1	1	1	1	1	1	1	1
√	√				√						√	√		
		√	√	√		√		√		√				√
		√				√								
		√	√	√		√		√	√	√	√			
√					√	√		√		√	√			√
						√								√
√	√	√			√	√		√	√	√	√	√		√
		√				√		√	√	√	√	√		√
					√			√	√	√	√	√	√	
√	√	√	√	√		√	√	√	√	√	√	√	√	√
				√		√	√	√	√	√	√		√	√
√					√	√		√						√
√		√		√	√								√	√
√	√	√	√	√	√	√	√	√	√	√	√	√	√	√
√						√					√			
√		√				√	√	√			√	√		√
√		√				√	√	√	√			√		√
√		√			√	√		√	√					
								√						
														√
		√				√	√	√	√					√
									√			√	√	

TABLE 6.1 (Continued)

Country	Australia	Austria	Belgium	Canada	Czech R.	Denmark	Finland	France	Germany
Tax on Non-Deposit Containers				√		√			
Packaging Charge			√		√			√	√
User Charges									
Charges for Visits to National Parks	√		√						
Fee for Landscape & Nature Protection		√							
Hunting & Fishing Tax		√		√		√	√		
Volumetric Charge for Water Abstracted		√	√	√	√	√		√	√
Volumetric Charge for Water Disposed		√	√		√			√	√
Charge on Waste Producers Based on Quantity				√		√	√	√	
Charges for Mineral Extraction				√					
Charges for Logging or Tree Removal		√		√					
Road Pricing		√	√						

Notes

Australia	Rates vary by state. Not all states have a waste disposal fee. Emissions charges to water not levied by type of emission in all states.
Austria	Some taxes are only applied locally. Tree cutting charge applied in Vienna if no replanting is done.
Belgium	Excise taxes cover coal and other fossil fuels as well. Water charge is only for groundwater Emissions to water are taxed on basis of toxicity in flanders. Waste disposal tax also applies to waste incinerated.
Canada	Taxes vary by province. Water abstraction charge varies widely by type of use.
Czech Republic	Air pollution fees vary by size of source. Abstraction charge applies to groundwater.
Denmark	Container tax is not only for non-deposit containers. Nitrogen fertilizer tax is for households only. Tax on pesticides/fertilizers includes taxes in antibiotics and growth promoters.
Germany	Taxes on products include taxes on tubes, pipes, foils etc. containing phthalates. Abstraction and wasted disposal rates vary by Länder. Tax on energy includes a special nuclear tax.
Italy	Road pricing consists of a congestion tax in Milan.
Japan	Tax on fossil energy includes a tax on coal.
Korea	Air emissions charges are only for excess emissions. Logging charges are levied on projects that caused damage to the environment including deforestation.

Italy	Japan	Korea	Mexico	N'lands	Norway	Poland	Portugal	Slovak R.	Slovenia	Spain	Sweden	Switzerland	UK	USA
		√			√							√		
√	√				√	√	√		√			√		
			√											
			√			√	√				√			√
	√	√	√	√		√			√	√		√		
√			√							√				
√	√	√					√		√		√	√		
											√		√	√
		√				√								√
√											√			

Mexico	A surcharge is imposed on petrol sold in Mexico City. Water effluent charges are imposed on effluents exceeding permissible standards.
Netherlands	Fuel/energy tax includes a tax on coal. Tax on abstraction is only for groundwater.
Norway	Taxes are also levied on some other pollutants such as tetrachloreten (PER) and trichloreten (TRI).
Poland	Forest charges are levied on premature harvesting of forests. List of air pollution charges is very comprehensive.
Slovak Republic	Air pollution charges are classified by pollutant class and are not all identifiable by chemical. The same applies to effluents to water.
Slovenia	Details of water and air effluent charges by chemical are not available.
Spain	Taxes vary by province. Effluent charges are classified by pollution unit and details by chemical. The same applies to effluents to water. Charges also levied on environmental damage caused by Department Stores and on installation of cables.
Sweden	Aircraft charges cover more than noise. Road pricing relates to a congestion tax in Stockholm. Water pollutiuon fee relates to oil spills.
Switzerland	Some taxes vary by canton. CO_2 levy is on heating and process fuels. Aircraft charges are both for emissions and noise. Sulfur is taxed via its content in heating oil and motor fuel.
United Kingdom	The carbon tax is a climate levy with different rates of carbon taxes by fuel.
United States	Taxes vary considerably by state. A timber severance tax is levied in some states. Air emissions charges are levied only in Maine.

Source: Adapted from the OECD website <http://www2.oecd.org/ecoinst/queries>

First, the environmental effects of the taxes are estimated to be positive but small (but with some notable exceptions). This is largely due to low rates at which the taxes are levied and the myriad exemptions that have been granted, on the basis of hardship, possible employment and competitiveness effects, etc. A good example of how an environmental tax becomes diluted in its effect can be seen by looking at the carbon tax (Box 6.1).

In addition, the design of the taxes has given more emphasis to revenue-raising than to the incentive effects (which would require much higher taxes in most cases). The revenues are often earmarked for specific environmental measures, so that the government can address certain environmental problems. However, revenue generation through environmental taxes is still a minor part of total government taxes (see Chapter 5). As a percentage of total tax revenue they range from a low of 0.3 percent (Portugal) to a high of 5.9 percent (the Netherlands). Energy taxes, on the other hand (which also have environmental impacts), are more significant – ranging from 3.2 to 8.4 percent of the total. Together the two taxes can add to as much as 10 percent of total tax revenue.

The incentive effects of resource charges are limited because of the way the charge is levied. For example, if a user charge is levied on water, and is paid based on the size of the house, there is little incentive to reduce water consumption, as the amount paid does not depend on the level of consumption.[4] Metering for water is still not widespread, making water charges a cost-recovery instrument rather than an incentive-based one. Charges based on amounts of waste water generated are now beginning to be introduced and some countries levy additional waste water taxes, at rates that vary considerably across countries.

For waste the same problem arises as far as incentive effects are concerned; rarely are charges related to amounts of waste generated, although variable charging is being introduced by some municipalities. There are landfill taxes on waste disposal in several countries. These may have some incentive effects as the charges paid by the municipalities encourage them to recycle and find other ways to reduce the waste generated. Rates on landfill range from €3–30 (US$4–40) per ton. A full assessment of the impact of these taxes on amounts sent to landfill sites has not been carried out but earlier studies in the USA on the "pay-by-the-bag" programs found significant reductions in the amounts generated.[5]

A handful of countries impose taxes on agricultural inputs – pesticides and fertilizers. Some, however, provide incentives for increased use by, for example, exempting them from VAT. Those countries that have imposed taxes on these inputs have seen a decline in their use (e.g. the Netherlands, Denmark).

BOX 6.1 CARBON TAXES IN DENMARK AND THE UK

Danish carbon tax

The Danish government introduced a carbon tax in 1996, with different rates for heavy and light processes and for space heating. By 2000 the taxes ranged from between US$4 and US$14 per ton of CO_2. There were, however, considerable exemptions to the taxes, with energy-intensive industries in heavy processes paying less than even the lower end of this range.

The carbon tax was recycled through four channels: employers' contributions to social security (reductions in the payroll tax); employers' contributions to pensions (reductions in the ATP); subsidies for investment in new energy-efficient technology; and a special fund for small enterprises. The Danish government reviewed the experience of the tax and came up with the following findings:

- The CO_2 reductions from the carbon tax in 2005 were estimated at around 2 percent, which is a relatively small contribution. The fact that it is so small is probably the result of significant tax reductions to energy-intensive industries (50 percent of emissions are caused by energy-intensive industries that pay only 20 percent of energy taxes). At the same time, however, another 1.8 percent reduction in CO_2 emissions was attributed to the subsidies mentioned above.
- The impacts on employment were not reported, but are estimated to be positive and small.
- The tax differentiations outlined above were considered necessary to maintain international competitiveness in the energy-intensive sectors.
- The administrative costs of the tax to companies amounted to 1–2 percent of the revenue, but the costs of applying for the subsidies were around 3–9 percent of the amount of the subsidies.

UK climate levy

In April 2001, the UK introduced a tax on businesses called the Climate Change Levy (CCL). The CCL was an approximation to a carbon tax in one sector of the economy, but also had aspects of an energy tax.

The levy applied to industry, commerce, agriculture and the public sector, via their energy bills. The transport and domestic sectors were exempt, as were very small businesses. The rates of the levy amounted to around US$1.7 per ton of CO_2 from gas and US$3.8 per ton of CO_2 from coal. Typically, observers estimate that the levy added between 10 percent and 15 percent onto most industry energy bills. The government offered a reduction of 80 percent of the levy to organizations that entered into an agreement to meet strict energy-efficiency targets. These agreements were called "Climate Change Agreements" (CCAs). CCAs were only available to industrial sites covered by Integrated Pollution Prevention and Control Agreements.

The CCL was designed to be "revenue-neutral" for the government. The government returned to industry and commerce an amount of money that matched the amount that the government collected through the levy, in three ways: (1) a reduction in the rate paid by employers of a payroll tax called "National Insurance" (the majority was returned this way), (2) a fund for energy efficiency, and (3) a scheme of reductions in company tax.

It would need a sophisticated analysis of the levy to really determine its impacts and this has not been carried out. Before the above changes to electricity prices, the government's Regulatory Impact Assessment projected that the levy would save 5 MtC a year by 2010, with 2.5 MtC coming from the negotiated agreements. But an *ex post* study indicates a reduction of around 1 MtC was achieved.

In 2001, the Association for the Conservation of Energy evaluated the CCAs that industrial trade associations had negotiated with the government for 14 sectors of industry. It concluded that the CCAs were too lenient on industry. One reason for this was because the level of energy-efficiency improvements that had been agreed was too low. The Association for the Conservation of Energy's figures indicate that the agreements may have given the affected sectors of industry an 80 percent rebate on the levy in return for little improvement in energy intensity, or none at all, over improvements that would have occurred without the agreements.

Taxes on products for environmental reasons are growing in popularity (most have been introduced since the late 1990s). The purpose is mainly to defray the costs of disposal of the products, including, in some cases, handling illegal disposal. Incentives to avoid improper disposal and to recycle are provided by "Take Back Schemes" and "Deposit Refund Schemes," which are used for batteries, disposable containers, lamp bulbs, refrigerators and some kinds of packaging. In earlier US studies these instruments have been found to reduce the amounts of waste and the costs of waste management significantly.

Overall, therefore, environmental taxes have not had strong incentive effects, but case studies carried out showed that they can have an important impact and even a small tax can have an awareness effect, which is hard to measure but which may, nevertheless, be quite real.

Examples from developing countries

There are fewer cases of environmental charges in developing countries. Like the developed world, taxes on petroleum products are very common but everywhere these are mainly driven by a desire to raise revenue and not to correct for environmental damages caused. The use of resource charges to cover the costs of providing water supply and sewerage services and decent waste disposal is limited by the ability of households to pay for these services. Hence an element of subsidy is often needed. At the same time, poor households often pay exorbitant amounts for commodities such as water from private vendors and the failure of supply from municipal sources is partly an institutional failure of pricing the service correctly and using the funds efficiently to provide the promised service.[6]

In general the argument that taxes to correct for underpricing of environmental services are more of a burden on the poor than the rich is overstated. This rationale has been invoked to keep fuel taxes low and even to subsidize the use of some energy products in developing countries. A recent study has looked at the taxation of fuels in Eastern and Southern Africa.[7] In general countries in this region have relatively high taxes on fuels (with the exception of a few oil exporting countries). Recently, however, some of them have being subsidizing fuels to cushion the effects of increases in international oil prices. In Mozambique the government decided to subsidize petroleum prices in 2008 and in Ethiopia the government has systematically kept fuel prices down. This has resulted in a situation where some petroleum products like kerosene are sold below cost.

An analysis of the distributional effects of fuel taxes on transport needs to look at the impacts of such taxes on both private and public transport. As far as private transport is concerned fuel taxes in developing countries are highly progressive: the upper income deciles spend much more of their income on private transport than the lower deciles. In the case of public transport the highest income shares are among the middle income classes so the pattern is not quite so progressive, but taken together expenditure on transport is slightly progressive in these countries. Moreover this progressivity remains even if one includes expenditure on kerosene. Thus the argument for a subsidy on fuels on distributional grounds is not justified.

Developing countries are also moving to adopt some of the tax instruments that have become more popular in developed countries. There is a greater awareness of the need to cover costs of provision of water supply and waste disposal services and the use of volume-based charges to achieve that goal is increasing. The goals of cost recovery and ability to pay are partly reconciled by using increasing marginal rates for supply of water and electricity so that those who use more of the service pay a higher average cost per unit.[8] Other examples of increased use of taxes and charges include the following:

* Fishing licenses sold in accordance with sustainable catch limits or export taxes to discourage overfishing generate revenues for the governments in countries such as Uganda, Namibia and Tanzania.[9]
* Taxes on plastic bags have been introduced in several countries in Eastern and Southern Africa and South Africa has introduced an incandescent light bulb levy.[10]
* In Colombia the pollution control authority (CORINARE) set a target of 50 percent reduction in organic discharges through taxes on BOD and TSS. Even though rates were not that high (around US$28/ton of BOD and US$12/ton of TSS) they had a notable impact: in the first six months of the scheme BOD discharges in the Rio Negro fell by 52 percent and TSS discharges by 16 percent.[11]
* In China pollution charges for air and water effluents were introduced as long ago as 1979 and the scheme has expanded considerably over the last 30 years. About 80 percent of funds are used to finance pollution prevention and control. The system is not ideal in that emissions are charged only if they exceed the standards and only the pollutant that most seriously violates standards is charged. It has been estimated, however, that the system has had an incentive effect: each 1 percent increase in the water pollution levy has reduced the intensity of organic water

pollution by 0.8 percent and each 1 percent air pollution levy has cut the pollution intensity of suspended particulates from industrial sources by 0.4 percent.[12]

- In the Philippines pollution in Lake Laguna, the second largest inland water body in Southeast Asia, had become a serious problem in the 1990s. To address this, the government introduced pollution charges for selected plants at two rates: a lower rate for emissions below the permissible level and a higher rate for emissions above that level. While previous attempts at managing the lake had not worked, this program resulted in an 88 percent reduction from the pilot plants over two years.[13]

- In Malaysia the growth of the palm oil industry in the 1960s and 1970s resulted in serious pollution problems as the mills discharged their waste into the waterways. The government started to address this in 1974 with a combination of command and control standards as well as a fee of MS10 (US$4) per ton of organic effluent discharged into the water for emissions within the limit. Emissions over the limit were charged at MS100 (US$40) per ton. The combined measures reduced the problem within a single year: effluents per mill fell from 220 tons to 125 tons. Over time the higher charge was abandoned and the limits became mandatory. No one has analyzed how much the success of the program was due to the fees and how much to the legally imposed standards but the combination certainly worked and the costs of compliance were not a deterrent to the palm oil industry in this competitive sector.

- South Africa introduced in 2010 a CO_2 tax on emissions from new vehicles at €7.45 per gram CO_2/km for CO_2 emissions above 120 g CO_2/km. The tax can be seen as a means of encouraging the purchase of low-emitting vehicles not dissimilar to taxes on vehicles in developed countries.[14]

The reduction of environmentally damaging subsidies

One area where we have not made much progress is in reducing subsidies that are environmentally damaging. This is particularly true of energy subsidies, many of which apply to fossil fuels and which result in increased emissions of harmful local pollutants, more greenhouse gases and a general misallocation of resources (see, for example, Box 3.5). Even subsidies to renewable energy have been questioned in terms of their environmental impacts. The Global Subsidies Initiative, for example, documents the significant nitrate runoff from biofuel subsidies in the USA.[15]

Estimates of the magnitude of fossil fuel subsidies are difficult, but globally, fossil fuel consumption subsidies amounted to US$557 billion in 2008 (see Box 3.5).[16] Production subsidies accounted for an additional US$100 billion. Together, these subsidies account for roughly 1 percent of world GDP. Removal of such perverse incentives would therefore boost energy savings substantially. For example, phasing out all fossil fuel consumption and production subsidies by 2020 could result in a 5.8 percent reduction in global primary energy demand and a 6.9 percent fall in greenhouse gas emissions, and would save around 1 percent in global GDP.

Yet, despite these considerable economic and environmental benefits of removing fossil fuel subsidies, these and many other harmful subsidies in agriculture, water, transport and other key economic sectors remain in place throughout the world. As explained in Chapter 3, vested political interests and transaction costs are a major reason for this policy intransigence. Overcoming such obstacles remains an important objective, if we are to achieve a truly greener world economy that is both more efficient and less environmentally damaging.

Environmentally motivated subsidies

In addition to the various charge schemes, there are also many environmentally motivated subsidies. It is difficult to keep track of these subsidies, as the level of reporting is very uneven. Nevertheless Table 6.2 provides some indication of the subsidy schemes in operation in OECD countries.[17] From the 30 countries that provide data, there are 245 schemes, divided into the following three categories:[18]

- tax credits and rebates of various kinds,
- grants and subsidies, and
- feed-in tariffs or renewable portfolio standard for renewable energy.[19]

Not included in Table 6.2 are three types of subsides that are pretty well universal: for research and development in cleaner technologies, for public transport, and for information and awareness-raising.

Feed-in tariffs or renewable portfolio standards

Of the categories considered in Table 6.2 the most common are the feed-in tariffs (FITs) or Renewable Portfolio Standards (RPS) for renewable energy. Not only do 25 of the 34 OECD countries have them but they are also used in 17 other countries, ranging as widely in their economic development as China and Brazil at one end and Mongolia at the other. Although they are very popular, it is not clear that they offer the most effective way of achieving a reduction in carbon and other polluting emissions. As has been noted by those working in this area the ideal solution to addressing the environmental problems associated with energy generation is to tax the damages caused by the emissions at the same time as subsidizing research and development to the extent that there are spillover benefits from this activity. A modest subsidy to generation from renewable sources such as wind and solar is also justified to the extent that there are some gains from "learning by doing."[20] In practice governments find it difficult if not impossible to tax emissions (or to impose an equivalent effective cap on emissions) at the marginal damage they cause and there is a need to rely on other instruments. In this context policies such as feed-in tariffs do provide a means of reducing fossil-fuel based generation. But the benefits of this depend on what is being replaced (coal is better than gas). Furthermore, with government subsidies used to pay the FITs or subsidize the producers of renewable electricity in an RPS scheme, the price of energy does not rise, reducing any incentives for conservation[21] that a price increase would imply. In general the evidence shows that FITs have been more effective than RPS in terms of cost, and they provide more incentives for the less proven technologies but both schemes can place a burden on the public budget, which creates welfare costs of its own.

Subsidies for energy efficiency

The other area where subsidies are widespread is to encourage the adoption of energy-efficient appliances among households. Most developed countries have some such schemes and spend quite a lot on them. Indeed there is a very wide range of such subsidies, ranging from support for passive housing to home insulation and installation of solar water heaters to subsidies for the purchase of more energy-efficient consumer durables. Yet their cost-effectiveness remains in question, principally due to two effects: the energy paradox and the rebound effect. The energy paradox arises from the fact that despite the obvious appeal of energy-efficiency investments, empirical evidence suggests that many consumers overlook opportunities for making such investments and reducing their energy bills now and in the future. A possible explanation for this phenomenon includes high discount rates, a lack of information about the energy performance of appliances and durables, liquidity constraints, and skepticism about the energy savings estimated by "official"

TABLE 6.2 Instruments used to provide environmentally motivated subsidies in selected OECD countries

Country	Australia	Belgium	Canada	Chile
Tax Discounts				
Tax Discount when Investing in Pollution Abatement	1			
Rebates for Mining Site Rehabilitation	1			
Donations to Environmental NGOs Tax Deductible	1	1	1	
Tax Discount for Home Insulation, Energy Efficiency		1	1	
Tax Discount for Renewable Energy/Energy Saving		1	1	
Tax Discount for Cleaner Vehicles		1	1	
Tax Discount for Biofuels			1	
Tax Credits to Travellers for Public Transport			1	
Tax Discounts for Environmentally Sensitive Areas			1	
Tax Discount on CO_2 Tax for Lower Emissions				
Grants/Soft Loans				
Grants/Soft Loans for Recycling	1		1	
Subsidies for Nature Conservation		1	1	
Subsidies for Environmental Elements in Agriculture		1	1	1
Subsidies to Industry/Gov. for Environmental Improvements		1	1	1
Subsidies to Industry/Gov. for Renewable Energy/GHG Reduction				1
Subsidies for Remediation of Contaminated Soils/Sites		1		
Subsidies for Water Infrastructure/Management		1	1	1
Subsidies for Waste Management		1	1	
Subsidies for Cleaner Vehicles/Cleaner Fuels			1	1
Household Energy Efficiency/Renewable Energy Subsidies		1	1	1
Subsidies for Soundproofing & Other Environmental Goals		1		
Subsidy for Energy Efficiency in Public Sector		1	1	
Subsidy for Water Saving Devices			1	
Subsidies for Forest Management	1			
Tariff Subsidies for Renewable Electricity				
Subsidy via Guaranteed Purchase Price (FIT or RPS)	1	1	1	1

Source: Adapted from the OECD website <http://www2.oecd.org/ecoinst/queries>

Czech R.	Denmark	Finland	Israel	Italy	Japan	Korea	Lux'burg	N'lands	Poland	Slovenia	Spain	Sweden	Switzerland	Turkey	UK	USA
		1		1	1	1	1	1			1					1
1			1													
1																1
1				1							1		1			
1		1	1	1			1				1		1		1	1
		1		1							1					1
		1									1					1
				1							1					
1		1						1								1
	1	1														
1						1		1								1
1	1	1					1	1				1	1		1	1
1	1	1		1		1	1	1			1	1	1		1	1
1	1	1	1		1	1	1	1	1	1		1	1	1	1	1
1	1			1	1	1	1	1	1	1		1	1		1	1
1								1					1			
1		1	1								1	1	1			1
1											1		1		1	1
	1	1	1	1	1							1		1	1	1
1	1	1		1		1	1	1	1	1			1		1	1
1								1					1			
1																1
1															1	
	1	1						1				1	1			
1	1	1	1	1		1	1	1		1	1		1	1	1	1

engineering approaches. These issues were noted in BGE over 20 years ago and they still remain largely unresolved.[22]

The rebound effect results from the fact that energy-efficiency improvements result in lower costs and consumer prices and therefore increase consumption. This can arise directly (the lower price increases the demand for energy), or indirectly (the change increases the demand for other goods that use energy). A recent review of this issue[23] concludes that the econometric evidence on the topic has considerable limitations, but it does, nevertheless, indicate that such effects can be substantial, especially for technology changes in the transport sector, where the rebound effect of a 100 percent increase in efficiency (which would halve energy use from an activity) would be to increase energy demand by around 22 percent. Less confidence is expressed in estimates of the rebound effect on energy in the case of space heating and even less for space cooling and other devices. In all cases, however, some rebound effect is found to exist. Issues that are often missing in studies that have estimated the effects include: (1) not accounting sufficiently for the capital costs of measures that allow the user to take advantage of the lower energy costs, and (2) not allowing for the time costs involved in making the transition.

For both these reasons one has to be wary of subsidy schemes that promote energy efficiency through subsidies to households and even to firms. This is not to say that such programs can never be successful but they need to be examined carefully and also need to be accompanied by programs on information that are based on known knowledge gaps. Greater importance needs to be given to social and psychological factors that influence purchasing decisions than has been the case in the past.

Subsidies have unintended consequences

Finally we note that subsidies can have negative side effects that are not taken into account when they are designed. We have already remarked on the fact that reducing the cost of a subsidized good reduces its price, which results in more use being made of it. This applies not only to energy but also to water and waste disposal services, where the greater demand under subsidized conditions generates more environmental burdens. Other examples of unintended consequences include:[24]

- Biofuel subsidies that increase nitrate pollution and increase the international price of staple foods, with negative implications for poor households in developing countries.

- FITs for wind are offered irrespective of where the turbines are located. This can favor high wind areas remote from transmission lines, with the result that more lines are constructed increasing environmental pressures.
- Grants for clean coal technologies have increased the demand for coal, including that with a high ash and sulfur content.
- Irish and EU subsidies for peat-fired power plants resulted in destruction of peat bogs and questionable CO_2 savings.

In addition to these examples two other important factors need to be taken into consideration. First, one has to remember that subsidies have to be paid from public funds and there is a welfare cost in raising such funds. Even if the subsidy takes the form of a tax rebate, there is a potential loss of public revenue that has to be made good from some other source given a constant level of public expenditure. Second, subsidies create a rent that is captured by some sections of society and that makes it difficult to eliminate later when the original justification no longer holds. For all these reasons the sound advice remains that it is better to avoid, whenever possible, the use of subsidies to correct for environmental damages.

Tradable permit schemes

An alternative to taxing harmful emissions is to put a cap on the amount of emissions that are permitted and allocate these to the emitters. They are then able to trade them – buy some if their allocation is less than their need or sell them if the opposite is the case. Because different polluters have different costs of abatement such a scheme is a cost-effective way of achieving a given reduction in emissions. In BGE we discussed the potential role of this instrument and even then there were some examples of its application at the local level in the United States. Since then tradable permits have been used a lot more. Particularly important cases are the sulfur trading scheme in the USA, the EU emission trading scheme and the use of banking and biodiversity credits to compensate for damages caused by the loss of biodiversity when undertaking infrastructure development. We examine each of these but before doing so let us consider the comparative advantage of taxes and tradable permits.

Taxes or tradable permits?

The question of which is a better way of getting to a desirable level of emission control – taxes or tradable permits – has been discussed at length.

Under perfect certainty about the costs of abatement and damages the two should be equivalent. But because that is not the case taxes and permits have different consequences in practice. In particular if we use a tax the resulting reduction in emissions is uncertain whereas if we use a permit scheme the resulting costs to emitters are uncertain.[25]

In the context of achieving a reduction in global carbon emissions, experience with the European emissions trading scheme has been mixed (see below) and the need to engage the USA and other large emitters and fast-growing countries has led some economists to suggest a global carbon tax as a possible way around the impasse.[26]

A recent study has examined how uncertain abatement costs and uncertain climate sensitivity (which ultimately reflects on climate damages) affect optimal choices when a stabilization target is imposed through a tax instrument and compared it to the case when a tradable permit scheme is adopted.[27] While the presence of uncertain abatement costs pushes risk-adverse individuals to prefer the price instrument, the randomness of climate damages introduces an opposite bias towards the quantity instrument. The paper analyzes how these two competing forces combine and comments on the resulting optimal policy choices for a risk-adverse individual. Results show that uncertainty leads to GDP and consumption with higher means and lower variances under the price instrument than under the quantity instrument. In this sense the tax instrument stochastically dominates the quantity instrument with respect to GDP and consumption. It is particularly interesting that this result is not reversed when uncertainty on climate damages is introduced into the model. Emissions on the other hand are of course constant under the cap-and-trade scenario, while they adjust to random differences in abatement costs under the carbon tax scenario, not necessarily satisfying the limits sought by a stabilization target.

Thus while the tax option dominates with respect to GDP and consumption, it does less well with respect to achieving emissions reduction targets. The costs of not achieving the emissions targets, however, do not turn out to be that high: even in the case of higher than expected climate damages, the penalty for non-compliance to the environmental target is relatively small when carbon taxes are very high as in the stringent stabilization scenario considered here. This stems from the fact that one of the results of greatly reducing carbon emissions is precisely that of hedging against worse than expected climate change consequences by keeping carbon concentrations under control. Inter-temporal discounting further reduces the cost of slightly missing the environmental target. These issues, together, make the penalty rather small. Energy research and development investments appear to be higher under the tax scenario but to display higher variance under the cap-and-trade scenario.

Finally, investments in renewables for electricity generation show a higher mean and variance under the quantity instrument although the difference with the price instrument is not large.

In the light of this discussion one would argue in favor of taxes over permits. Yet permits have some advantages. Simply because they are not a tax they have a better chance of being accepted politically in some countries. Second, permits can be allocated to existing polluters (in practice some of them usually are), so if a reduction of, say, 30 percent is required all existing polluters are issued with permits equal to 70 percent of their current emissions. Such a scheme is called grandfathering and although it has some problems of its own it results in less opposition from industry to the introduction of the controls. Lastly we note (see Box 6.1) that taxes are subject to special pleading and exemption, which make them less effective. For all these reasons the case for taxes over permits remains complex and each situation has to be evaluated in its own historical and institutional context.

We consider below three tradable permit schemes: the US sulfur trading, the EU emissions trading and the biodiversity credits schemes.

The US Acid Rain Program

As part of its Acid Rain Program the USA has had a permit trading scheme for SO_2 since 1995, when the first phase was initiated involving 445 units. This was followed by a second phase in 2000 which involved over 2000 units. The aim was to reduce SO_2 emissions by 10 million tons below 1980 levels.[28] Most allowances were allocated initially on a grandfathering basis, although some were also auctioned later. The scheme resulted in high initial prices, which fell as participants discovered abatement opportunities.

There is a strong view that emissions have declined significantly under the program. The Environmental Protection Agency (EPA) estimates that emissions would have been slightly higher in 2010 than they were in 1990 in the absence of the program and in fact SO_2 emissions declined by 8 million tons (from 17.3 to 9.3), nitrous oxide by 2.7 million tons (from 7.6 to 5), and mercury by 10 tons (from 52 to 42) over that period.[29] It is hard to know how much lower the costs of achieving these reductions through permit trading have been compared to other instruments but a comparison of the costs against the benefits in terms of less health and ecosystem damages indicates a significant net gain[30] with a benefit cost ratio of over 40. At the same time some skeptics remain, who say that direct regulations have achieved bigger reductions in the EU and other factors are also responsible for the US reductions, including low sulfur coal being more economical owing to reduced transportation costs. What is not questioned, however, is the overall benefit of making the reduction and the fact that the permit scheme did offer emitters flexibility and choice in meeting the reduction requirements.

The EU Emissions Trading Scheme (ETS)

The EU ETS derives from a directive issued in 2003, which mandated an initial three-year trading period for 2005–7, often called the pilot or trial phase, to be followed by a second five-year trading period for 2008–12 that corresponds to the First Commitment Period under the Kyoto Protocol, and subsequent post-2012 trading periods. The second trading period covered about 46 percent of all CO_2 emissions in the EU. Transport, household and agriculture are major areas that are not covered. There is extensive literature that analyzes the performance of the EU ETS,[31] which has noted three key features of the scheme: its price volatility, the level of emission trading and the impact of the allocation of permits.

The price of permits has fluctuated quite widely over the period, starting with a rapid rise at the start in 2005 and more or less a collapse in 2006. The initial high prices are common to cap-and-trade schemes and something similar was also observed in the US sulfur scheme. They reflect uncertainty in a new market, especially with regard to how abatement activity will respond to the price for permits. The collapse in 2006, however, was also partly a result of the fact that the first phase came to an end in 2007 and no carryover of permits (known as banking) was allowed. The second notable feature was the volume of trades. These were quite small initially but have been growing. The third feature was the over allocation of permits. These were made by the national authorities to the major polluters at the start of the first phase and because they were generous, many of the participating companies did not need to buy any additional permits to carry on their operations. As a consequence the emission reduction in the trial period was not higher than 2 percentage points. However, as has been noted, the primary goal during the trial period was not to achieve significant reductions but to develop the market infrastructure, which has by and large been achieved.

Probably the most difficult aspect of the market is going to be the future allocation of permits. Phase 1 allowances were distributed free of charge and some sectors, particularly power companies, enjoyed enormous windfall profits. In Phase 2, free allowances to power generators were cut more than other sectors. Phase 3 seems to be leading to greater auctioning in the power sector and protective measures to sectors at risk of "carbon leakage." Carbon leakage occurs when firms exercise the option of relocating outside the jurisdictions where emissions are regulated (possibly to developing countries). There is a growing interest in determining how big the carbon leakage problem might be and how preventive policies can be implemented. Some of the preventive policies suggested include cost-containment measures, international sectoral agreements, allocation rebates or border tax adjustments.

In summary, the ETS was a major attempt to introduce a market-based instrument to achieve an important environmental goal. The early stages had some teething problems but there has been considerable learning as well, and the expectation is that it will expand (currently the scheme has been extended to cover emissions from airlines, which is causing some international conflicts) and be an effective means of achieving the transition to a low-carbon economy in the European Union. At the same time it will never be possible to cover all CO_2 emissions through an ETS and there will always be a role for complementary instruments to deal with the rest, including possibly carbon taxes.

Biodiversity offsets

Another growing area of trading is biodiversity offsets and one important and successful application has been wetland banking.[32] The concept goes back to 1983 when the US Fish and Wildlife Service supported the establishment of "banks" where anyone who wished to drain a wetland could purchase credits from someone who had restored or created a wetland elsewhere and "deposited" it in a "wetland bank." This was found to be more effective than direct mitigation requirements from developers who were involved in wetland drainage and has been expanded significantly over the past 30 years, with support from the EPA, which has provided guidance on the establishment, use and operation of such banks. The fact that these banks have legal status has been critical to their adoption and use for many development projects. In 2004, the Society of Wetland Scientists released a position paper describing mitigation banking as a sound mechanism which can improve compensatory mitigation success and contribute to the goal of no net loss of wetlands and other aquatic resources; and in the Water Resources Development Act (WRDA) of 2007 identified mitigation banking as the preferred mechanism for offsetting unavoidable wetland impacts associated with Corps Civil Works projects. The scheme is widely regarded as a success and the number of banks has grown from 46 in 1992 to over 450 in 2005 with another 198 at the proposal stage. In its 2001 critique of compensatory mitigation, the National Research Council concluded that third-party compensatory mitigation such as these wetland banks offered a number of advantages over permittee-responsible mitigation in the fulfillment of regulatory goals. One such advantage identified by NRC is the consensus-driven, inter-agency review process used to approve banks. Another is the flexibility and cost-effectiveness of the compensating mechanism.

The idea of biodiversity offsets is expanding to other areas and countries. Habitat banking has been applied under German law since the 1990s and the Environment Bank in the UK[33] offers the possibility of habitat banking in that country. The aim is to cover a wider range of biodiversity impacts than just wetlands through the use of "conservation credits." These are based on "a series of 'metrics' as relative measures of the biodiversity value of an area identified for development." The same metrics are then used to identify other sites that can be rehabilitated. The difficulty with the extension of the scheme in this way is that biodiversity is not a commodity and there are problems of comparability between the sites being lost against the sites being used as compensation. One measure of comparability would be the monetary value of the habitats but this is not being used in this context.

Other schemes with similar objectives are also emerging outside of wetlands and are being introduced in some developing countries. The Business and Biodiversity Offsets Program is one such scheme,[34] which has pilot projects in Africa (Ghana, Madagascar and South Africa), the United States and New Zealand, involving mining companies and local municipalities that are undertaking developments with wider impacts on the local biodiversity than just wetlands. These impacts are offset through investments in rehabilitating damaged ecosystems elsewhere. The schemes involved are voluntary, which makes them less effective as instruments of conservation than if they had legal force, but they are nevertheless a start.

Payments for Environmental Services (PES)[35]

The concept behind PES

A development in economic instruments that has taken place since BGE is the use of payments for environmental services. In contrast to the polluter pays principle the idea here is that the beneficiary pays the parties whose activities are damaging the environment to modify their behavior. In practice there are frequently occasions where both parties can gain from such a transaction. A simple and not untypical example would be a river basin where the downstream area is highly urbanized and relatively wealthy and the upstream area rural and relatively poor. Farming practices upstream are damaging the source of water supply downstream and both parties can gain if payments are made to the upstream farmers to adopt less polluting agricultural methods.

In principle there is no reason why such schemes should not be adopted and they are in no way inferior to ones passed on the polluter pays principle. The difference between the two is a matter of equity, which can favor either PES or the PPP, depending on who the polluters and beneficiaries are. PES mechanisms are based on the realization that, without due compensation for the services generated by their land, landowners or other agents who use natural resources will not act in a "socially optimal" way. Such mechanisms are generally payments to land use, which attempt to internalize the benefits of ecosystems in terms of the services they offer, thus creating the missing incentives for landowners and users to maintain functioning ecosystems on their land. In addition to providing landowners and other users the right incentives to maintain a healthy ecosystem, PES schemes have the additional advantage of providing a new source of income for landowners, helping them improve their livelihoods. Finally, by selling the services provided by ecosystems, PES aim at generating resources that can be used to finance conservation projects.

Broadly speaking PES schemes have been divided into three main categories, on the basis of the type of payment mechanisms involved: voluntary contractual agreements (VCAs), public payment schemes (PPS) and trading schemes (TS). VCAs are typically between private parties, while government involvement is usually limited to enforcement of property rights and contractual agreements (although in some cases public entities may also be involved). In order for VCAs to be a viable option, and to be effective in their implementation, it is necessary that (1) there is a clear assignment of property rights, and (2) that contracts voluntarily stipulated among contracting parties are negotiable. There are few examples of VCAs, because of the nature of environmental services – which are often of a public good nature.

PPS are arrangements between the government and other entities (governmental or non-governmental agencies, community-based organizations, private companies or individuals). In these cases, the government plays a central role in determining payment levels, as well as in collecting and disbursing funds and setting priorities. In a public payment scheme, the government or a public entity can mobilize funding for compensating service providers through fees or taxes. The government may also create an institutional arrangement to provide or maintain watershed services (contracts with

NGOs or universities, mandating agencies). Changes in legislation are often needed for the implementation of PPS, such as the establishment of new water tariffs or fees, means to provide incentives to landowners, new monitoring and enforcement activities and powers, and the establishment of non-compliance fees.

TS involve the government in creating a demand for environmental and ecological services by establishing standards and targets, which provide a basis for making individual allocations that can be traded. Since we have considered tradable permits as a separate category of instrument we will not examine them much further here except to provide examples where relevant. Certainly one can look at tradable permit schemes as a form of PES as well.

International experience with PES

The main PES schemes are in the areas of watershed protection, biodiversity conservation, carbon sequestration and landscape and beauty services. There are several applications of each: a review cites 61 examples of watershed management schemes, 72 of biodiversity conservation, 75 of carbon sequestration and 50 of landscape and beauty services.[36] We consider each of these types of PES.

Markets for watershed protection

Hydrological services are among the most valuable ecosystem services – and in many cases investment in sustainable watershed management may be substantially cheaper than investing in new water supply and treatment facilities. Generally speaking, in the realm of water management PES can be most successfully implemented in maintaining water quality and water flow for drinking water and hydroelectric power generation. Such schemes work best when dealing with small watersheds where relatively small numbers of providers and beneficiaries are involved. In larger watersheds problems arise when more parties may be involved and linkages between upstream land use and downstream water impacts are weak and uncertain. The situation is further exacerbated when cross-border issues arise and the above survey of international schemes has only one example of a PES involving cross-border deals – that between Bolivia and Argentina.

Funds are usually generated through user fees to finance improved land-use management upstream – and therefore require the development of sophisticated hydrological models to link management practices with the generation of the water service, to ensure that the PES system is providing the service for which beneficiaries are paying. One of the key challenges to the maintenance of watershed services is the pressure for changing land-use patterns in the upper watershed: payments to landowners must therefore cover the opportunity cost of alternative land uses, such as agriculture.

PES schemes for protecting watersheds are increasingly substituting the more traditional approach of establishing protected areas upstream under a command and control regulatory regime. They have been implemented in the United States, Mexico, Colombia, Ecuador, Costa Rica, Honduras and Brazil. The private sector is heavily involved in these schemes (private individuals and corporations account for 60 percent of the buyers, while, among service providers it is individual landowners who are the main actors).[37] Watershed services are more often bought by those who use water as an input in their production activities, or by those who need to offset polluting discharges. The government also acts as a buyer of services as well as playing an intermediary role of setting up the legislative and regulatory requirement arrangements. Box 6.2 provides examples of PES schemes involving watersheds.[38]

Markets for biodiversity conservation

Biodiversity services provided under PES schemes include the protection of ecosystems of particular value, natural habitats, species and genetic resources. Contrary to the watershed protection case, PES schemes for biodiversity can be at a local, national or global scale – but, as in the case of watershed services, biodiversity commodities are not traded directly: instead, specific land uses that are thought to protect species, ecosystems or genetic diversity are sold. The reason is that an accepted measure of biodiversity is still lacking, with critical implications for the development of markets for such services, as they rely on proxies correlated to biodiversity.[39]

Payment for biodiversity services are often implemented as part of development projects, and involve both financial resources and non-monetary benefits such as training, technical assistance and the provision of equipment. Transfers of funds occur globally from the rich industrialized countries to the developing ones. Local payments for conservation are less common, but innovative examples are found, for instance, in Brazil, where there is a proposal for tradable reserve requirements in the Amazon.

A review identified 72 payment schemes implemented in 33 countries and involving biodiversity services, excluding PES schemes where biodiversity services are traded alongside other EES.[40] The majority, however, are quite small and experimental. Major buyers of "biodiversity conservation" are

---

BOX 6.2 EXAMPLES OF NEGOTIATED AGREEMENTS AND TRADING SCHEMES INVOLVING WATERSHEDS

Negotiated agreements: farmers have initiated negotiated agreements with upstream land users in several countries, with the aim of ensuring sustainable and sufficient water supply for irrigation. Examples include the Cauca Valley and Gubas River schemes in Colombia and the FONAG (Fondo Nacional del Agua) scheme in Ecuador. The former has led to the adoption of conservation measures in over one million hectares of land, and raises US$600,000 in revenues from water user fees. The FONAG scheme involves water users, including the municipality of Quito and a hydroelectric power utility. In Brazil, Sao Paulo's water utility has agreed to contribute 1 percent of its revenues to fund conservation and forest restoration activities in the Corumbatai watershed (Pagiola et al., 2002). In France, the deal between Vittel and dairy farmers and forest owners saw Vittel compensating farmers for adopting better land and water management practices.

In the United States, the city of New York has initiated a land acquisition program, coupled with conservation payments to farmers and forest producers to remove environmentally sensitive land from production or adopt sustainable land-use regimes (Isakson, 2002); in Brazil, municipalities in the states of Paranà and Minas Gerais receive 5 percent of the state sale tax to finance upper watershed protection activities, while in Mexico Semarnat (Secretaría de Medio Ambiente y Recursos Naturales) has initiated PES pilot projects in six watersheds.

Trading schemes: in the USA, a system of tradable effluent emission permits was set up to protect water quality, and in Australia the state of New South Wales has set up a scheme to reduce water salinity in which the State Forest earns salinity reduction credits by planting trees or other vegetative cover, and sells them to farmers downstream.

---

international or national organizations, foundations and conservation NGOs. Private actors – for instance, pharmaceutical companies – may also be involved, but it is rather difficult to estimate the value of biodiversity, and match demand with supply. Governments are generally the main suppliers, but the private sector and local communities are increasingly involved. Box 6.3 presents some examples of negotiated agreements for biodiversity conservation.[41]

BOX 6.3 EXAMPLES OF PES SCHEMES FOR BIODIVERSITY SERVICES

Negotiated agreements: in Brazil, rubber tappers receive payments for forest conservation services provided by their resource management practices, with the government directly involved in the payment scheme (Rosa et al., 2003; Payments for Environmental Services: Brazil. The Ford Foundation and Fundación PRISMA). In Guyana, Conservation International obtained from the government a conservation concession for 20,000 acres of forest. In the USA, farmers receive payments for removing sensitive land from production to prevent land degradation.

Markets for carbon sequestration

Several PES schemes focus on carbon sequestration services: active absorption of carbon through reforestation, and avoided emissions through conservation of forest cover. As in the case of biodiversity services, carbon sequestration markets may involve local, national or global actors – although the majority of the schemes are at the global level. The markets are competitive and quite well developed with falling transaction costs. The full development of carbon markets is, however, affected by uncertainty regarding the Kyoto Protocol.[42]

A review found 75 examples of payments for carbon sequestration services in 27 countries, showing that, despite the uncertainties related to the Kyoto Protocol, the market is growing fast. In fact, 20 of such schemes are registered under the Kyoto Protocol's "Activities Implemented Jointly."[43]

In terms of payment mechanisms, the markets for carbon offsets are characterized by a widespread use of less traditional approaches (such as investment funds, futures markets, etc.), with the accompanying emergence of ancillary systems, including insurance, legal and advisory services. The market for carbon offsets is increasingly dominated by the private sector, which is the largest player in demanding and supplying the service, as well as in terms of provision of ancillary services, reflecting confidence that the carbon market will continue expanding.

Another interesting feature of carbon markets is that there has been a shift from smaller, ad hoc deals, towards the establishment of large-scale trading schemes and exchange mechanisms offering trading and clearing functions for carbon offsets. Investment funds are another innovative payment mechanism, an example being the World Bank Prototype Carbon Fund, while over-the-counter trading has become increasingly popular thanks to the emergence of standardized carbon offsets. In Costa Rica, this system has been in place since 1996 as part of the clearing-house system managed by the Costa Rican Office for Joint Implementation, but it has been experimented also in the Netherlands, in Canada, Denmark and Australia.

Similar to the biodiversity services market, payments for carbon offsets are closely related to international cooperation activities, being mostly rooted in the UNFCC and related protocols that define the market. Yet, there is still little detailed guidance as to how to develop an effective carbon market. At a lower level of governance, carbon offset deals rely on cooperation between private and non-governmental entities, which help spread the risks and transaction costs associated with market development – and examples of market supporting alliances abound.[44]

There are two risks associated with PES for carbon sequestration that need to be addressed: perverse incentives may lead to natural forests being replaced by plantation forests, or to financing conservation where no deforestation would have occurred in the first place. Carbon sequestration projects must therefore be carefully defined to avoid such perverse outcomes. Examples of carbon sequestration are provided in Box 6.4.[45]

Despite this limited experience in PES involving carbon sequestration, perhaps one of the most important developments in recent years has been the

BOX 6.4 EXAMPLES OF PES INVOLVING CARBON SEQUESTRATION

Examples of PES schemes in this field include the Bioclimatic Fund established in Mexico to manage funds collected under the Scolel Té project, a carbon sequestration scheme based on agroforestry practices which involved more than 300 coffee and corn farmers planting trees on 20 percent of their land.

One of the largest forest-based carbon projects in the world is found in Bolivia, where Nature Conservancy, the Bolivian government, US-based energy companies and other NGOs developed a scheme to sequester 26 million tons of carbon over 15 years in the Noel Kempff Mercado National Park.

establishment of the nascent UN program to reduce emissions from defor-estation and forest degradation (REDD). Establishment, financing and expansion of REDD has become a priority of recent international negotiations on climate change, notably at Cancun in 2010 and Dugan in 2011. In Chapter 7, we examine the REDD initiative and its potential effectiveness as a global PES market in combating both tropical deforestation and sequestrating carbon.

Landscape services

Landscape services are associated with the aesthetic and cultural value of a specific site, and may involve the protection of cultural sanctuaries, natural heritage sites or even traditional livelihoods. The difficulties involved in valuing landscape beauty services mean that very few such schemes exist, although they are increasingly introduced within other PES schemes as an item of cultural consciousness. Markets for landscape beauty have the longest history, with the emergence of eco-tourism. Yet this market is far from the most advanced because, even though simple payment systems for scenic beauty have existed for decades, the evolution to more sophisticated mechanisms has been slow.

A review identifies around 50 examples of PES schemes for landscape beauty, but in all cases the market was found to be immature and character-ized by significant constraints, including the lack of sophisticated payment mechanisms, and the low willingness to pay for the services.[46] Most of the transactions involve site-specific negotiation by independent agencies, such as short- or long-term access agreements, entrance permits or forest manage-ment contracts. In some cases, the government has attempted to establish payment schemes at the national level (e.g. in the EU, Canada or in Nepal).

Conclusions on PES

This survey has shown how PES has grown to be an important instrument in achieving the goals of environmentally sustainable development. It is still evolving and lessons are being learnt but even now a lot has been achieved and more can be expected in the future.

The main problems remain in the areas where the services are hard to define (such as biodiversity) and where the scheme is driven more by gov-ernment aims and objectives and less by local needs. In such cases payments often do not guarantee the environmental improvements in spite of large outlays. Two major schemes in China – the Sloping Land Conversion Program (SLCP) initiated in 1999 and the Forest Ecosystem Compensation

Fund (FECF) – have not achieved their desired targets[47] largely because they were too much directed from the center and not enough account was taken of local interests or incentives to motivate behavior of the providers of the services. This can be avoided by making sure that schemes are based on full participation of all relevant parties and proper account is taken of how providers will respond to the incentives offered.

Voluntary mechanisms

The last area where major developments have taken place over the past two decades is in the use of voluntary mechanisms to promote higher environmental standards. This has undoubtedly benefitted from the greater public availability of information on environmental quality, something we noted in Chapter 2, where we commented on the importance of international conventions such as the Aarhus Convention on Access to Information, Public Participation in Decision-making and Access to Justice in Environmental Matters, which applies in Europe and Central Asia. But even in other regions of the world there has been an opening up of information about developments that affect the environment and of reporting environmental quality more openly and honestly. This is the case even in countries with weaker democratic institutions such as China and Russia. Civil society groups are increasingly active everywhere and are holding the authorities to account when standards are not met.

Perhaps the most famous example of public information being used in a public–private partnership to obtain better compliance with environmental standards was the PROPER scheme in Indonesia. The environmental authority there (BAPEDAL) was having little success in enforcing standards in discharges from industrial plants in the 1990s and there was serious concern about the environmental damages that were being caused as a result of this. The solution adopted by BAPEDAL was to introduce a program for rating individual plants according to their environmental performance and making this information public through a color-coded score. A black indicated that the plant had made no effort to control pollution, a red that that it had made some effort but that the plant was still not meeting the standard, a blue that minimum standards were being met, a green for plants that significantly exceeded national standards and a gold for plants that were attaining world-class standards in terms of clean technology, waste minimization and pollution prevention.[48]

The scheme was a notable success. When it started in early 1995 two-thirds of the 187 plants in the program did not meet national regulations.

By the end of 1996 only one plant was rated as black and non-compliant plants in total had fallen to under half. The program ran to 1998 and a careful analysis of the data shows that it was indeed responsible for most of the improvements in emissions reductions during that period.[49] There were legal difficulties in its continued implementation (some plants challenged their ratings) but there is general agreement that public disclosure improved accountability. Careful design and consultation with stakeholders were also important in its success. A similar scheme was introduced in the Philippines in 1997 and countries such as Mexico and Colombia have developed public programs to report environmental performance at the plant level. Even where such programs do not exist, the presence of well-informed civil groups acts as a strong incentive for compliance.

The other voluntary area where important developments have taken place is in product labeling. This has been a powerful force in promoting products that are environmentally more benign and most countries now have some form of green labeling scheme and a number of studies have shown that they do result in some switch in consumption to the labeled products.[50] Possibly one of the best examples of how labeling can change demand and have a positive environmental impact is organic agriculture. While there is not universal agreement on the environmental and sustainability benefits, the balance of the studies does find areas with significant gains in these respects (see Box 6.5).[51]

Conclusions

This chapter has covered a very wide field of developments since BGE: those relating to incentives to promote sustainable development, especially through prices and other market-based instruments. There has been a veritable explosion of these in the last two decades and mostly we would conclude that they have been a force for the good. The increased use of charges has brought flexibility and reduced the cost of meeting environmental standards. More could be done to raise the charges to reflect true damages and we would encourage a move in that direction. The use of subsidies remains more difficult. Environmentally damaging subsidies still contribute significantly to the environmental burdens we face and there is little indication that they are going down. The use of subsidies that are environmentally motivated has helped in some areas but they are not always a cost-effective instrument and great care is needed when introducing them. Indeed we need more research on how and when such incentives do work and what complementary measures are needed to make them work.

BOX 6.5 ORGANIC AGRICULTURE

Organic agriculture is one of the fastest growing forms of agriculture in the world. Data from the International Federation of Organic Agriculture Movements show that in 2002 the market for organic products was around US$23 billion and 24 million hectares were under organic production. By 2009 the market had risen to US$55 billion and the area had gone up to 37 million hectares. Thus although the market for organic products is around 1 percent of the food market in the EU and 1–2 percent in the USA it is rapidly growing in spite of the price premium that organic products command.

The environmental claims of organic agriculture have been subject to considerable study and while such agriculture does not meet all claims made for it (the health benefits for example are the most contested) there are gains in terms of lower nutrient inputs and absence of synthetic pesticides. Results for carbon emissions are less clear: while organic agriculture has lower emissions per hectare they are higher on a per unit output basis in some studies.

Other instruments that have grown in popularity include tradable permits and PES schemes. These have also contributed to making it easier to achieve the goals of sustainable development. There remain challenges in their application but these can be addressed and gradually we are making progress in doing so. Finally we have the very important contribution that public disclosure and product labeling have made to promote cleaner products. The role of civil society has been a major positive development and while some claims of labeled products are questionable many do make a valuable contribution to improving our lives and promoting sustainable livelihoods.

7

TOWARDS A GREEN
GLOBAL ECONOMY

Over 2008–9, the world was confronted with the worst economic crisis since the Great Depression of the 1930s. This "Great Recession" was characterized by economic imbalances and market instability. It was also preceded by a period of rapid energy and commodity price rises that has added to unease over the future of global energy and food security. Similarly, concerns over ecological scarcity have grown in recent years, and there is now widespread belief that increasing resource use, environmental degradation and carbon dependency in the world economy are precipitating damaging ecological and climatic change on a global scale. Major environmental catastrophes, such as the 2010 BP oil spill in the Gulf of Mexico and the 2011 Japan earthquake, tsunami and nuclear reactor meltdown, have raised additional questions about current global economic, energy and environmental policies. Uncertainties have been further heightened by political instability and conflict in the Middle East – the main source of global fossil fuel reserves – as well as the failure to conclude a new global climate change agreement before the Kyoto Treaty expires in 2012.

As the world economy continues its slow and shaky recovery from the 2008–9 recession, the perception is that there will be further economic, ecological and energy crises, unless these crises are tackled simultaneously. For the first time, international policy makers are seriously considering "greening" economies as the way of accomplishing this goal. For example, an important global policy response to the economic recession was the acknowledgment that measures to reduce carbon dependency and other environmental improvements could have a role in the economic recovery.[1] A report by the United Nations Environment Programme (UNEP) proposes a series of policies and investments for a long-term transition to a green global economy, with the aim of "increasing human well-being and social equity, and reducing environmental risks and ecological scarcities."[2]

The purpose of the following chapter is to explain the case for policies to enable the transition to a greener global economy. Throughout this book, we have argued that sound economic and environmental policies are essential to efficient and sustainable management of natural capital. The failure to do so undermines long-term economic welfare and human well-being. We have shown how environmental degradation and welfare losses are directly related to mismanagement of this vital source of economic wealth. The economic values and benefits generated by environmental assets are significant, and are equally as important as marketed goods and services when considering environmental management decisions.

As we have suggested, these arguments in favor of environmentally sustainable development have changed little over the two decades since *Blueprint for a Green Economy* (BGE) was published. But now, with the world facing multiple economic, environmental and energy crises, there is an even more powerful argument in support of greening economies: it may not only be necessary for the sustainable management of natural capital but also essential for sustainable *economic* development. If the imminent threats posed by climate change, energy insecurity, deteriorating ecosystems and environmental catastrophes are to be reduced significantly, then policies to improve environmental management must be broadened into a comprehensive strategy to overcome ecological scarcity and the inherent unsustainability and instability of the world economy. To develop such a long-term green economy transition requires looking further at the role of complementary pricing policies, creating global markets and devising long-term green development strategies.

The green legacy of the Great Recession

The multiple crises that continue to plague the world economy, and the failure of conventional economic policies to reduce these threats, have clearly boosted support for "greening" the global economy. As suggested by UNEP:

> This recent traction for a green economy concept has no doubt been aided by widespread disillusionment with our prevailing economic paradigm, a sense of fatigue emanating from the many concurrent

crises and market failures experienced during the very first decade of the new millennium, including especially the financial and economic crisis of 2008. But at the same time, we have seen increasing evidence of a way forward, a new economic paradigm – one in which material wealth is not delivered perforce at the expense of growing environmental risks, ecological scarcities and social disparities.[3]

From the beginning of the 2008–9 recession, UNEP has been promoting such a comprehensive global "green" economic strategy, beginning with its "Global Green New Deal" initiative (see Box 7.1).

Initially, the response of the world community seemed positive. For example, at the 24–25 September 2009 Pittsburgh Summit, the G20 leaders pledged to enhance global climate change initiatives and negotiations, improve energy security, including phasing out fossil fuel subsidies, and reduce the economic vulnerability of the world's poor.[4] By the end of 2009, several G20 economies had incorporated a sizable "green fiscal" component in their recovery spending (see Figure 7.1). Such measures included support for renewable energy, carbon capture and sequestration, energy efficiency, public transport and rail, improved electrical grid transmission and environmental protection. However, the G20 failed to instigate a worldwide "green recovery," as envisioned by the Global Green New Deal plan (Box 7.1).

Governments – almost exclusively members of the G20 – did spend over US$520 billion on green stimulus during the recession, comprising 16 percent of all fiscal spending and 0.7 percent of the G20 gross domestic product (GDP).[5] Although this sounds like quite a lot, the green spending fell short of the 1 percent of GDP recommended in the Global Green New Deal. More importantly, only a handful of economies devoted much of their total fiscal spending to green stimulus. South Korea launched a "Green New Deal" as its fiscal response to the global recession, which when supplemented by additional green stimulus spending comprised 5 percent of its GDP. China apportioned around a third of its total fiscal spending to green measures, or 3 percent of GDP. Although low-carbon investments accounted for the majority of fiscal spending by the European Union, total EU fiscal spending in general was small (US$22.8 billion), only 0.2 percent of GDP. Green stimulus amounted to just 12 percent of total fiscal stimulus of the United States and 0.9 percent of GDP.

Overall, most G20 governments were cautious in making low-carbon and other environmental investments during the 2008–9 recession, and some did not implement any green stimulus measures. Important emerging market and developed economies that did not enact any green stimulus include

BOX 7.1 UNEP'S GLOBAL GREEN NEW DEAL

On 2–3 December 2008, the United Nations Environment Programme (UNEP) convened a meeting in Geneva to instigate its "Global Green New Deal" initiative. The need for such a comprehensive global strategy seemed self-evident: in 2008, the world was confronted with multiple crises – fuel, food and financial – and by December the result was the worst economic recession since the Great Depression of the 1930s. Overcoming these crises required a package of policy measures similar to Roosevelt's New Deal, but at the global scale and embracing a wider vision. A "Global Green New Deal" (GGND) encapsulates such a timely mix of polices, which aim to stimulate economic recovery and create jobs while enhancing the livelihoods of the world's poor and lessening carbon dependency and environmental degradation. At its Governing Council in February 2009, UNEP unveiled its consultancy report on the GGND.[6] The report was the key background document for UNEP's Global Green New Deal: Policy Brief, which was released in March 2009.[7] A revised and expanded version of UNEP's GGND report was eventually published as a book.[8] The package of policy, investment and incentive measures comprising the proposed GGND had three principal objectives:

- Revive the world economy, create employment opportunities and protect vulnerable groups.
- Reduce carbon dependency, ecosystem degradation and water scarcity.
- Further the Millennium Development Goal of ending extreme world poverty.

But achieving these goals would require a commitment to global governance, especially by the world's largest and richest economies – the Group of 20 (G20).[9] Thus, the GGND recommended an expenditure of 1 percent global GDP on green initiatives over several years. The GGND argued that G20 countries should prioritize energy efficiency and clean-energy investments, and developing countries should aim to improve agricultural productivity, freshwater management and sanitation. Such investments should be accompanied by a swath of domestic and international policies – from removing perverse agricultural, fishing and energy subsidies to taxing or trading carbon emissions, instigating tax credits for low-pollution cars and other clean-energy innovations, financing the transfer of green technologies to developing countries and creating a global carbon market through climate change negotiations.

Argentina, Brazil, Greece, the Netherlands, Portugal, Russia and Switzerland. The reasons for this caution in implementing green stimulus are still difficult to discern; they ranged from skepticism about the effectiveness of the measures in delivering both jobs and environmental improvement, lack of political will, concerns about increasing government budget deficits and simple short-sightedness.[10]

However, relying on green stimulus alone is not enough to instigate a "green" recovery, let alone usher in a more sustainable world economy over the long term. Fossil fuel subsidies and other market distortions, as well as the lack of effective environmental pricing policies and regulations, will continue to diminish the impacts of G20 green stimulus investments on long-term investment and job creation in green sectors.[11] Without correcting existing market and policy distortions that underprice the use of natural resources, contribute to environmental degradation and worsen carbon dependency, public investments to stimulate clean energy and other green sectors in the economy will be short-lived. The failure to implement and coordinate green stimulus measures across all G20 economies also limits their effectiveness in "greening" the global economy.

BOX 7.2 WHAT IS A GREEN ECONOMY?[12]

UNEP defines a green economy as

> one that results in improved human well-being and social equity, while significantly reducing environmental risks and ecological scarcities. In its simplest expression, a green economy can be thought of as one which is low carbon, resource efficient and socially inclusive. In a green economy, growth in income and employment should be driven by public and private investments that reduce carbon emissions and pollution, enhance energy and resource efficiency, and prevent the loss of biodiversity and ecosystem services. These investments need to be catalysed and supported by targeted public expenditure, policy reforms and regulation changes. The development path should maintain, enhance and, where necessary, rebuild natural capital as a critical economic asset and as a source of public benefits, especially for poor people whose livelihoods and security depend on nature.

Finally, over 2008–9, the G20 devoted less effort to assisting developing economies that suffered from worsening poverty and environmental degradation as a result of the global recession. Nor did the G20 take a leadership role in facilitating negotiations towards a new global climate change agreement to replace the Kyoto Treaty that will expire in 2012.

Why a global green economy now?

Box 7.2 outlines the broad objective of a green economy, as envisioned by UNEP. There are several reasons why such a global policy initiative is urgent.

First, problems such as climate change, energy insecurity and ecological scarcity are not short term but pervasive. Unless specific policies are devised to tackle these problems, they will continue to pose a threat to future global prosperity and well-being.

Given the current fossil fuel dependency of the world economy, once global growth returns to long-term trends, energy prices could rise significantly. Projections by the International Energy Agency (IEA) suggest that, over the long run, fossil fuel demand will rise by 45 percent, and the oil price could reach US$180 per barrel. The remaining oil reserves will be concentrated in fewer countries, the risk of oil supply disruptions will rise, and oil supply capacity will fall short of demand growth.[13] Such factors may influence fossil fuel prices even in the short and medium term. For example, events over 2010–11, such as political instability in the Middle East and the nuclear reactor catastrophe in Japan, combined with the nascent world recovery, quickly pushed the price of oil to over US$100 per barrel.

The impact of higher fossil fuel prices will be felt throughout the global economy, but especially by the poor. In 2008, rising fuel prices cost consumers in developing economies US$400 billion in higher energy expenditures and US$240 billion in dearer food. The accompanying rise in food prices increased global poverty by between 130 million and 155 million people.[14] Increasing energy prices will exacerbate the widespread problem of global energy poverty. Billions of people in developing countries have no access to modern energy services, and those consumers who do have access often pay high prices for erratic and unreliable services. Among the energy poor are 2.4 billion people, who rely on traditional biomass fuels for cooking and heating, including 89 percent of the population of Sub-Saharan Africa, and another 1.6 billion people who do not have access to electricity.[15]

Even if demand for energy remains flat until 2030, just to offset the effect of oilfield decline the global economy will still need 45 million barrels per day of additional gross production capacity – an amount approximately equal to four times the current capacity of Saudi Arabia.[16] But with long-term world economic growth, fossil fuel demand is unlikely to stay constant, despite the rise in energy prices. Increasing consumption of fossil fuels will worsen global energy security concerns, which will be exacerbated by the increased concentration of the remaining oil reserves in a fewer number of countries, the risk of oil supply disruptions, rising energy use in the transport sector worldwide, and rapid demand growth from emerging market economies.[17] From 2007 to 2035, global energy consumption is expected to increase from 495 to 739 quadrillion Btu, with non-OECD countries accounting for the vast majority of this nearly 50 percent projected increase in energy use.[18]

As growth in the world economy revives fossil fuel consumption, it will also accelerate global climate change. As shown in Box 7.3, projections indicate that the growth in GHG emissions for most economies and regions will continue in coming decades. These trends suggest that, despite encouraging signs that the GHG intensity of many large economies is declining, the overall carbon dependency of the global economy is actually increasing. In 2030, a carbon-dependent world economy will produce close to 60 percent more GHG emissions from energy combustion than it does today. Growth in emissions will occur in the high-income OECD economies, but just 17.4 percent higher than today. Japan's emissions might fall, and the European Union's emissions may increase by less than 6 percent. Much of the growth in OECD emissions is likely to come from the USA, which may show a 19 percent increase. However, the large increase in global GHG emissions is likely to come from transition and developing economies. Emissions by 2030 will more than double for developing economies, led by large increases in India and China. Emissions from transition economies will rise by nearly 30 percent, led by Russia. By 2030, China's share of GHG emissions could be close to one-third the world total, and all developing economies could account for the majority of emissions.

The 2008–9 economic crisis may have temporarily slowed these trends in GHG emissions, but projections such as those indicated in Box 7.3 have clear implications. As long as global economic development remains fundamentally tied to increasing fossil fuel use, the overall carbon dependency of the world's economy will not be reduced significantly. The energy sector currently accounts for over three-quarters of the world's GHG emissions, and almost all is from the combustion of fossil fuels. As global populations increase, the world economy grows and poorer countries develop, the increased use of fossil fuel energy will cause GHG emissions to rise.

BOX 7.3 GLOBAL GREENHOUSE GAS EMISSIONS (MILLION TONNES OF CO$_2$ EQUIVALENT), 2005–2030[a]

	2005	2030	Change	Average annual growth (%)	Total growth (%)	Share of 2030 world total (%)
World	26,620	41,905	15,285	1.8	57.4	
OECD[b]	12,838	15,067	2,229	0.6	17.4	36.0
European Union	3,944	4,176	232	0.2	5.9	10.0
Japan	1,210	1,182	−28	−0.1	−2.3	2.8
United States	5,789	6,891	1,102	0.7	19.0	16.4
Transition economies[c]	2,538	3,230	692	1.0	27.3	7.7
Russia	1,528	1,973	445	1.0	29.1	4.7
Developing economies[d]	10,700	22,919	12,219	3.1	114.2	54.7
China	5,101	11,448	6,347	3.3	124.4	27.3
India	1,147	3,314	2,167	4.3	188.9	7.9

Notes

[a] International Energy Agency (IEA) projections from energy sources of greenhouse gas (GHG) emissions only.

[b] Organization for Economic Cooperation and Development.

[c] Economies of the former Soviet Union and Eastern Europe.

[d] Low- and middle-income economies from Africa, Asia, Latin America and the Middle East.

Source: Climate Analysis Indicators Tool (CAIT) Version 6.0. 2008. World Resources Institute, Washington, DC.

Thus, growth in a carbon–dependent world economy will simply contribute to both the rising demand for and combustion of fossil fuels and increased GHG emissions.

Without a change in the carbon dependency of the global economy, the atmospheric concentration of GHG could double by the end of this century, and lead to an eventual global average temperature increase of up to 6°C.[19] Such a scenario is likely to cause a sea-level rise between 0.26 and 0.59 meters, and severely disrupt freshwater availability, ecosystems, food production, coastal populations and human health.[20] With 5–6°C warming, the world economy could sustain losses equivalent to 5–10 percent of global GDP, with poor countries suffering costs in excess of 10 percent of GDP.[21] Across all cities worldwide, about 40 million people are exposed to a one in 100-year extreme coastal flooding event, and by the 2070s the population exposed could rise to 150 million.[22]

The world's poor are especially vulnerable to the climate-driven risks posed by rising sea level, coastal erosion and more frequent storms. Around 14 percent of the population and 21 percent of urban dwellers in developing countries live in low elevation coastal zones that are exposed to these risks.[23] The livelihoods of billions – from poor farmers to urban slum dwellers – are threatened by a wide range of climate-induced risks that affect food security, water availability, natural disasters, ecosystem stability and human health. For example, many of the 150 million urban inhabitants that are likely to be at risk from extreme coastal flooding events and sea-level rise are likely to be the poor living in developing country cities.[24]

Global ecosystems and freshwater sources are also endangered by the widespread environmental degradation that will accompany current patterns of economic development. Over the past 50 years, ecosystems have been modified more rapidly and extensively than in any comparable period in human history, largely to meet rapidly growing demands for food, freshwater, timber, fiber and fuel. The result has been a substantial and largely irreversible loss in biological diversity. Approximately 60 percent of the major global ecosystem services have been degraded or used unsustainably, including freshwater, capture fisheries, air and water purification, and the regulation of regional and local climate, natural hazards and pests.[25]

Poor people in developing countries will be most affected by the continuing loss of critical ecological services worldwide. The rural poor in developing regions tend to be clustered in areas of ecologically fragile land, which are already prone to degradation, water stress and poor soils.[26] In addition, by 2019, half of the developing world will be in cities, and by 2050, 5.33 billion people, or 67 percent of the population in developed countries, will inhabit urban areas.[27] This brisk pace of urbanization means that the growing populations in the cities will be confronted with increased congestion and pollution and rising energy, water and raw material demands. Although such environmental problems are similar to those faced by industrialized countries, the pace and scale of urban population growth in developing countries are likely to lead to more severe and acute health and welfare impacts.

As in the case of climate change, the link between ecological scarcity and poverty is well established for some of the most critical environmental problems. For example, for the world's poor, global water scarcity manifests itself as a water poverty problem. One in five people in the developing world lacks access to sufficient clean water, and about half the developing world's population, 2.6 billion people, do not have access to basic sanitation. More than 660 million of the people without sanitation live on less than US$2 a day, and more than 385 million on less than US$1 a day.[28] If worldwide economic development fails to tackle the emerging problem of global water scarcity, or if it makes the problem worse, then more and more of the world's poor will be unable to afford improved access to clean water and sanitation.

In sum, given the disproportionate impacts on the world's poor of increasing ecological scarcity, including climate change, the claim that perpetuating the same pattern of global economic growth will reduce poverty significantly is questionable. Although from 1981 to 2005 the number of extreme poor fell globally by slightly over 500 million, from 1.9 billion to 1.4 billion, it may be more difficult to make further inroads on reducing poverty simply through growing the world economy without addressing its underlying structural problems.[29] One problem is the number of extreme poor keeps growing due to demographic trends. For example, estimates suggest that, by 2015, there will be nearly 1 billion people living on less than US$1 a day and almost 3 billion living on less than US$2 a day.[30] But another factor, which is ignored in current global development strategies, is that improving the livelihoods of the remaining poor may be an intractable problem unless their vulnerability to ecological scarcity is reduced. One reason is where many of the poor are located and how they survive. In general, about twice as many poor people live in rural than in urban areas in the developing world.[31] Well over 600 million of the rural poor currently live on lands prone to degradation and water stress, and in upland areas, forest systems and drylands that are vulnerable to climatic and ecological disruptions.[32] A global economic development strategy that does not also address directly the problems of energy and water poverty, climate change and ecological risks will have little impact on improving the livelihoods of many of the world's poor.

If these imminent threats posed by climate change, energy insecurity, growing freshwater scarcity, deteriorating ecosystems and, above all, worsening global poverty are to be reduced significantly, then worldwide development efforts must be broadened into a comprehensive strategy to overcome ecological scarcity in the world economy. To develop such a long-term strategy requires:

- adopting green pricing policies,
- creating global markets, and
- devising long-term green development strategies.

Green pricing policies

Pricing policies to enhance the effectiveness of and sustain policies to combat environmental degradation were a major feature of the sustainable development strategy outlined in *Blueprint for a Green Economy*. For example, BGE maintained that "price is a powerful weapon in the pursuit of the environmental policies needed for sustainable development because it allows resource users to respond in the same way as they do to the price signals elsewhere in the market."[33] Throughout this book, we have also stressed the importance of pricing policies in improving environmental management in today's economies (see especially Chapter 6). Such policies include both additional taxes, tradable permits and other market-based instruments for providing the correct incentives for reducing carbon dependency and ecological scarcity and the removal of perverse subsidies and other market distortions that inhibit these objectives.

As discussed in Box 7.4, there are also other longer-term economic benefits arising from green pricing policies. Combined with technological push policies, such as public support for clean energy research and development (R&D), carbon taxes or tradable permit systems could provide significant

---

BOX 7.4 INDUCED TECHNOLOGICAL CHANGE AND PUBLIC POLICY FOR REDUCING CARBON DEPENDENCY

A report for the Pew Center on Global Climate Change highlights the role of public investment and policies for promoting induced technological change to reduce carbon dependency. Induced technological innovation can be efficiently promoted through combining "direct emission policies," such as a cap-and-trade system, with "technology-push policies," such as research and development (R&D) subsidies for encouraging private sector investment. As the table below indicates, other direct emissions and technology-push policies could be combined to provide maximum induced technological innovation in the private sector.

Studies for reducing greenhouse gas emissions in the United States, Europe and other OECD economies show that combining the two policies substantially lowers the costs of meeting targets compared to relying just on a technology-push approach, such as an R&D subsidy for low-carbon energy options and energy efficiency.[34] Although the optimal portfolio of policies invariably includes some form of emissions price and subsidies for technology R&D and learning, carbon pricing and direct emissions policies are generally the most efficient policy option if only a single economy-wide policy can be adopted. For example, as one study concludes from an analysis of the US electricity sector: "We find that for anything beyond very small emissions reduction targets, the emissions price is the most efficient single policy for reducing emissions, since it simultaneously gives incentives for fossil energy producers to reduce emissions intensity, for consumers to conserve, and for renewable energy producers to expand production and to invest in knowledge to reduce their costs."[35]

Public policies for reducing carbon dependency

Direct emissions policies	Technology-push policies
Carbon taxes	Subsidies to R&D in low-carbon technologies
Carbon quotas	Public-sector R&D in low-carbon technologies
Cap-and-trade for greenhouse gas (GHG) emissions	Government-financed technology competitions (with awards)
Subsidies to GHG emission abatement	Strengthened patent rules

Source: Adapted from Goulder, L. 2004. "Induced Technological Change and Climate Policy." Pew Center on Global Climate Change, Arlington, VA, box 1.

---

incentives for induced technological innovation in reducing carbon dependency. The revenues earned, or financial subsidies saved, from complementary pricing policies could also pay for any additional fiscal stimulus measures and other public expenditures in support of green sector development. This would alleviate concern about green public investments adding to chronic government debt over the long term.

To the extent that green pricing policies help revive economies while reducing carbon dependency and improving energy security, they may also assist in correcting the problem of structural imbalances for oil-importing economies with large current account deficits, such as the United States, and for fossil fuel exporting economies with accumulating foreign reserves.[36] For trade surplus countries, such as emerging market economies, green pricing policies should be part of the development strategy that shifts these economies to reorient domestic savings toward clean energy investments, increase imports of low-carbon technologies and capital, and expand output of tradables to satisfy growing domestic demand. To the extent that such measures rebalance the pattern of economic growth in these economies by expanding imports of capital goods in key sectors and absorbing more savings domestically, they could help reduce chronic trade surpluses in Asian and other emerging market economies.[37] Increased domestic spending on education and health care, government insurance mechanisms and safety net programs could also help reduce the precautionary motives for high levels of saving by households in these economies.[38]

As outlined in Chapter 6, green pricing policies and market reforms in developing economies have also been important for enhancing the sustainable and efficient use of natural resources and production processes dependent on them, and to ensure that the financial returns generated from these activities are reinvested in the industrial activities, infrastructure, health services, and the education and skills necessary for long-term economic development. Removing subsidies and other incentive distortions and implementing, where appropriate, market-based instruments and other measures to improve the efficiency of water delivery and utilization will be essential to managing growing water demand as global populations grow.

As economies and governments become more familiar with the use of green pricing policies, they tend to develop these policies, improve their effectiveness and extend them to a variety of environmental management areas. As a result, the transaction costs of implementing new pricing policies and other market-based instruments start to fall as they become more widespread and common. An assessment by the European Environment Agency, for example, found that since 1996 the increased use of a variety of market-based instruments across a growing number of sectors and economies is developing an emerging "environmental tax base." Box 7.5 illustrates the spread of environmental taxes in Europe since the mid-1990s. A long-run global development strategy that relies on green pricing policies could also encourage more economies to develop and enhance a similar environmental tax base for sustaining a healthy and efficient green economy of the future.

BOX 7.5 THE EMERGING ENVIRONMENTAL TAX BASE IN SELECTED EUROPEAN ECONOMIES

	Austria	Belgium	Denmark	Finland	France	Germany
Air/energy						
CO_2			*	*		**
SO_2			**		*	
NO_x					*	
Fuels	*	*	*	*	*	*
Sulfur in fuels		***	*	***		
Transport						
Car sales and use	*	*	*	*	*	*
Differentiated car tax			**			**
Water						
Water effluents	*	*	*	*	*	*
Waste						
Waste-end	**	***	*	**	**	
Dangerous waste			*	*		*
Noise						
Aviation noise						*
Products						
Tires	*		**	**		
Beverage containers		*	*	*		
Packaging	**		*		***	
Bags			*			
Pesticides		**	*			
CFCs	*		*			
Batteries	**	**	*			
Light bulbs			*			
PVCs			**			
Lubrication oil				*		
Fertilizers			**			
Paper and board			**		*	
Solvents			**			
Resources						
Raw materials		***	*			

Notes
* In 1996 ** New after 1996 *** New after 2000
Source: Based on and updated from European Environment Agency (EEA). 2005.
The European Environment – State and Outlook 2005: Part A: Integrated Assessment.
EEA, Copenhagen, figure 10.2, p. 236.

Greece	Iceland	Ireland	Italy	Lux.	Neth.	Norway	Portugal	Spain	Sweden	UK
		***	**		*	*			*	***
			*			***				
			*						*	
*	*	*	*	*	*	*	*	*	*	*
					***	*			*	***
*	*	*	*	*	*	*	*	*	*	
						**				
		*	*		*	*			*	
**			**		*	**		***	**	*
	*									
			*		*	*				
					**					
						*			*	
			**			***				
	*	***	*							
						**			*	
	***		**						*	
			*			**		***		
			**						*	
	*									
						**				
			***						*	***

Creating global markets

However, perhaps the greatest policy challenge in the long term is to address the lack of markets for the most pervasive environmental impacts. Most of the impending environmental crises facing the world economy – climate change, ecological scarcity and declining availability of water – are examples of market failure on a global scale. That is, those who emit greenhouse gases, destroy ecosystem services and threaten water availability inflict damages on others without paying for these losses. In the case of climate change, the uncompensated damages are truly global, in that all economies are contributing to the problem, without paying fully for the costs, and the economic consequences of the market failure will be felt worldwide. In the case of ecological scarcity, it is the scale and pace of the loss of ecosystems and their services that have created a global market failure. And, finally, in the case of freshwater scarcity, it is the chronic underpricing of vital water resources worldwide, and the increasing dependence of many countries on shared sources of water supply.[39]

The most efficient solution for combating such worldwide market failures is to create global markets. To provide the best incentives for all economies worldwide to invest in clean energy technologies and reduce their carbon dependency requires establishing a long-term and credible price signal for carbon across world markets. To ensure that ecosystems yielding valuable services are more likely to be conserved rather than destroyed requires establishing a system of international payment of ecosystem services that allows individuals in one part of the world who value these services to compensate those in other parts of the world for managing ecosystems. To tackle transboundary water allocation, which is becoming increasingly critical to global supply, will require a renewed commitment by countries sharing these resources to cooperate on governance and pricing arrangements to manage joint supply relative to demand.

One example is the need to reach agreement on a post-Kyoto global climate change framework. Many of the low-carbon investments and innovations needed to reduce the carbon dependency of the world economy will be affected by the growing uncertainty over the future global carbon market after 2012 when the Kyoto treaty expires. Both uncertainty over future global climate policy and the delay caused by inaction also increase sharply the costs of an agreement. Delay in adopting effective climate policies will affect the cost of future agreements that will be required to abate an even larger amount of greenhouse (GHG) emissions. Such inaction in the short term increases significantly the costs of compliance in the long term, which is compounded by the effects of uncertainty on investment and policy decisions.

Even if a post–Kyoto agreement fails, it is essential that any new international climate policy achieves two aims: the enhancement of global carbon emissions trading and reform of the Clean Development Mechanism (CDM).[40] In lieu of an inclusive international climate agreement, the continued existence of a global carbon market that would allow developing economies to finance their mitigation measures would still allow attainment of global GHG emission reduction targets, which usually set goals for 2020 or 2030. Guaranteeing the future of a global carbon market and CDM mechanism after 2012 is therefore not only essential to the success of many green recovery actions proposed for the next several years but also for the attainment of ambitious GHG targets for 2020 and beyond.

The world economy has made tentative steps towards international trading in GHG emissions but it is not there yet by any means. By establishing the first regional carbon market with its Emissions Trading System (ETS), the European Union has demonstrated how international trading can function to provide regional incentives for reducing GHG emissions: a European-wide carbon price has been created; businesses began incorporating this price in their decisions; and the market infrastructure for multilateral trading in carbon has been set up. But expansion and reform of the ETS is needed if it is to become the basis of a global trading scheme.[41] Similarly, the CDM has become the basis for establishing projects and investments for large emerging market economies, such as Brazil, China, India, South Korea and Mexico, effectively linking them into global GHG emissions trading and financing. As with the ETS, however, reform and expansion of the CDM is essential to cover a broader range of GHG reduction projects and developing economies, if it is truly to be the basis for a global carbon market.[42] A number of important economies, such as Australia, Canada, Japan, New Zealand, Norway and Switzerland, have proposed or implemented cap-and-trade systems, which could link into the larger international trading network. In addition, GHG trading has been established in the northeastern US states, although cap-and-trade legislation for the entire United States still seems to be unlikely for political reasons. The basis for a global carbon market is clearly emerging, but it needs to become a major priority not only for enhancing efforts to green the present economic recovery but also to provide the incentives for long-term targets to reduce carbon dependency in the world economy.

A second example is the funding challenge for global ecosystem and biodiversity conservation. There remains a huge gap between the global benefits that humankind receives from ecosystems and what we are willing to pay to maintain and conserve them. For example, David Pearce pointed out that the global benefits of ecosystem goods and services are likely to be "hundreds of billions of dollars," yet currently the world spends at most US$10 billion annually on ecosystem conservation.[43] Overcoming this funding gap is critical if we are to stop the current decline in global ecosystems and the benefits they provide. But there are a number of economic disincentives that have so far prevented successful international negotiation and agreement to halt biodiversity loss and ecosystem degradation worldwide. Financing and implementing international mechanisms to combat this global funding problem is a major obstacle.

The wide gap between the global benefits that humankind receives from ecosystems and what we are willing to pay to maintain and conserve them is a critical symptom of how oblivious we are to the risks arising from the excessive ecological deterioration arising from the current pattern of economic development. Yet, there are many disincentives working against the creation of such schemes. Although progress has been made in establishing international payments for global ecosystem services, most notably through a nascent financial mechanism to reduce emissions from deforestation and forest degradation (REDD), several important concerns have arisen. Monitoring and verifying changes in deforestation rates in developing countries and their impacts on carbon emissions could increase substantially the transaction costs of implementing a REDD scheme on a global scale. In addition, a carbon market for avoided deforestation may not necessarily be the best way of protecting forests that yield other global ecosystem services. There is also concern over the high opportunity costs faced by many developing countries from losses in forgone agricultural and timber benefits. These issues need to be resolved if there is to be a successful REDD financial mechanism implemented on a global scale.

With regard to negotiating and implementing a more comprehensive international scheme to cover a wider range of ecosystems yielding global benefits, the best outcome that we can hope for currently is a scheme that is underwritten by only a handful of rich countries, and which is capable of providing a level of global ecosystem protection that is only slightly more than current efforts. Although they may be supported through multilateral and bilateral assistance, developing countries will continue to bear the direct and opportunity costs of ecosystem conservation for the foreseeable future. Clearly, this perpetuates the unsustainability problem, especially given rising global ecological scarcity. But to overcome the economic disincentives that are reinforcing such an outcome, the international community needs to think more creatively as to how to agree, design, implement and verify international mechanisms for payment of ecosystem services. We also need to develop more innovative ways of financing such schemes, other than the traditional methods of development assistance or transfers.

Box 7.6 outlines actual and potential funding mechanisms for global ecosystem conservation. One of the funding sources, the Global Environmental Facility (GEF) of the United Nations, has been in operation since 1991. To date the GEF has allocated US$10.7 billion, supplemented by more than US$47 billion in co-financing, for over 2,700 projects in 165 developing economies.[44] One type of scheme for international payment of ecosystem services (IPES) is the REDD mechanism, which has been operating as a pilot initiative with a budget of US$118 million.[45] The other financing mechanisms listed in Box 7.6 have yet to be implemented, but have been discussed and debated as potential ways of providing substantial additional funding for the GEF, REDD and new IPES schemes, or possibly a direct source of financing ecosystem conservation globally.

Such additional funding is clearly needed in the case of the GEF. Although the multi-donor funding mechanism made a promising start in providing additional financing for a variety of global public goods in developing countries, since 1994 its total budget allocation has declined in real terms.[46] Thus, concerns have been raised about its future role, as well as the need to raise additional funds other than conventional development assistance.[47] Increasing significantly the resources of the GEF is essential if it is to be transformed into an innovative mechanism for delivering global ecosystem benefits, which can only be accomplished if the GEF has sufficient funds to compensate developing countries for land-use change and other economic activities that are the cause of ecological degradation worldwide. Currently, the GEF is incapable of doing the latter. As one observer has remarked, "The GEF's capacity to fund new initiatives and sustain results during the long term is questionable without a gradual but predictable increase in the flow of resources."[48]

IPES and REDD in particular may represent new sources of financing of global ecosystem conservation. For example, some of the funds raised through a global cap-and-auction system for greenhouse gas emissions among wealthy nations could be diverted to fund international payment for ecosystem services, with the financing apportioned to targeted countries in accordance with how well they meet specific criteria for the provision of global ecosystem services.[49] Similarly, in the case of REDD, the annual cost of reducing global deforestation by 10 percent may be around US$0.4–1.7 billion but the additional financing through carbon markets could earn developing

BOX 7.6 FINANCING MECHANISMS FOR FUNDING GLOBAL ECOSYSTEM CONSERVATION

Mechanism	Description
Global Environmental Facility (GEF)	A multi-donor global mechanism to meet the additional costs of developing countries in achieving global environmental benefits from biological diversity, climate change, international waters, ozone layer depletion, reduced land degradation and abatement of persistent organic pollution.
Adaptation Fund	A fund financing adaptation projects and programs in developing countries; funded with 2% of the Certified Emission Reduction credits issued for projects of the Clean Development Mechanism and from other sources.
International Payment for Ecosystem Services (IPES)	A global mechanism for raising and distributing funds from beneficiaries of ecosystem services to those who conserve them.
Reduced emissions from deforestation and forest degradation (REDD+) scheme	A specific IPES aimed at reducing GHG emissions from deforestation and forest degradation in developing countries.
Global carbon cap-and-auction system	A cap-and-auction scheme for GHG emissions; funds are raised by auctioning the initial emission permits.
Global carbon tax	Taxes applied to carbon-equivalent GHG emissions.
International Finance Facility (IFF)	Mobilize financing from international capital markets by issuing long-term bonds repaid by donor countries.
Sovereign Wealth Fund (SWF)	A proportion of a country's foreign exchange reserves set aside for investment purposes.

Financial Transaction Tax (FTT)	Tax applied to the sale of specific financial assets, such as stock, bonds or futures.
Currency Transaction Tax (CTT or Tobin tax)	Tax applied to currency exchange transactions.
Airline travel tax	Tax applied to international airline ticket sales.
Aviation or shipping fuel tax	Tax applied to international aviation and shipping fuel use.
Arms trade tax	Tax applied to international exports of armaments.
Tobacco excise tax	Tax applied to sales of tobacco products, a proportion of which is allocated to global funds.

countries US$2.2–13.5 billion annually.[50] But the same disincentives that work against negotiating an international agreement for IPES mechanisms would also have to be overcome to set up an international cap-and-auction system for GHG emissions.[51]

An alternative to raising funds through an international cap-and-auction scheme would be to implement a global carbon tax on GHG emissions.[52] Under such a tax regime, countries set market penalties on GHG emissions at levels that are equalized across different regions and industries. The tax would be set low initially, and rise steadily over time to reflect the rising damages from global warming. Estimated revenues from such a scheme could range from US$318 to US$980 billion by 2015 (in 2005 prices) and US$527 to US$1,763 billion by 2030.[53] Conceivably, some of these revenues could be used to finance IPES schemes, the GEF and other global initiatives for ecosystem conservation. However, as the economist William Nordhaus has pointed out, international agreements on harmonized taxes on GHG emissions are proving to be more elusive than for IPES or carbon cap-and-trade: "Economists often point to harmonized carbon taxes as a more efficient and attractive regime, but these have been generally shunned in negotiations, particularly in the United States, because of the taboo on considering tax-based systems."[54]

The idea of an International Finance Facility (IFF) is to mobilize resources from international capital markets by issuing long-term bonds that are repaid by donor countries over 20 to 30 years. This approach has already been applied to the IFF for Immunization (IFFIm), which was launched in 2006 by the UK and supported by France, Italy, Spain, Sweden, the Netherlands, Norway and South Africa. These countries have pledged to contribute US$5.9 billion over 23 years.[55] IFFIm raises finances by issuing bonds in the capital markets to convert these long-term government pledges into funds for immediate investment. The government pledges are then used to repay the IFFIm. So far IFFIm bonds have raised US$3.6 billion through bonds, which receive a triple-A rating. The investments are disbursed through the Global Alliance on Vaccines and Immunization (GAVI), a public–private partnership of major stakeholders in immunization in the developing world. Since inception, IFFIm has approved immunization programs of US$2 billion and disbursed US$1.2 billion to support vaccine purchases and delivery to 70 developing countries. The World Bank acts as financial advisory and treasury manager to the IFFIm.

One of the perceived advantages of the IFF approach is that, unlike other potential new sources of global financing or mechanisms, it can be started by a handful of donor countries without the need of an international agreement involving many countries.[56] On the other hand, if the IFFIm is any guide, the funds raised are more likely to be in the tens of billions rather than hundreds of billions. Doubts have therefore been raised over the ability of the IFF approach to overcome on its own major shortfalls in international assistance, such as for global ecosystem conservation.[57] Still, an IFF for global ecosystem protection would be an innovative and potentially viable financial mechanism, and as the IFFIm has shown, can easily work with existing development institutions, such as the World Bank. A similar funding relationship could easily be worked out between any IFF and the GEF, or possibly a new IPES scheme such as REDD.

Some US$4.3 trillion in global foreign exchange reserves, including US$3.5 trillion in developing countries, are held in sovereign wealth funds (SWFs). UNCTAD proposes that developing economies invest 1 percent of their funds in regional development banks, which could in turn facilitate a wide range of sustainable development initiatives.[58] Allocating 1 percent of SWFs in G20 countries would raise at least US$40 billion annually for global environment and development investments.[59] However, to be effective, such a mechanism would require international agreement concerning the transfer of SWFs and their disbursement.

A financial transaction tax (FTT) is gaining ground as one possible long-term funding source for global public goods, such as ecosystem conservation.[60] A FTT is a tax collected on the sale of specific financial assets, such as stock, bonds or futures. A variant is a currency transaction tax (CTT), or Tobin tax, named after the economist James Tobin who first proposed it in the 1970s. This is a tax applied to any foreign currency exchange transaction.

An FTT is usually seen as a tax that would be implemented nationally, and in fact such taxes already exist, as in the case of the stamp duty tax in the United Kingdom. However, the 2008–9 global recession has renewed impetus in establishing a global tax. For example, the UN-sponsored Leading Group on Innovative Financing for Development has concluded that a CTT is the most desirable and feasible option for overcoming the chronic underfunding of global public goods, partly because it would be relatively easy and cheap to implement.[61] In addition, a very small tax rate could raise substantial funds globally for public goods, such as ecosystem conservation. For example, a small tax of 0.10 percent on equities and 0.02 percent on bonds could bring in about US$48 billion from G20 member states.[62] Foreign exchange transactions total around US$800 trillion annually, which means that a CTT of only 0.05 percent could raise US$400 billion in revenues for aid to poor economies, climate change mitigation and ecosystem conservation.[63]

Instead, the major obstacle to an international FTT is implementation. Any global FTT or CTT would still involve some form of negotiated international agreement involving many countries. France and Belgium have adopted CTT legislation, but its implementation is contingent on other EU countries adopting the tax, which is still an unlikely prospect. Initially, then, an FTT or CTT is likely to be collected nationally, with a proportion of revenues transferred to international agencies, such as the World Bank or GEF, for disbursement. But that means the most likely priority for their revenues is to support national public budgets, including reducing chronic fiscal deficits in some countries, which in turn would limit the proceeds available for ecosystem conservation and other global public goods. As an alternative, proceeds from a CTT or FTT could be channeled to a global solidarity fund, which would then use the proceeds to fund international conservation and similar investments. Negotiating and establishing another international funding mechanism would be yet another international policy challenge.

Taxes could be imposed on the arms trade, tobacco products, airline travel and aviation or shipping fuel to fund global environment and development initiatives. For example, a 10 percent tax on global arms exports could raise up to US$5 billion annually.[64] Additional tobacco sales taxes in G20 and other EU countries could generate US$10.8 billion, global aviation fuel taxes an extra US$27 billion, and shipping fuel taxes US$37 billion.[65] However, such taxes are not negligible, could be diverted for domestic spending, are difficult to implement politically and would create problems of smuggling, especially for tobacco products, small arms and light weapons. Airline travel, transport fuel and tobacco products are already taxed substantially by some governments. Any of these additional taxes would require a negotiated international agreement, which could be difficult to negotiate successfully.

Global green development strategies

For many developing economies, sustaining long-term growth prospects will require a reorienting of their development and industrial strategies to encourage expansion in the output of modern tradable goods and services, mainly to meet growing domestic demand and to absorb high rates of saving in these economies. An advocate of this policy, the economist Dani Rodrik, has argued that this was largely the development strategy and rapid structural transformation undertaken by "high-growth" economies in past periods, such as Japan from 1950 to 1973, South Korea from 1973 to 1990 and China from 1990 to 2005.[66] In the past, high-growth emerging market economies expanded their output of tradable industrial goods through promoting their export with policies such as undervalued exchange rates. But with the world economy still recovering from the 2008–9 Great Recession, Rodrik argues that emerging market and other developing economies should encourage growth in the output of tradable commodities but through industrial policies, including targeted subsidies, which will allow these goods and services to be consumed domestically.

Policies to target and develop clean energy, sustainable transport and other green sectors could achieve these objectives by serving as the new growth poles in emerging market and other developing economies. Moreover, these sectors would be at the forefront of fostering modern tradable goods and services to meet expanding domestic demand. To overcome critical capital, technological and skills gaps, developing economies should encourage the importation of low-carbon capital and technology goods. In the medium and long term, the transfer of new technologies and skills will facilitate the development of an indigenous technological capacity and workforce that enables future innovations and long-term adoption of low-carbon technologies. Such strategies to promote "green growth" can form the basis of a new and sustainable, long-run development path for these economies.

Some key Asian economies appear to have endorsed this view that greening their economies may be crucial both to economic recovery and ensuring long-run growth. For example, as noted above, the major Asia-Pacific economies, Australia, China, Japan and South Korea, invested heavily in promoting energy efficiency, low-carbon power and other environmental improvements through green stimulus during the 2008–9 recession. The recovery policies adopted by China and South Korea in particular reflect the belief that investments in clean energy technologies can have a major impact on growth, expanding exports and creating employment.

For example, one reason that China has focused on clean energy invest-ments is that its renewable energy sector already has a value of nearly U$17 billion and employs close to 1 million workers. Other green initiatives included promoting fuel-efficient vehicles, rail transport, electricity grid improvements and pollution control. China has also raised taxes on gasoline and diesel and reduced the sales tax on more fuel-efficient vehicles. In addi-tion, China is the world's largest recipient of carbon emission reduction cred-its under the Clean Development Mechanism (CDM), currently earning US$2 billion from these credits. Overall, China views promotion of green sectors as sound industrial policy; it aims to be the world market leader in solar panels, wind turbines, fuel-efficient cars and other clean energy industries.[67]

South Korea also sees its industrial strategy tied to green growth. South Korea's "Green New Deal" of US$60 billion amounted to nearly 80 percent of the fiscal stimulus during the recession, and comprised investments over five years in a variety of clean energy and environmental projects. In addition to the Green New Deal, the South Korean government plans to establish a US$72.2 million renewable energy fund to attract private investment in solar, wind and hydroelectric power projects. In July 2009, South Korea launched a five-year Green Growth Investment Plan, spending an additional US$60 billion on reducing carbon dependency and environmental improve-ments, with the aim of creating 1.5–1.8 million jobs and boosting economic growth through 2020.[68]

Ultimately, long-run development in the global economy must focus on policies to promote the transition to low-carbon and clean energy use in all advanced and emerging market economies. The right mix of investments and policies today could not only reduce carbon dependency and improve the environment, but also create jobs and stimulate innovation and growth in key economic sectors. For example, Box 7.7 summarizes a study by the Union of Concerned Scientists (UCS), which analyzes such a long-run clean energy policy strategy for the United States. The UCS finds that the most beneficial policies can reduce US GHG emissions to 56 percent below 2005 levels by 2030, have only minimal impacts on long-run economic growth in the United States, increase nonfarm employment slightly, and yield net cumulative savings of US$1.7 trillion. Carbon pricing and complementary sectoral policies that encourage development of clean energy over the long term are clearly key to such a strategy. A study of expansion and reform of the European Union's Emissions Trading System (ETS) confirms that economy-wide cap-and-trade has the capacity to induce substitution in electricity generation to clean energy technologies, including nuclear power.[69]

For most low- and middle-income economies, improving the sustainability of primary production must also be considered part of a long-term sustainable development goal. The main policy priorities should be ensuring that primary production activities generate sufficient investible funds for diversifying the economy, building up human capital, and investing in social safety nets and other investments targeted at the poor. Policies aimed at these objectives should also be the basis for devising a global strategy for alleviating poverty and enhancing sustainable development in resource-dependent economies over the next several decades, with the overall aim of achieving the United Nations' Millennium Development Goal of ending extreme world poverty by 2025.

However, promoting clean energy and energy efficiency also has a role to play in low- and middle-income economies. In developing economies, every US$1 invested in improving the energy efficiency of electricity generation saves more than US$3 in operating costs. Small hydropower, biomass and solar photovoltaics (PV) already provide electricity, heat, water pumping and other power for tens of millions of people in many rural areas. Developing economies currently account for 40 percent of existing global renewable resource capacity, 70 percent of solar water heating capacity and 45 percent of biofuels production. Expansion of these sectors may also be critical for increasing the availability of affordable and sustainable energy services for the poorest households in these economies.[70]

BOX 7.7 THE 2030 BLUEPRINT FOR A CLEAN ENERGY ECONOMY FOR THE UNITED STATES

A study by the Union of Concerned Scientists (UCS) analyzes a long-run policy strategy for establishing a clean energy economy in the United States.[71] The main aim of the strategy is to reduce US greenhouse gas emissions to 26 percent below 2005 levels by 2020 and 56 percent below by 2030. The UCS finds that the most beneficial policies for attaining these targets is an economy-wide cap-and-trade system combined with complementary policies targeted at industry, buildings, electricity and transportation. As indicated in Figure 7.1, the UCS study estimates that these policies could achieve the 2020 and 2030 GHG emission reductions targets through constraining cumulative emissions in the US economy to 180 billion tonnes of CO_2 equivalent between 2000 and 2030. The price of carbon allowances starts at US$18 per tonne of CO_2 in 2011, rises to US$34 in 2020 and then to US$70 in 2030. In addition, the study estimates that the savings for households and businesses from reductions in electricity and fuel use will more than offset the costs of any additional investments arising from the strategy. By 2030 the net savings will be US$255 billion. Although administering and implementing the policies will cost US$8 billion, auctioning carbon allowances will generate US$219 billion revenues that should be recycled to consumers and business. Overall, the strategy should yield US$465 billion in savings by 2030. Net cumulative savings from 2010 to 2030 amounts to US$1.7 trillion. Finally, the strategy has only minimal impacts on long-run economic growth. Under full implementation of the policies, GDP increases by at least 81 percent between 2005 and 2030. In the reference case, the US economy grows by 84 percent. Employment trends are virtually identical in the two scenarios, although nonfarm employment is slightly higher under the clean energy strategy compared to the reference case.

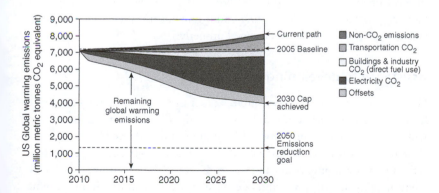

FIGURE 7.1 Emissions reductions under the US 2030 Blueprint for a Clean Energy Economy

Source: Cleetus, Rachel, Steven Clemmer, and David Friedman. 2009. Climate 2030: A National Blueprint for a Clean Energy Economy. Union of Concerned Scientists (UCS), Cambridge, MA, figure 7.1.

There are two additional ways in which a long-term global green economic strategy can more directly improve the livelihoods of the poor. The first is to provide financing directly, through involving the poor in payment for ecosystem services schemes and other measures that enhance the environments on which the poor depend. Payments for the conservation of standing forests or wildlife habitat are the most frequent type of compensation programs used currently in developing countries, and they have been mainly aimed at paying landowners for the opportunity costs of preserving natural landscapes that provide one or more diverse services: carbon sequestration, watershed protection, biodiversity benefits, wildlife protection and landscape beauty.[72] Wherever possible, the payment schemes should be designed to increase the participation of the poor, to reduce any negative impacts on nonparticipants while creating additional job opportunities for rural workers, and to provide technical assistance, access to inputs, credit and other support to encourage poor smallholders to adopt the desired land-use practices. More effort must be devoted to designing projects and programs that include the direct participation of the landless and near landless.

The second is to target investments directly to improving the livelihoods of the rural poor, thus reducing their dependence on exploiting environmental resources. For example, in Ecuador, Madagascar and Cambodia poverty maps have been developed to target public investments to geographically defined subgroups of the population according to their relative poverty status, which could substantially improve the performance of the programs in term of poverty alleviation.[73] A World Bank study that examined 122 targeted programs in 48 developing countries confirms their effectiveness in reducing poverty, if they are designed properly.[74]

Assistance to developing countries

Low- and middle-income economies will clearly need continuing assistance from the international community in achieving these long-term goals. This will require that the international community also reorient development assistance and financing to improve the sustainability of primary production activities in developing countries, the livelihoods of the poor living in fragile environments, and the provision of ecosystem services on which the extreme poor depend. To achieve the goal of halving the proportion of the population without access to clean water and sanitation, aid flows would need to double to this sector, rising by US$3.6–4 billion annually.[75]

Developing economies will especially need considerable long-term assistance in overcoming the capital, skills and technological gaps that prevent them from adopting low-carbon and clean energy technologies, and may also limit the dissemination of simpler renewable energy technologies to poor households that lack access to basic energy services.[76] Developing economies face similar challenges in implementing sustainable transport strategies, including improving access to basic transport facilities by the poor. For example, improving sustainable transport and access requires an increase in investments in developing economies of about US$1.2 billion annually from now to 2030, with about one-sixth of the financing coming from development assistance.[77]

There is also an urgent need to establish a long-term global vulnerability fund that would be used to finance in developing economies a comprehensive and targeted safety net for the poor, investments in infrastructure including low-carbon technology projects, support for small and medium-sized enterprises and micro-finance institutions, and financing for food assistance, nutritional support for poor households and sustainable agricultural development.[78] To adapt to the impacts of climate change, developing countries are estimated to need around US$15–30 billion in additional development assistance to 2020.[79] This would include investments in knowledge, preparation and planning, disaster management and proactive/urgent adaptation.

In sum, there appear to be two broad priority areas for increased international assistance to developing economies: (1) overcoming the shortfalls in aid for low-carbon energy investments, sustainable transport, primary production and improvements in water and sanitation; and (2) financing for food assistance and nutritional support, sustainable primary production methods, safety net programs targeted at poor households, and adaptation to climate change impacts. Current aid efforts in these areas are not sufficient to address the critical development problems facing developing economies and the poor. Reorienting current development assistance to these priority areas is essential to achieving a more sustainable and equitable world economy over the next several decades.

Conclusion

In their communiqué at the 2 April 2009 London Summit, the leaders of the G20 stated: "We will make the transition towards clean, innovative, resource efficient, low carbon technologies and infrastructure.... We will identify and work together on further measures to build sustainable economies."[80] As part of their efforts to boost aggregate demand and growth, some G20 governments adopted expansionary policies that also incorporated a sizable "green fiscal" component. Such measures included support for renewable energy, carbon capture and sequestration, energy efficiency, public transport and rail, and improving electrical grid transmission, as well as other public investments and incentives aimed at environmental protection. The impetus for such "green recovery" efforts came from studies showing that such "green stimulus" policies could foster a more sustainable, low-carbon economic development in the medium term while creating growth and employment in "clean energy" sectors.

However, as we have argued in this chapter, the temporary green stimulus measures enacted during the 2008–9 recession are not enough to instigate a "green" recovery, let alone usher in a more sustainable world economy over the long term. Without a comprehensive and long-term strategy of implementing green pricing policies and effective environmental regulations, existing market and policy distortions will continue to underprice the use of natural resources, contribute to environmental degradation and worsen carbon dependency in the global economy. In addition, tackling global environmental crises – climate change, ecological scarcity and declining freshwater availability – will require creating global markets for carbon, ecosystem services and water. Targeting and developing clean energy, sustainable transport and other green sectors could serve as the new growth poles in emerging market and developing economies. Long-run development in the global economy must also focus on policies to promote the transition to low-carbon and clean energy use in all advanced and emerging market economies. For most low- and middle-income economies, improving the sustainability of primary production must also be considered part of a long-term sustainable development goal, which should include targeting investments and payments for ecosystem services directly to the poor. Development assistance from the international community needs to be reoriented to meeting these new green development goals, such as reducing carbon dependency, poverty and ecological scarcity.

If the G20, as well as the broader international economy, is truly committed to building a more sustainable world economy, then progress must be made soon. The major twenty-first-century economic and environmental problems of climate change, ecological scarcity, freshwater availability, energy insecurity and poverty are beyond the ability of any single country to tackle alone. The resulting costs and risks are also global, and will further exacerbate the economic instability and market instability brought on by the Great Recession and its aftermath. These problems stem from the failure of the world economy to address fundamental environmental scarcities. Devising a strategy to overcome these scarcities is not difficult. But perhaps the more limiting factors are time and political will.

8
CONCLUSION

Published over 20 years ago, *Blueprint for a Green Economy* (BGE) identified the key policies necessary for making economies more environmentally sustainable. The book's widespread appeal had much to do with its novel approach to integrating environmental and economic policies. As we stated in its Preface:

> environmental policy matters not just for the quality of life in general, nor just because natural environments have values "in themselves," but because environments and economies are not distinct. Treating them as if they were is the surest recipe for unsustainable development.[1]

More than two decades later, this central theme of BGE is still crucial. Perhaps the biggest obstacle to attaining sustainable development is the erroneous view that the "environment" is, at best, peripheral and, at worst, irrelevant to economic development.

As discussed in Chapter 1, we need to recognize that there is a fundamental economy–environment tradeoff between the economic benefits of development and any resulting environmental and welfare impacts arising from natural resource depletion, pollution and ecological degradation. Rather than ignore this tradeoff, we need to ensure that the maximum economic benefits are attained with the minimum environmental costs. The failure to consider the environmental and welfare consequences of present-day development is the main reason why economies remain inherently sustainable.

In BGE, we argued that to make economies more sustainable requires progress in valuing the environment, accounting for the beneficial services of natural capital and creating incentives for environmental improvement. The aim of this book has been, first, to review what has been achieved since BGE in implementing policies and other measures to improve environmental valuation, accounting and incentives, and second, to explain what more needs to be done to generate a truly "green economy" in the twenty-first century. Over 20 years on, although much has been accomplished, additional advances in policy are still required to green economies successfully.

As indicated in Chapters 1 and 2, we have certainly become more aware of the environmental challenges that face us. Today, with the threat of global warming, the decline in major ecosystems and their services, and fears over energy security, achieving the environmental policy goals outlined in this book is even more vital. There has even been progress, as Chapter 2 documents, with improvements in air quality globally, greater access to safe drinking water by the poor, and improvements in lakes and rivers in the developed world. Yet the major environmental problems – climate change, degradation of ecosystems, biodiversity loss, freshwater scarcity and increased impacts from natural hazards – still need to be urgently addressed.

Compared to 20 years ago, sustainable development is more widely accepted as an essential economic goal, and we have also become clearer about the environmental policies required to achieve it (see Chapter 3). However, despite many important economic and environmental gains, efforts to improve the management of natural resources, pollution and ecological degradation are often thwarted by vested interests and institutional inertia, obstacles to instigating economic policy and technological change that can be formidable, especially with regard to how we use the environment. Powerful vested interests in particular seem to perpetuate policy outcomes that are not only inefficient and environmentally unsustainable but also inequitable.

Environmental valuation is a key tool in formulating better policies for attaining sustainable development (see Chapter 4). As many environmental benefits are not marketed, including vital goods and services provided by ecosystems, then estimating these values is essential to assessing the economy–environment tradeoff underlying many development choices. Environmental valuation has become more accepted as having an important role in informing policy decisions, and there has been considerable progress in valuing many environmental benefits. Further progress is necessary, especially in the area of biodiversity and ecosystem services, if we are to continue to take into consideration the benefits and costs of economic activity with respect to the environment.

Related to environmental valuation is accounting for the environment. As discussed in Chapter 5, an important development since BGE has been to create wealth accounts that allow us to track the sustainability of economies. Included in such accounts has been some measure of the economic depreciation of "natural capital," especially forests, minerals, fossil fuels and other economically important natural resources. In developing countries, such natural capital can comprise over a quarter of a nation's overall economic wealth. In developed countries, the total wealth share of natural capital may be only 2 percent, but it is often worth more than the natural assets of poor countries. In addition, a wide range of indicators of environmental performance and sustainability have been developed to provide guidance as to how economies are impacting the environment. What is now needed is further progress and agreement on what wealth and sustainability indicators should be used by economies, and for these indicators to be used more routinely to guide economic and environmental policies.

Market-based instruments and other price incentives are used more extensively than ever to achieve environmental objectives, such as reducing pollution, managing natural resources more efficiently and controlling ecological degradation (see Chapter 6). Public disclosure and product labeling have also contributed significantly to promoting cleaner products and production processes. However, environmentally damaging subsidies still contribute significantly to the environmental burdens we face, and there is little indication that they are going down. We seem to be at an important crossroads with pricing the environment. There has been considerable progress in prices and incentives for environmental improvement, but we have yet to use such mechanisms on a sufficient economy-wide basis to provide the necessary market signals for attaining greater sustainability. We are also reluctant to use such instruments to tackle major environmental problems, such as reducing carbon use, improving energy security, controlling water use and mitigating biodiversity and ecological loss.

As we argue in Chapter 7, if the imminent threats posed by climate change, energy insecurity, deteriorating ecosystems and environmental catastrophes are to be reduced significantly, then policies to improve environmental management must be broadened into a comprehensive strategy to overcome ecological scarcity and the inherent unsustainability and instability of the world economy. To ensure a transition to a greener world economy requires complementary pricing policies, creating global markets and devising long-term green development plans for poorer economies. Unless at least all the major economies, developed and developing, implement green pricing policies and effective environmental regulations, existing market and policy distortions will continue to underprice the use of natural resources, contribute to environmental degradation and worsen carbon dependency in the global economy.

Recently, the United Nations Environment Programme (UNEP) has proposed a comprehensive strategy comprising policies and investments for a long-term transition to a green global economy, with the aim of "increasing human well-being and social equity, and reducing environmental risks and ecological scarcities."[2] Such a transition strategy is clearly not costless, and will require substantial commitment by all economies. For example, UNEP estimates that public and private investments of around US$1.3 trillion (around 2 percent of global GDP) are required annually to green the global economy. Over time investing in a green economy will actually enhance long-term economic performance, through improved management of renewable resources and ecosystems, reducing environmental risks and rebuilding capacity to generate future prosperity. There will also be considerable improvements in the livelihoods of the poor in developing regions. But the question remains: Will policy makers view sustainable development as a sufficiently important economic goal to make the necessary investments, let alone implement the critical policies to achieve this goal?

As an encouraging sign, green growth, the promotion of energy efficiency and clean energy technologies and sustainable development are increasingly viewed as complementary goals by international policy makers. For example, at the conclusion of the November 2010 Group of 20 (G20) summit comprising the 20 richest and largest economies of the world, the G20 leaders stated:

> We recognize that sustainable green growth, as it is inherently a part of sustainable development, is a strategy of quality development, enabling countries to leapfrog old technologies in many sectors, including through the use of energy efficiency and clean technology. To that end, we will take steps to create, as appropriate, the enabling environments that are conducive to the development of energy efficiency and clean energy technologies, including policies and practices in our countries and beyond, including technical transfer and capacity building.[3]

However, such talk needs urgently to be followed up with concrete action. The world cannot wait another 20 years to implement the type of policies for a green economy advocated in this book. We have a blueprint for a green economy. It is time to put it into practice.

NOTES

Preface

1 World Commission on Environment and Development. 1987. *Our Common Future*. Oxford University Press, Oxford and New York.
2 Pearce, D.W., A. Markandya and E.B. Barbier. 1989. *Blueprint for a Green Economy*. Earthscan Publications, London, p. xv.
3 Visser, W. 2009. *The Top 50 Sustainability Books*. Greenleaf Publishing, Sheffield, UK, a publication of University of Cambridge's Programme for Sustainability Leadership as part of the 800th anniversary celebrations of the University of Cambridge and the 20th anniversary of the Cambridge Programme for Industry (CPI).

1 Introduction

1 For instance, in the early 1970s, Freeman, A.M. III, R.H. Haveman and A.V. Kneese. 1973. *The Economics of Environmental Policy*. John Wiley, New York, p. 20, proposed that the environment should be considered a "capital good" for the diverse "services" that it generates: "[We] view the environment as an asset or a kind of nonreproducible capital good that produces a stream of various services for man. Services are tangible (such as flows of water or minerals), or functional (such as the removal, dispersion, storage, and degradation of wastes or residuals), or intangible (such as a scenic view)."
2 For example, as Daily, G.C., T. Söderqvist, S. Aniyar, K. Arrow, P. Dasgupta, P.R. Ehrlich, et al. 2000. "The Value of Nature and the Nature of Value." *Science* 289:395–96 state (p. 395), "the world's ecosystems are capital assets. If properly managed, they yield a flow of vital services, including the production of goods (such as seafood and timber), life support processes (such as pollination and water purification), and life-fulfilling conditions (such as beauty and serenity)."

3 Pearce, D.W., A. Markandya and E.B. Barbier. 1989. *Blueprint for a Green Economy*. Earthscan Publications, London, p. 1.
4 World Commission on Environment and Development (WCED). 1987. *Our Common Future*. Oxford University Press, Oxford and New York.
5 The UK prime minister at the time that BGE came out, Margaret Thatcher, caught the idea of sustainability very well when she stated that we who are alive today are tenants with a full repairing lease on the planet.
6 Pearce et al., 1989, *op. cit.*, p. 19.
7 Pearce et al., 1989, *op. cit.*, p. 23.
8 This definition of *ecological scarcity* was first developed in Barbier, E.B. 1989. *Economics, Natural Resource Scarcity and Development: Conventional and Alternative Views*. Earthscan Publications, London, pp. 96–97: "The fundamental scarcity problem…is that as the environment is increasingly being exploited for one set of uses (e.g., to provide sources of raw material and energy, and to assimilate additional waste), the quality of the environment may deteriorate. The consequence is an increasing *relative scarcity* of essential natural services and ecological functions…. In other words, if 'the environment is regarded as a scarce resource', then the 'deterioration of the environment is also an economic problem.'"
9 Pearce et al., 1989, *op. cit.*, p. 3.
10 In some circumstances, we can create economic wealth to help recover or protect the environment. These are the green growth options we discuss in Chapter 7.
11 Pearce et al., 1989, *op. cit.*, p. 22.
12 Pearce, D.W., ed. 1991. *Blueprint 2: Greening the World Economy*. Earthscan Publications, London, p. 2.
13 Pearce et al., 1989, *op. cit.*, p. 81.
14 Millennium Ecosystem Assessment. 2005. *Ecosystems and Human Well-being: Synthesis*. Island Press, Washington, DC.
15 Pearce et al., 1989, *op. cit.*, pp. 5–7.
16 *Ibid.*, p. 94.
17 *Ibid.*, p. 93.
18 For example, the World Bank updates and publishes its adjusted net savings indicator for many countries as part of its annually released *World Development Indicators*.
19 Pearce et al., 1989, *op. cit.*, p. 170.
20 Pearce, D.W. and E.B. Barbier. 2000. *Blueprint for a Sustainable Economy*. Earthscan Publications, London, p. 157.
21 UNEP. 2011. *Towards a Green Economy: Pathways to Sustainable Development and Poverty Eradication – A Synthesis for Policymakers*. UNEP, Nairobi. <www.unep.org/greeneconomy> In this report, UNEP estimates that the additional sustainability investments amounted to 2 percent of global GDP per year over 2010–50, across a range of sectors to build capacity, adopt new technologies and management techniques, and scale up green infrastructure.
22 Pearce et al., 1989, *op. cit.*, p. 160.

2 *Blueprint for a Green Economy* in the twenty-first century

1 Data are from the World Bank indicators and from <http://cdiac.ornl.gov/ftp/ndp030/CSV-FILES/>
2 Halsnaes, K., A. Markandya and P. Shukla. 2011. "Introduction: Sustainable Development, Energy and Climate Change." *World Development* 39(6):983–86.

3 In the long run economic development is associated with a "decarbonization" of the economy, in that each dollar of GDP needs less and less carbon to be emitted. In the USA, this rate is estimated to be around 1.3 percent per annum. Moreover, it has remained quite steady over 200 years as a long-term trend. Unfortunately, such a rate is not enough to attain the goal of halving emissions by 2050. See Nakicenovic, N. 2002. "Technological Change and Diffusion as a Learning Process." In A. Grubler, N. Nakicenovic and W.D. Nordhaus, eds. *Technological Change and the Environment*, Resources for the Future and International Institute for Applied Systems Analysis, Washington, DC.

4 Stern, N. 2006. The Economics of Climate Change: The Stern Review. [Electronic Version]. <http://www.hm-treasury.gov.uk/stern_review_report.htm> (accessed July 10, 2011).

5 Pimm, S.L., G.J. Russel, J.L. Gittleman and T.M. Brooks. 1995. "The Future of Biodiversity." *Science* 269:347–50.

6 The source of Figure 2.1 is WWF. 2010. *Living Planet Report 2010: Biodiversity, Biocapacity and Development*. WWF, Gland, Switzerland.

7 Newman, D.J. and G.M. Cragg. 2007. "Natural Products as Sources of New Drugs Over the Last 25 years." *Journal of Natural Products* 70:461–77.

8 "Traditional Medicine." World Health Organization website. <http://www.who.int/mediacentre/factsheets/fs134/en/index.html> (accessed July 27, 2011).

9 For a brief review see ten Brink, P., ed. 2011. "Rewarding Benefits Through Payments and Markets." *The Economics of Ecosystems and Biodiversity in National and International Policy Making*. Earthscan Publications, London, chapter 5.4.

10 See Purvis, A. and A. Hector. 2000. "Getting the Measure of Biodiversity." *Nature* 405 (May 11):212–19, and Mace, G.M., J.L. Gittleman and A. Purvis. 2003. "Preserving the Tree of Life." *Science* 300:1707–9.

11 Millennium Ecosystem Assessment (MEA). 2005. *Ecosystems and Human Well-being: Current State and Trends*. Island Press, Washington, DC.

12 ten Brink, 2011, *op. cit.*

13 MEA, 2005, *op. cit.*

14 Alkemade, R., M. Blackens, R. Bobbin, L. Miles, C. Nellermann, H. Simons and T. Mecklenburg. 2006. "GLOBIO 3: Framework for the Assessment of Global Biodiversity." In MNP, *Integrated Modeling of Environmental Change. An Overview of IMAGE 2.4*. NEAA/MNP, Bilthoven, pp. 171–86.

15 For a discussion of the limitations and advantages of the MSA approach see Markandya, A. and A. Chiabai. (forthcoming). "Economic Loss of Ecosystem Services from 1900 to 2050." In B. Lomborg, ed. *Economics of Human Challenges*. Cambridge University Press, Cambridge.

16 Source: Netherlands Environmental Assessment Agency. PBL. 2010. *Rethinking Global Biodiversity Strategies: Exploring Structural Changes in Production and Consumption to Reduce Biodiversity Loss*. Netherlands Environmental Agency. <http://www.pbl.nl/en/publications/2010/Rethinking_Global_Biodiversity_Strategies.html>

17 *Ibid.*

18 In 2007 average per capita income for the different income groups was as follows: low income, US$574; lower middle income, US$1,904; middle income, US$2,910; upper middle income, US$7,107; and upper income, US$37,572.

19 Source: World Bank. World Development Indicators.

20 Grossman, G. and A. Krueger. 1995. "Economic Growth and the Environment." *Quarterly Journal of Economics* 110(2):353–77.

21 Source: World Resources Institute, <http://www.wri.org>
22 Mario Molina, <http://www.slideshare.net/wildfoundation/climate-change-current-status-impacts-and-solutions-by-mario-molina> (accessed August 21, 2011).
23 <http://www.ucar.edu/news/releases/2005/drought_research.shtml> (accessed August 21, 2011).
24 <http://www.beta.undp.org/undp/en/home/mdgoverview/mdg_goals/mdg7/where_do_we_stand.html> (accessed August 21, 2011).
25 Mario Molina, *op. cit.*
26 <http://www.beta.undp.org/undp/en/home/mdgoverview/mdg_goals/mdg7/where_do_we_stand.html>
27 Source: Eurostat, Waterbase – Rivers. <http://www.edis.sk/ekes/Eurowaternet_final_low_res.pdf>
28 <http://www.emdat.be/database>
29 *Ibid.*
30 *Ibid.* World Bank. 2010. "Natural Hazards, Unnatural Disasters: The Economics of Effective Protection." World Bank, United Nations, Washington, DC.
31 <http://en.wikipedia.org/wiki/Aarhus_Convention> (accessed August 21, 2011).
32 Former centrally planned economies had a complex set of pollution charges as long ago as the 1970s but these did not really serve as incentives to adopt cleaner technologies. For details see Bluffstone, R. and B. Larson, eds. 1997. *Implementation of Pollution Charge Systems in Transition Economies.* Edward Elgar, Cheltenham.

3 Sustainable development

1 World Commission on Environment and Development (WCED). 1987. *Our Common Future.* Oxford University Press, Oxford and New York.
2 Pearce, D.W., A. Markandya and E.B. Barbier. 1989. *Blueprint for a Green Economy.* Earthscan Publications, London, p. 28.
3 The term *ecological resilience* or *robustness* usually refers to an ecosystem's ability to absorb large shocks or sustained disturbances and still maintain internal integrity and functioning. This concept of resilience is usually attributable to Holling, C.S. 1973. "Resilience and Stability of Ecological Systems." *Annual Review of Ecological Systems* 4:1–23, who maintains that ecosystems are characterized by multiple locally stable equilibria, or different *ecological regimes.* Hence, a *regime shift* can occur if the ecosystem undergoes a sudden change from one stable equilibrium to another. The resilience of an ecosystem can therefore be thought of as the extent to which it can sustain shocks or disturbances before the ecosystem "flips" to an alternative stable state, or ecological regime.
4 See Barbier, E.B. 1987. "The Concept of Sustainable Economic Development." *Environmental Conservation* 14(2):101–10, figure 1.
5 *Ibid.*, p. 104.
6 As Bishop, R.C. 1993. "Economic Efficiency, Sustainability and Biodiversity." *Ambio* 22(2–3):69–73 has pointed out, stated in this way the objective of "sustainability" is different from that of the standard economic goal of "efficiency." That is, there are potentially an infinite number of development paths for an economy, only some of which are sustainable. Efficiency therefore does not guarantee sustainability, as some efficient paths are not sustainable.

At the same time, there is no reason why an economy could not be both efficient and sustainable.

7 See, for example, Pezzey, J.C.V. 1989. "Economic Analysis of Sustainable Growth and Sustainable Development." Environment Department Working Paper No. 15. World Bank, Washington, DC.

8 Pearce et al., 1989, *op. cit.*, p. 3.

9 An early distinction between weak and strong sustainability appears in the essay by Turner, R.K. 1993. "Sustainability Principles and Practice." In R.K. Turner, ed. *Sustainable Environmental Management: Principles and Practice*, 2nd ed. Belhaven Press, London, pp. 3–36.

10 Note, however, that rapid population growth may imply that the value of the per capita aggregate capital stock is declining even if the total value stays the same. Moreover, even if the per capita value of the asset base were maintained, it may not imply non-declining welfare of the majority of people. These considerations also hold for the strong sustainability arguments discussed below.

11 These principles are inspired conceptually by Hartwick's rule (1977), which is often also referred to as the Hartwick–Solow rule, in recognition that Solow (1974) first derived the principle that reinvestment of the rents generated from the intertemporally efficient use of exhaustible natural resources can be reinvested in reproducible capital in order to ensure a constant stream of consumption over time. Solow (1993) provides an excellent summary of the implications of Hartwick's rule for economic sustainability. Hartwick, John. 1977. "Intergenerational Equity and the Investing of Rents from Exhaustible Resources." *American Economic Review* 67:972–74; Solow, Robert M. 1974. "Intergenerational Equity and Exhaustible Resources." *Review of Economic Studies*, Symposium on the Economics of Exhaustible Resources, 29–46; Solow, Robert M. 1993. "Sustainability: An Economist's Perspective." In Robert Dorfman and Nancy S. Dorfman, eds. *Economics of the Environment: Selected Readings*, 3rd ed. W.W. Norton, New York, pp. 179–87.

12 Dasgupta, P. 2008. "Nature in Economics." *Environmental and Resource Economics* 39:1–7, p. 3.

13 See, for example, Dixit, A. 1996. *The Making of Economic Policy: A Transaction-Cost Politics Perspective*. MIT Press, Cambridge, MA; Hodgson, G.M. 1998. "The Approach of Institutional Economics." *Journal of Economic Literature* 36(1):166–92; McCann, L., B. Colby, K.W. Easter, A. Kasterine and K.V. Kuperan. 2005. "Transaction Cost Measurement for Evaluation Environmental Policies." *Ecological Economics* 52:527–42; North, D.C. 1990. "A Transaction Cost Theory of Politics." *Journal of Theoretical Politics* 2(4):355–67; Williamson, O.E. 2000. "The New Institutional Economics: Taking Stock, Looking Ahead." *Journal of Economic Literature* 38(3):595–613.

14 See, for example, Grubb, M., T. Chapuis and M. Ha Duong. 1995. "The Economics of Changing Course: Implications of Adaptability and Inertia for Optimal Climate Policy." *Energy Policy* 23:417–32; Micahaelowa, A. and F. Jotzo. 2005. "Transaction Costs, Institutional Rigidities and the Size of the Clean Development Mechanism." *Energy Policy* 33:511–23; and Schwoon, M. and R.S.J. Tol. 2006. "Optimal CO_2-Abatement with Socio-economic Inertia and Induced Technological Change." *The Energy Journal* 27(4):25–59.

15 The figure in Box 3.4 is adapted from McCann et al., 2005, *op. cit.*, figure 1.

16 See, for example, Easter, K.W. and S. Archibald. 2002. "Water Markets: The Global Perspective." *Water Resources Impact* 4(1):23–25; Hellegers, P.J.G. and

C.J. Perry. 2006. "Can Irrigation Water Use Be Guided by Market Forces? Theory and Practice." *Water Resources Development* 22(1):79–86; McCann, L. and K.W. Easter. 2004. "A Framework for Estimating the Transaction Costs of Alternative Mechanisms for Water Exchange and Allocation." *Water Resources Research* 40:1–6; McCann et al., 2005, *op. cit.*

17 See, for example, Aidt, T. 1998. "Political Internalization of Economic Externalities and Environmental Policy." *Journal of Public Economics* 69:1–16. Barbier, E.B. 2010. "Corruption and the Political Economy of Resource-based Development: A Comparison of Asia and Sub-Saharan Africa." *Environmental Resource Economics* 46:512–37; Barbier, E.B., R. Damania and D. Léonard. 2005. "Corruption, Trade and Resource Conversion." *Journal of Environmental Economics and Management* 50:276–99; Fredriksson, P.G. 2003. "Political Instability, Corruption and Policy Formation: The Case of Environmental Policy." *Journal of Public Economics* 87:1383–1405; López, R. and S. Mitra. 2000. "Corruption, Pollution, and the Kuznets Environmental Curve." *Journal of Environmental Economics and Management* 40:137–50; Wilson, J.K. and R. Damania. 2005. "Corruption, Political Competition and Environmental Policy." *Journal of Environmental Economics and Management* 49:516–35.

18 IEA/OPEC/OECD/World Bank. 2010. *Analysis of the Scope of Energy Subsidies and the Suggestions for the G-20 Initiative*. Joint Report Prepared for Submission to the G-20 Summit Meeting Toronto (Canada), 26–27 June 2010.

19 Chomitz, K.M. with P. Buys, G. De Luca, T.S. Thomas and S. Wertz-Kanounnikoff. 2007. *At Loggerheads? Agricultural Expansion, Poverty Reduction, and Environment in the Tropical Forests*. World Bank, Washington, DC; Food and Agricultural Organization of the United Nations (FAO). 2001. *Forest Resources Assessment 2000: Main Report*. FAO Forestry Paper 140. Rome, FAO; Food and Agricultural Organization of the United Nations (FAO). 2003. *State of the World's Forests 2003*. Rome, FAO.

20 Rudel, T.K. 2007. "Changing Agents of Deforestation: From State-initiated to Enterprise-driven Process, 1970–2000." *Land Use Policy* 24:35–41, p. 40. See also, Barbier, E.B. 2005. *Natural Resources and Economic Development*. Cambridge University Press, Cambridge and New York; Chomitz et al., 2007, *op cit.*; FAO, 2001 and 2003, *op. cit*; Rudel, T.K. 2005. *Tropical Forests: Regional Paths of Destruction and Regeneration in the Late 20th Century*. Columbia University Press, New York; and Wassenaar, T., P. Gerber, P.H. Verburg, M. Rosales, M. Ibrahim and H. Steinfeld. 2007. "Projecting Land Use Changes in the Neotropics: The Geography of Pasture Expansion into Forest." *Global Environmental Change* 17:86–104.

21 Barbier, 2005 *op. cit.* and Barbier, E.B. 2010. "Poverty, Development and Environment." *Environment and Development Economics* 15:635–60.

22 Comprehensive Assessment of Water Management in Agriculture. 2007. *Water for Food, Water for Life: A Comprehensive Assessment of Water Management in Agriculture*. Earthscan, London, and International Water Management Institute, Colombo, Sri Lanka and World Bank. 2003. *World Development Report 2003*. World Bank, Washington, DC.

23 Population Division of the United Nations Secretariat. 2008. *World Urbanization Prospects: The 2007 Revision: Executive Summary*. United Nations, New York.

24 Chen, S. and M. Ravallion. 2007. "Absolute Poverty Measures for the Developing World, 1981–2004." *Proceedings of the National Academy of Sciences* 104(43):16757–62.

25 McGranahan, G., D. Balk and B. Anderson. 2007. "The Rising Tide: Assessing the Risks of Climate Change and Human Settlements in Low Elevation Coastal Zones." *Environment and Urbanization* 19(1): 17–37.

26 Organization for Economic Cooperation and Development (OECD). 2008. *Costs of Inaction on Key Environmental Challenges*. OECD, Paris, and United Nations Development Programme (UNDP). 2008. *Human Development Report 2007/2008. Fighting Climate Change: Human Solidarity in a Divided World*. UNDP, New York.

27 Nicholls, R.J., S. Hanson, C. Herweijer, N. Patmore, S. Hallegatte, J. Corfee-Morlot, et al. 2007. *Ranking of the World's Cities Most Exposed to Coastal Flooding Today and in the Future: Executive Summary*. OECD Environment Working Paper No. 1. OECD, Paris.

28 United Nations Development Programme (UNDP). 2006. *Human Development Report 2006. Beyond Scarcity: Power, Poverty and the Global Water Crisis*. UNDP, New York.

29 Modi, V., S. McDade, D. Lallement and J. Saghir. 2005. *Energy Services for the Millennium Development Goals*. International Bank for Reconstruction and Development/World Bank and the United Nations Development Programme, Washington, DC and New York.

4 Progress in valuing the environment

1 Pearce, D.W., A. Markandya and E.B. Barbier. 1989. *Blueprint for a Green Economy*. Earthscan Publications, London, p. 81.

2 Millennium Ecosystem Assessment. 2005. *Ecosystems and Human Well-being: Current State and Trends*. Island Press, Washington, DC.

3 Critics of this approach claim that a measure based on willingness to pay is "income constrained" and therefore inequitable. But that is true of all allocation decisions made by households, not just environmental ones. We may wish to change the allocation of resources to make it more equitable but this does not prevent us using values based on willingness to pay as one input to decide on priorities. Of course if we then find the resulting decisions unfair or inequitable we can and should take that into account as an additional criterion.

4 Millennium Ecosystem Assessment. 2005. *Ecosystems and Human Well-being: Synthesis*. Island Press, Washington, DC.

5 Barbier, E.B. 2007. "Valuing Ecosystems as Productive Inputs." *Economic Policy* 22:177–229.

6 National Research Council (NRC). 2005. *Valuing Ecosystem Services: Toward Better Environmental Decision Making*. National Academies Press, Washington, DC, p. 2.

7 Polasky, S. and K. Segerson. 2009. "Integrating Ecology and Economics in the Study of Ecosystem Services: Some Lessons Learned." *Annual Review of Resource Economics* 1:409–34, p. 422.

8 From Environmental Protection Agency (EPA). 2009. *Valuing the Protection of Ecological Systems and Services*. A Report of the EPA Science Advisory Board. EPA, Washington, DC, p. 12.

9 Adapted from NRC, 2005, *op. cit.*, figure 7–1.

10 Another component of value, *option value*, is commonly referred to as a non-use value in the literature. However, option value arises from the difference between

valuation under conditions of certainty and uncertainty, and is a numerical calculation, not a value held by people per se. See NRC, 2005, *op. cit.*, ch. 6 for further discussion.

11 There is now an extensive economics literature that discusses in some detail how these standard valuation methods are best applied to various ecosystem services, emphasizing in particular both the advantages and the shortcomings of the different methods and their application. See, for example, Barbier, 2007, *op. cit.*; EPA, 2009, *op. cit.*; Freeman, A.M. III. 2003. *The Measurement of Environmental and Resource Values: Theory and Methods*, 2nd ed. Resources for the Future, Washington, DC; Hanley, N. and E.B. Barbier. 2009. *Pricing Nature: Cost-Benefit Analysis and Environmental Policy*. Edward Elgar, London; Kumar, P., ed. *The Economics of Ecosystems and Biodiversity: Ecological and Economic Foundations*. Earthscan Publications, London; Mendelsohn, R. and S. Olmstead. 2009. "The Economic Valuation of Environmental Amenities and Disamenities: Methods and Applications." *Annual Review of Environment and Resources* 34:325–47; NRC, 2005, *op. cit.*

12 Naylor, R. and M. Drew. 1998. "Valuing Mangrove Resources in Kosrae, Micronesia." *Environment and Development Economics* 3:471–90, p. 488.

13 Carlsson, F., P. Frykblom and C. Lilijenstolpe. 2003. "Valuing Wetland Attributes: An Application of Choice Experiments." *Ecological Economics* 47:95–103.

14 Bateman, I.J., B.H. Day, A.P Jones and S. Jude. 2009. "Reducing Gain–Loss Asymmetry: A Virtual Reality Choice Experiment Valuing Land Use Change." *Journal of Environmental Economics and Management* 58:106–18.

15 See, for example, Christie M., N. Hanley, J. Warren, K. Murphy, R. Wright and T. Hyde. 2006. "Valuing the Diversity of Biodiversity." *Ecological Economics* 58(2):304–17.

16 See, for example, Barbier, E.B. 1994. "Valuing Environmental Functions: Tropical Wetlands." *Land Economics* 70:155–73; Barbier, 2007, *op. cit.* and McConnell, K.E. and N.E. Bockstael. 2005. "Valuing the Environment as a Factor of Production." In K.-G. Mäler and J.R. Vincent, eds. *Handbook of Environmental Economics*, Vol. 2. Elsevier, Amsterdam, pp. 621–69.

17 Freeman, 2003, *op. cit.*, p. 259.

18 See, for example, Barbier, E.B. 2000. "Valuing the Environment as Input: Applications to Mangrove–Fishery Linkages." *Ecological Economics* 35:47–61; Barbier, 2007, *op. cit.*; Freeman, 2003, *op. cit.*, ch. 9; and McConnell and Bockstael, 2005, *op. cit.*

19 From Barbier, 2007, *op. cit.*

20 In the case of air pollution see Markandya, A., A. Bigano and R. Porchia. 2010. *The Social Costs of Electricity: Scenarios and Policy Implications*. Edward Elgar, London.

21 In the EU the impact pathway approach has influenced several directives, including Draft directive on non-hazardous waste incineration (2000/76/EC); Large combustion plant directive (LCPD, 2001/80/EC); EU strategy to combat acidification (COM (97)88); and The CAFE Programme – Implementation of the Thematic Strategy on Air Pollution.

22 Chong, J. 2005. *Protective Values of Mangrove and Coral Ecosystems: A Review of Methods and Evidence*. IUCN, Gland, Switzerland.

23 Shabman, L.A. and S.S. Batie. 1978. "Economic Value of Natural Coastal Wetlands: A Critique." *Coastal Zone Management Journal* 4(3):231–47.

24 Byström, O. 2000. "The Replacement Value of Wetlands in Sweden." *Environmental and Resource Economics* 16:347–62.

25 See, for example, Barbier, 1994 and 2007, *op. cit.*; Ellis, G.M. and A.C. Fisher. 1987. "Valuing the Environment as Input." *Journal of Environmental Management* 25:149–56; Freeman, 2003, *op. cit.*; Shabman and Batie, 1978, *op. cit.*

26 Barbier, 2007, *op. cit.*

27 Barbier, 2007, *op. cit.*; Freeman, 2003, *op. cit.*, pp. 243–47.

28 Johnston, R.J., T.A. Grigalunas, J.J. Opaluch, M. Mazzotta and J. Diamantedes. 2002. "Valuing Estuarine Resource Services Using Economic and Ecological Models: The Peconic Estuary System." *Coastal Management* 30(1): 47–65.

29 For a review, see Tschirhart, J. 2009. "Integrated Ecological–Economic Models." *Annual Review of Resource Economics* 1:381–407.

30 Finnoff, D. and J. Tschirhart. 2003. "Protecting an Endangered Species while Harvesting its Prey in a General Equilibrium Ecosystem Model." *Land Economics* 70:160–80; Finnoff, D. and J. Tschirhart. 2003. "Harvesting in an Eight-Species Ecosystem." *Journal of Environmental Economics and Management* 45:589–611; and Sanchirico J.N., M.D. Smith and D.W. Lipton. 2008. "An Empirical Approach to Ecosystem-based Fishery Management." *Ecological Economics* 64:586–96.

31 Finnoff, D. and J. Tschirhart. 2008. "Linking Dynamic Economic and Ecological General Equilibrium Models." *Resource and Energy Economics* 30:91–114.

32 Nelson, E., G. Mendoza, J. Regetz, S. Polasky, H. Tallis, et al. 2009. "Modeling Multiple Ecosystem Services, Biodiversity Conservation, Commodity Production, and Tradeoffs at Landscape Scales." *Frontiers in Ecology and Environment* 7(1):4–11.

33 Settle, C. and J.F. Shogren. 2006. "Does Integrating Economic and Biological Systems Matter for Public Policy? The Case of Yellowstone Lake." *Topics in Economic Analysis & Policy* 6(1): art. 9. Available at: <http://www.bepress.com/bejeap/topics/vol6/iss1/art9>

34 See, for example, Bateman, I.J. and A.P. Jones. 2003. "Contrasting Conventional with Multi-level Modeling Approaches to Meta-analysis: Expectation Consistency in UK Woodland Recreation Values." *Land Economics* 79:235–58; Brander, L.M., R.J.G.M. Florax and J.E. Vermaat. 2006. "The Empirics of Wetland Valuation: A Comprehensive Summary and a Meta-analysis of the Literature." *Environmental and Resource Economics* 33:223–50; Brander, L.M., P. van Beukering and H.S.J. Cesar. 2007. "The Recreational Value of Coral Reefs: A Meta-analysis." *Ecological Economics* 63:209–18; Johnston, R.J., M.H. Ranson, E.Y. Besedin and E.C. Helm. 2006. "What Determines Willingness to Pay Per Fish? A Meta-analysis of Recreational Fishing Values." *Marine Resource Economics* 21:1–32; Smith, V.K. and Y. Kaoru. 1990. "Signals or Noise? Explaining the Variation in Recreation Benefit Estimates." *American Journal of Agricultural Economics* 72:419–33; Woodward, R.T. and Y.-S. Wui. 2001. "The Economic Value of Wetland Services: A Meta-analysis." *Ecological Economics* 37:257–70; Zandersen, M. and R.S.J. Tol. 2009. "A Meta-analysis of Forest Recreation Values in Europe." *Journal of Forest Economics* 15:109–30. The use of *meta-analysis* in environmental valuation is explained by Woodward and Wui, 2001, *op. cit.*, p. 260: "The basic approach used in most valuation meta-analyses is the same. A set of studies is selected yielding a number of values that become the dependent variable. The independent variables are the characteristics of each study and study site. If a single study reports numerous values, then several data points are obtained. Meta-analysis allows the evaluation of the effect of changes in the

underlying environmental attribute on value. Such analysis is usually not possible in the context of a single study since most such attributes are held constant."

35 Zandersen and Tol, 2009, *op. cit.*

36 Bateman, I.J., A.A. Lovett and J.S. Brainard. 2005. *Applied Environmental Economics: A GIS Approach to Cost-Benefit Analysis.* Cambridge University Press, Cambridge, ch. 2–4.

37 From Willis, K.G., G. Garrod, R. Scarpa, N. Powe, A.A. Lovett, I.J. Bateman, et al. 2003. *The Social and Environmental Benefits of Forests in Great Britain.* Report to Forestry Commission, UK Forestry Commission, Edinburgh, Scotland. Note that Box 4.10 also indicates a high value for the biodiversity of remaining non-coniferous forests in Great Britain. However, this estimated biodiversity value for forests in Britain should be treated with caution. According to Willis et al., 2003, *op. cit.*, pp. 14–15, "non-use biodiversity values are particularly difficult to capture. Both CV and stated choice (SC) experiments encounter difficulties in deriving biodiversity values. These problems arise for a number of reasons. First, people have widely different preferences for wildlife, so the variance of the mean WTP value is large. Second, people's WTP for biodiversity in different types of British woodland is a very small fraction of income; whilst WTP variation between individuals is mainly driven by taste for different forms of wildlife, vis-à-vis other goods, rather than by income. Because taste is difficult to measure, the variation in WTP between individuals is difficult to explain. Third, biodiversity is a difficult concept for people to grasp, and people find it difficult to trade-off species importance within fungi, plants, invertebrates, birds, and mammals, and to trade-off species importance between these groups. They also find it difficult to trade-off changes in numbers in a particular species against changes in the number of species represented in a habitat. Thus biodiversity is a complex issue over which many people struggle to form preferences. These preferences, once formed, seem to vary widely."

38 Zandersen, M., M. Termansen and F. Søndergaard Jensen. 2007. "Testing Benefits Transfer of Forest Recreation Values over a Twenty-Year Time Horizon." *Land Economics* 83(3):412–40.

39 Aksornkoae, S. and R. Tokrisna. 2004. "Overview of Shrimp Farming and Mangrove Loss in Thailand." In E.B. Barbier and S. Sathirathai, eds. *Shrimp Farming and Mangrove Loss in Thailand.* Edward Elgar, London, and Food and Agricultural Organization of the United Nations (FAO). 2003. "Status and Trends in Mangrove Area Extent Worldwide" (by M.L. Wilkie and S. Fortuna). *Forest Resources Assessment Working Paper No. 63.* Forest Resources Division, FAO, Rome.

40 Based on Barbier, 2007, *op. cit.*

5 Accounting for the environment and sustainability

1 Commission on the Measurement of Economic Performance and Social Progress. <http://www.stiglitz-sen-fitoussi.fr/en/index.htm> (accessed November 28, 2011).

2 J.E. Stiglitz et al. 2011. "Report by the Commission on the Measurement of Economic Performance and Social Progress." <www.stiglitz-sen-fitoussi.fr>

3 See Pearce, D. and G. Atkinson. 1993. "Capital Theory and the Measurement of Sustainable Development: An Indicator of Weak Sustainability." *Ecological Economics* 8(2):103–8.

4   We do not cover one area that has emerged recently, namely the measurement of happiness. It has resulted in indicators of well-being that are being taken seriously by politicians but its relationship to environment and sustainability are incidental. For a review of the idea and its applications see Layard, R. 2006. *Happiness. Lessons from a New Science*. Penguin, London.

5   For an up-to-date state of the guidelines see UN. 2011. "Revision of the System of Environment–Economic Accounts." United Nations, Department of Economic and Social Affairs, Statistical Division.

6   Another problem is whether to define the expenditures on the basis of the measures that the agency itself executes or whether the definition is on the basis of expenditures that the agency finances. The two are referred to as the abater and financing principle and can give different overall results.

7   The OECD provides a forum in which governments from mainly developed countries can work together to share experiences and seek solutions to common problems. It currently has 34 members, including all developed economies but some emerging countries such as Turkey, Mexico and Chile. Eurostat is the statistical office of the European Union situated in Luxembourg. Its task is to provide the European Union with statistics at a European level (not just EU member states) that enable comparisons between countries and regions.

8   Eurostat assembles similar information for a number of European countries but its tables also have a lot of gaps, either in the data on private expenditures or public expenditures. Only a few countries have information on both sources of spending and for a number of years.

9   An environmental tax is a tax whose tax base is a physical unit (or a proxy of it) of something that has a proven, specific negative impact on the environment. Total revenues for environmental taxes include taxes on transport, energy, pollution and resources. Included are taxes on emissions, different sources of energy, taxes on vehicles, fees on abstraction of water and taxes on extraction of raw materials. Not included are VAT taxes on any environmental goods and services.

10 See World Bank. 2006. *Where is the Wealth of Nations: Measuring Capital for the 21st Century*. World Bank, Washington, DC.

11 See Markandya, A. and M.L. Tamborra. 2006. *Green Accounting in Europe: The GARPII Project*. Edward Elgar, Cheltenham; see also <http://people.bath.ac.uk/hssam/greensense/home.html>

12 This is based on Barbier, E.B. 2011. "Tracking the Sputnik Economy." *The Economists' Voice* 8(1): art. 9. <http://www.bepress.com/ev/vol8/iss1/art9>

13 For an application see Gerlagh, R., R. Dellink, M. Hofkes and H. Verbruggen. 2002. "A Measure of Sustainable National Income for the Netherlands." *Ecological Economics* 41:157–74. This builds on earlier work by Hueting who, as long ago as 1980, measured the costs of meeting sustainability constraints and proposed that sustainable income was equal to the actual level of income less the costs of meeting these constraints. See Hueting, R. 1980. *New Scarcity and Economic Growth: More Welfare Through Less Production?* North-Holland, Amsterdam.

14 The Project was coordinated by Anil Markandya at Bath University, with Alistair Hunt, Pam Mason and Nick Dale and involved researchers from Germany, Italy and Spain. See <http://ec.europa.eu/research/environment/print.cfm?file=/comm/research/environment/newsanddoc/article_2086_en.htm> (accessed November 30, 2011). <http://people.bath.ac.uk/hssam/greensense/home.html>

15 See Croitoru, L. and M. Sarraf., eds. 2010. *The Cost of Environmental Degradation: Case Studies from the Middle East and North Africa.* World Bank, Washington, DC.

16 Gundimeda, H. and Sukhdev, P. 2008. "GDP of the Poor." Unpublished manuscript.

17 The details are mostly taken from the proceedings of the conference "Beyond GDP" organized by the European Commission in 2007. See European Commission. 2009. "Beyond GDP: Measuring Progress, True Wealth and the Wellbeing of Nations." 19–20 November 2007 Conference Proceedings. European Commission, Luxembourg.

6 Progress in prices and incentives for environmental improvement

1 Organization for Economic Cooperation and Development (OECD). 1975. *The Polluter Pays Principle: Definition, Analysis, Implementation.* OECD, Paris.

2 The OECD includes mainly advanced and emerging market economies from Europe: Austria, Belgium, Czech Republic, Denmark, Finland, France, Germany, Greece, Hungary, Iceland, Republic of Ireland, Italy, Luxembourg, the Netherlands, Norway, Poland, Portugal, Slovakia, Spain, Sweden, Switzerland, Turkey and the United Kingdom; and from other regions: Australia, Canada, Japan, Mexico, New Zealand, South Korea and the United States.

3 In order to keep Table 6.1 legible we have excluded the following countries: Chile, Estonia, Greece, Hungary, Iceland, Ireland, Israel, Luxembourg, New Zealand and Turkey.

4 In the examples included in Table 6.1 we have tried to exclude those cases where the user charges are not based on weight or volume. This is not always possible as the information provided by national governments can be quite limited.

5 See Repetto R., R.C. Dower, R. Jenkins and J. Geoghegan. 1992. "Green Fees: How a Tax Shift Can Work for the Environment and the Economy." World Resources Institute, Washington, DC; and OECD. 1993. "Environmental Taxes in OECD Countries: A Survey." OECD Monographs no. 71. OECD, Paris.

6 Somanathan, E. and T. Sterner. 2006. "Environmental Policy Instruments in Developing Countries." In R. López and M.A. Toman. *Economic Development and Environmental Sustainability.* Oxford University Press, Oxford.

7 Sterner, T. and D. Slunge. 2011. "Environmental and Fiscal Reform in Eastern and Southern Africa." *Rivista di Politica Economica* 7–9(11–58):XX.

8 *Ibid.*

9 *Ibid.*

10 *Ibid.*

11 World Bank. 2000. *Green Industry: New Roles for Communities, Markets and Governments.* World Bank, Washington, DC.

12 *Ibid.*

13 *Ibid.*

14 <http://www2.oecd.org/ecoinst/queries/>

15 See <http://www.globalsubsidies.org/files/assets/relative_energy_subsidies.pdf>

16 IEA/OPEC/OECD/World Bank. 2010. *Analysis of the Scope of Energy Subsidies and the Suggestions for the G-20 Initiative.* Joint Report Prepared for Submission to the G-20 Summit Meeting Toronto (Canada), 26–27 June 2010.

17 Of the 34 OECD countries no information was reported from Germany, Norway, Mexico and Portugal.

18 Countries that did not provide data and those that provided only cursory data have been excluded from Table 6.2.

19 A feed-in tariff (FIT) is a guaranteed price paid to a generator from a renewable source. A renewable portfolio standard (RPS) is a system that obliges utilities or consumers to source a certain percentage of their power from renewable energy sources. The USA has relied more on RPS although some states have FITs for small producers. The advantage of an RPS is that it provides flexibility in terms of how firms make investment and trading decisions. Obligations could be met through the trading of certificates that are allocated to operators of renewable energy plants. The disadvantage is that firms are vulnerable to uncertainty in future electricity and certificate prices.

20 See Fischer, C. and L. Peronas. 2010. "Combining Policies for Renewable Energy." Resources for the Future, DP 10–19.

21 *Ibid.*

22 See Hassett, Kevin A. and Gilbert E. Metcalf. 1995. "Energy Tax Credits and Residential Conservation Investment: Evidence from Panel Data." *Journal of Public Economics* 57:201–17.

23 UKERC. 2007. "UKERC Review of Evidence for the Rebound Effect: Technical Report 2: Econometric Studies." REF UKERC/WP/TPA/2007/010.

24 See the Global Subsidies Initiative for more details: <http://www.globalsubsidies.org/>

25 This result was stated originally by Martin Weitzman in 1974 and has been worked on since. See Pizer, W.A. 1999. "Optimal Choice of Policy Instrument and Stringency under Uncertainty: The Case of Climate Change." *Resource and Energy Economics* 21:255–87; and Newall, R.G. and W.A. Pizer. 2003. "Regulating Stock Externalities Under Uncertainty." *Journal of Environmental Economics and Management* 45:416–32.

26 See for example Stiglitz, J. 2006. "A New Agenda for Global Warming." *The Economists' Voice* 3(7).

27 Bosetti, V., C. Carraro, M. Galeotti, E. Massetti and M. Tavoni. 2006. "WITCH: A World Induced Technical Change Hybrid Model." *Energy Journal* 27(2) Special Issue on Hybrid Modeling of Energy–Environment Policies: Reconciling Bottom-up and Top-down, pp. 13–38.

28 See <http://www.epa.gov/airmarkets/progsregs/arp/s02.html>

29 Chestnut, L. G. and D.M. Mills. 2005. "A Fresh Look at the Benefits and Costs of the US Acid Rain Program." *Journal of Environmental Management* 20:1–15.

30 *Ibid.*

31 See Ellerman, A. D. and B. K. Buchner. 2007. "The European Union Emissions Trading Scheme: Origins, Allocation, and Early Results." *Review of Environmental Economics and Policy* 1:66–87, and Convery, F., A.D. Ellerman and C. De Perthuis. 2008. "The European Carbon Market in Action: Lessons from the First Trading Period: Interim Report." (March). Available at: <http://www.aprec.fr/documents/08-03-25_interim_report_en.pdf>

32 See <http://www.epa.gov/owow/wetlands/facts/fact16.html>

33 See <http://www.environmentbank.com/>

34 See <http://bbop.forest-trends.org/pilot.php>

35 The discussion in this section draws on Markandya A., L. Jian, Z. Lee and J. Leshan. 2009. "Fujian Sustainable Water Monitoring and Payment for Ecological Services (PES) Development." Report to the ADB.

36 See Landell-Mills, N. and I.T. Porras. 2002. *Silver Bullet or Fools' Gold: A Global Review of Markets for Forest Environmental Services and their Impact on the Poor.* International Institute for Environment and Development, London.

37 *Ibid.*

38 Some details are taken from Pagiola, S., A. Arcenas and G. Platais. 2005. "Can Payments for Environmental Services Help Reduce Poverty? An Exploration of the Issues and the Evidence to Date from Latin America." *World Development* 33:237; Pagiola, S. 2002. "Paying for Water Services in Central America: Learning from Costa Rica." In S. Pagiola, J. Bishop and N. Landell-Mills, eds. *Selling Forest Environmental Services: Market-based Mechanisms for Conservation.* Earthscan Publications, London, pp. 37–61; Isakson, R.S. 2002. *Payments for Environmental Services in the Catskills: A Socioeconomic Analysis of the Agricultural Strategy in New York City's Watershed Management Plan.* Ford Foundation and Fundación PRISMA.

39 See Pagiola, S., P. Agostini, J. Gobbi, C. de Haan, M. Ibrahin, E. Murgueitio, et al. 2004. "Paying for Biodiversity Conservation Services in Agricultural Landscape." World Bank Environment Department Working Paper 96.

40 Landell-Mills and Porras, 2002, *op. cit.*

41 Details draw on Rosa, H., S. Kandel and L. Dimas. 2003. "Compensation for Environmental Services and Rural Communities: Lessons from the Americas and Key Issues for Strengthening Community Strategies." PRISMA, San Salvador, and on Landell-Mills and Porras, 2002, *op. cit.*

42 See Mayrand, K. and M. Paquin. 2004. "Payment for Environmental Services: A Survey and Assessment of Current Schemes." UNISFERA. <http://unisfera. org/?ln=1&id_secteur = 4>

43 Landell-Mills and Porras, 2002, *op. cit.*

44 See Kumar, P. 2005. "Market for Ecosystem Services." International Institute for Sustainable Development (IISD).

45 Details are taken from Rosa et al., 2003, *op. cit.* and Cohen, S. 2002. *Pro-poor Markets for Environmental Services. Carbon Sequestration and Watershed Protection.* World Summit on Sustainable Development (WSSD).

46 Landell-Mills and Porras, 2002, *op. cit.*

47 See Sun Changjin and Chen Liqiao. 2006. "A Study of Policies and Legislation Affecting Payments for Watershed Services in China." Research Center of Ecological and Environmental Economics Beijing, and International Institute for Environment and Development, London. See Li Xiaoyun, Jin Leshan, Zuo Ting, et al., 2007. *Payment for Watershed Services: Role of Market and Government.* Social Science Academic Press, Beijing.

48 World Bank, 2000, *op. cit.*

49 Lopez, J.C., T. Sterner and S. Afsah. 2004. "Public Disclosure of Industrial Pollution: The PROPER Approach for Indonesia?" Resources for the Future DP04–34.

50 See Zarrilli, S., V. Jha and R. Vossenaar. 1997. *Ecolabelling and International Trade.* Macmillan Press, London.

51 There are many studies that cover these issues but the following two give a useful range of estimates. See DEFRA. 2003. "An Assessment of the Environmental Impacts of Organic Farming." A review for Defra-funded project OF0405. DEFRA, ADAS, Elm Farm Research Centre and IGER (May). <http:// www.defra.gov.uk/farm/organic/policy/research/pdf/env-impacts2.pdf> See also "Evaluation of Conventional and Organic Agricultural Production

in Relation to Primary Energy Inputs and Certain Pollution Gas Emissions."
2000. Commissioned by the Federal Ministry for Food, Agriculture and Forestry
(BML), Bonn. Federal Research Centre of Agriculture. <http://www.fcrn.org.
uk/pdf/dmb_summary.pdf>

7 Towards a green global economy

1 See, for example, the communiqué from the 2009 London Summit from the
leaders of the Group of 20 (G20) largest and richest economies: "London Summit
– Leaders' Statement 2 April 2009." <www.g20.org/pub_communiques.aspx>
2 UNEP. 2011. *Towards a Green Economy: Pathways to Sustainable Development and
Poverty Eradication – A Synthesis for Policymakers.* UNEP, Nairobi. <www.unep.
org/greeneconomy>
3 UNEP, 2011, *op. cit.*
4 From the "Leaders' Statement, The Pittsburgh Summit, September 24–25,
2009." <www.g20.org/pub_communiques.aspx>
5 For further details on green stimulus spending by country over 2008–9, see
Barbier, E.B. 2010. *A Global Green New Deal: Rethinking the Economic Recovery.*
Cambridge University Press, Cambridge; Robins, Nick, Robert Clover and
Charanjit Singh. 2009. *Taking Stock of the Green Stimulus.* 23 November. HSBC
Global Research, New York; and Robins, Nick, Robert Clover and D. Saravanan.
2010. *Delivering the Green Stimulus.* 9 March. HSBC Global Research, New York.
6 The original report was revised in April 2009. See Barbier, E.B. 2009. *Rethinking
the Economic Recovery: A Global Green New Deal.* Report prepared for the
Economics and Trade Branch, Division of Technology, Industry and Economics,
United Nations Environment Programme. Geneva, April.
7 The UNEP policy brief is available at: <http://www.unep.ch/etb/publications/
Green%20Economy/UNEP%20Policy%20Brief%20Eng.pdf>
8 Barbier, 2010, *A Global Green New Deal, op. cit.*
9 The members of the G20 include 19 countries (Argentina, Australia, Brazil,
Canada, China, France, Germany, India, Indonesia, Italy, Japan, Mexico, Russia,
Saudi Arabia, South Africa, South Korea, Turkey, the UK and the USA) plus the
European Union.
10 See, for example, "The Grass Is Always Greener." *The Economist.* April 2, 2009.
<http://www.economist.com/business-finance/economics-focus/displaystory.
cfm?story_id = E1_TPQDQVGR>, which cautions that "saving the planet and
creating jobs may be incompatible" and expresses concerns about the additional
deficit burden of green stimulus.
11 Barbier, 2010. *A Global Green New Deal, op. cit.* See also Strand, J. and
M. Toman. 2010. "'Green Stimulus', Economy Recovery, and Long-Term
Sustainable Development." Policy Research Working Paper 5163. World Bank,
Washington, DC.
12 From UNEP, 2011, *op. cit.*
13 International Energy Agency. 2008. *World Energy Outlook 2008.* Organization for
Economic Cooperation and Development and the International Energy Agency,
Paris.
14 World Bank. 2009. *Global Economic Prospects 2009. Commodities at the Crossroads.*
World Bank, Washington, DC.

15 Modi, Vijay, Susan McDade, Dominique Lallement and Jamal Saghir. 2005. *Energy Services for the Millennium Development Goals*. International Bank for Reconstruction and Development/World Bank and the United Nations Development Programme, Washington, DC and New York.

16 IEA, 2008, *op. cit.*

17 International Energy Agency (IEA). 2007. *Oil Supply Security 2007: Emergency Response of IEA Countries*. Organization for Economic Cooperation and Development and the International Energy Agency, Paris.

18 US Energy Information Agency (EIA). 2010. *International Energy Outlook 2010*. EIA, Washington, DC. OECD stands for the Organization for Economic Cooperation and Development, which includes, from Europe: Austria, Belgium, Czech Republic, Denmark, Finland, France, Germany, Greece, Hungary, Iceland, Republic of Ireland, Italy, Luxembourg, the Netherlands, Norway, Poland, Portugal, Slovakia, Spain, Sweden, Switzerland, Turkey and the United Kingdom; and from other regions: Australia, Canada, Japan, Mexico, New Zealand, South Korea and the United States. Non-OECD economies are the remaining economies of the world, most of which are low- and middle-income countries.

19 IEA, 2008, *op. cit.*

20 Intergovernmental Panel on Climate Change (IPCC). 2007. *Climate Change 2007: Synthesis Report. Contribution of Working Groups I, II and III to the Fourth Assessment*. Report of the Intergovernmental Panel on Climate Change [Core Writing Team, Pachauri, R.K and A. Reisinger, eds.]. IPCC, Geneva.

21 Stern, Nicholas. 2007. *The Economics of Climate Change: The Stern Review*. Cambridge University Press, Cambridge. Although these estimates of the economic damages of climate change by Stern are widely cited, any such estimates are affected by the choice of discount rate and equity weights, and are subject to large uncertainties. See, for example, Tol, Richard S.J. 2008. "The Social Costs of Carbon: Trends, Outliers and Catastrophes." *Economics: The Open-Access, Open-Assessment E-Journal* 2:2008–25. <http://www.economics-ejournal.org/economics/journalarticles/2008–25>, who finds that Stern's estimates are highly pessimistic, even compared to other studies that employ low discount rates on future damages.

22 Nicholls, R.J., S. Hanson, C. Herweijer, N. Patmore, S. Hallegatte, Jan Corfee-Morlot, et al., 2007. *Ranking of the World's Cities Most Exposed to Coastal Flooding Today and in the Future: Executive Summary*. OECD Environment Working Paper No. 1. OECD, Paris. According to the authors, the top 10 cities in terms of exposed population are Mumbai, Guangzhou, Shanghai, Miami, Ho Chi Minh City, Kolkata, Greater New York, Osaka-Kobe, Alexandria and New Orleans.

23 McGranahan, G., D. Balk and B. Anderson. 2007. "The Rising Tide: Assessing the Risks of Climate Change and Human Settlements in Low Elevation Coastal Zones." *Environment and Urbanization* 19(1):17–37.

24 Nicholls et al., 2007, *op. cit.* See also Organization for Economic Cooperation and Development (OECD). 2008. *Costs of Inaction on Key Environmental Challenges*. OECD, Paris, and United Nations Development Programme (UNDP). 2008. *Human Development Report 2007/2008. Fighting Climate Change: Human Solidarity in a Divided World*. UNDP, New York.

25 Millennium Ecosystem Assessment, 2005. *Ecosystems and Human Well-being: Synthesis*. Island Press, Washington, DC, table 1.

26 Barbier, E.B. 2010. "Poverty, Development, and Environment." *Environment and Development Economics* 15:635–60.

27 Population Division of the United Nations Secretariat (PDUN). 2008. *World Urbanization Prospects: The 2007 Revision Executive Summary*. United Nations, New York.

28 United Nations Development Programme (UNDP). 2006. *Human Development Report 2006. Beyond Scarcity: Power, Poverty and the Global Water Crisis*. UNDP, New York.

29 These demographic trends are from Chen, S. and M. Ravallion. 2008. *The Developing World is Poorer Than We Thought, But No Less Successful in the Fight against Poverty*. Policy Research Working Paper 4703. World Bank, Washington, DC.

30 Based on projections to 2015 of the share of world population living on US$1 a day and US$2 a day in International Labor Organization (ILO). 2004. *World Employment Report 2004–05*. ILO, Geneva, and 2015 mid-level projections of world population from Population Division of the Department of Economic and Social Affairs of the United Nations Secretariat (PDUN). 2006. *World Population Prospects: The 2006 Revision and World Urbanization Prospects: The 2005 Revision*. United Nations, New York.

31 Chen, S. and M. Ravallion. 2007. "Absolute Poverty Measures for the Developing World, 1981–2004." *Proceedings of the National Academy of Sciences* 104(43):16757–62. The authors estimate that the US$1-a-day rural poverty rate of 30 percent in 2002 is more than double the urban rate, and although 70 percent of the rural population lives on less than US$2 a day, the proportion in urban areas is less than half that figure.

32 Barbier, 2010, "Poverty, Development, and Environment." *op. cit.*

33 Pearce, D.W., A. Markandya and E.B. Barbier. 1989. *Blueprint for a Green Economy*. Earthscan Publications, London, p. 170.

34 See, for example, Blesl, M., T. Kober, D. Bruchof and R. Kuder. 2010. "Effects of Climate and Energy Policy Related Measures and Targets on the Future Structure of the European Energy System in 2020 and Beyond." *Energy Policy* 38(10):6278–92; Fischer, C. and R.G. Newell. 2008. "Environmental and Technology Policies for Climate Mitigation." *Journal of Environmental Economics and Management* 55:142–62; Goulder, L. 2004. "Induced Technological Change and Climate Policy." Pew Center on Global Climate Change, Arlington, VA; International Energy Agency (IEA). 2009. *Progress with Implementing Energy Efficiency Policies in the G8*. IEA, Paris; Pew Charitable Trusts. 2009. *The Clean Energy Economy: Repowering Jobs, Businesses and Investments Across America*. Pew Charitable Trusts, Washington, DC; and Popp, D. 2010. "Innovation and Climate Policy." NBER Working Paper 15673. National Bureau of Economic Research, Cambridge, MA.

35 Fischer and Newell, 2008, *op. cit.*, p. 160.

36 Barbier, Edward B. 2010. "Green Stimulus, Green Recovery and Global Imbalances." *World Economics* 11(2):149–75.

37 Cline, William R. 2009. "The Global Financial Crisis and Development Strategy for Emerging Market Economies." Remarks presented to the Annual Bank Conference on Development Economics, World Bank, Seoul, South Korea, 23 June 2009; Feldstein, Martin S. 2008. "Resolving the Global Imbalance: The Dollar and the U.S. Saving Rate." *Journal of Economic Perspectives* 22(3):113–25; International Monetary Fund (IMF). 2009. *World Economic Outlook April 2009: Crisis and Recovery*. IMF, Washington, DC; Park, Donghyun and Kwanho Shin. 2009. "Saving,

Investment, and Current Account Surplus in Developing Asia." *ADB Working Paper Series* No. 158. Asian Development Bank, Manila, Philippines, April 2009.

38 Feldstein, 2008, *op. cit.*

39 For example, two out of five people in the world live in international water basins shared by more than one country. The Amazon River has 9 countries sharing it, and the Nile 11 countries. Currently, 39 countries receive most of their water from outside their borders, and all but two are developing economies. See Barbier, 2010, *A Global Green New Deal*, *op. cit.*, box 21 and UNDP, 2006, *op. cit.*

40 The Clean Development Mechanism (CDM) is a provision of the Kyoto Protocol, which was designed originally as a bilateral mechanism through which entities in high-income economies could gain certified emission reductions (CERs) by investing in clean energy technologies in developing economies. A CER is equal to one metric tonne of CO_2 equivalent. In practice, the CDM has become an international institution through which low- and middle-income countries can earn income from reducing greenhouse gas (GHG) emissions through earning CER credits. In addition, by effectively setting an international price on carbon, the CDM has facilitated the commercial viability of low-carbon technology transfer, in terms of both equipment and know-how, reduced some barriers to information and capital flows necessary for investing in clean energy technologies in recipient countries and, finally, improved the quality of technology transfers to developing economies by providing assistance in project design and collaboration in management. See Barbier, 2010, *A Global Green New Deal*, *op.cit.* for further details and discussion of the necessary reforms for the CDM.

41 See, for example, Convery, F.J. 2009. "Origins and Development of the EU ETS." *Environmental and Resource Economics* 43:391–412; Demailly, D. and P. Quirion. 2008. "Changing the Allocation Rules in the EU ETS: Impact on Competitiveness and Economic Efficiency." Fondazione Eni Enrico Mattei (FEEM), Nota di Lavora 89.2008. FEEM, Milan; Ellerman, A.D. and P.L. Joskow. 2008. *The European Union's Emissions Trading System in Perspective.* Prepared for the Pew Center on Global Climate Change. MIT, Cambridge, MA; and Stankeviciutute, L., A. Kitous and P. Criqui. 2008. "The Fundamentals of the Future International Emissions Trading System." *Energy Policy* 36:4272–86.

42 See Barbier, 2010, *A Global Green New Deal*, *op. cit.*, box 25.

43 Pearce, D.W. 2007. "Do We Really Care about Biodiversity?" *Environmental and Resource Economics* 37:313–33.

44 From <www.theGeF.org> as of December 2011. The GEF partnership includes 10 international donor agencies: the UN Development Programme; the UN Environment Programme; the World Bank; the UN Food and Agriculture Organization; the UN Industrial Development Organization; the African Development Bank; the Asian Development Bank; the European Bank for Reconstruction and Development; the Inter-American Development Bank; and the International Fund for Agricultural Development.

45 From <http://www.climatefundsupdate.org/> (accessed November 30, 2011).

46 Clemençon, R. 2006. "What Future for the Global Environmental Facility?" *Journal of Environment & Development* 15:50–74.

47 *Ibid.* and Mee, L.D., H.T. Dublin and A.A. Eberhard. 2008. "Evaluating the Global Environmental Facility: A Goodwill Gesture or a Serious Attempt to Deliver Global Benefits?" *Global Environmental Change* 18:800–10.

48 Clemençon, 2006, *op. cit.*, p. 69.

49 Farley, J., A. Aquino, A. Daniels, A. Moulaert, D. Lee and A. Krause. 2010. "Global Mechanisms for Sustaining and Enhancing PES Schemes." *Ecological Economics* 69:2075–84.

50 Ebeling, J. and M. Yasué. 2008. "Generating Carbon Finance through Avoided Deforestation and its Potential to Create Climatic, Conservation and Human Development Benefits." *Philosophical Transactions of the Royal Society B* 363:1917–24, and Kindermann, G., M. Obersteiner, B. Sohngen, J. Sathaye, K. Andrasko, E. Rametsteiner, et al. 2008. "Global Cost Estimates of Reducing Carbon Emissions through Avoided Deforestation." *Proceedings of the National Academy of Sciences* 105(30):10302–7.

51 Aldy, J.E. and R. Stavins, eds. 2007. *Architectures for Agreement: Addressing Global Climate Change in the Post-Kyoto World.* Cambridge University Press, Cambridge, and Olmstead, S.M. and R.N. Stavins. 2006. "An International Policy Architecture for the Post-Kyoto Era." *American Economic Review: Papers & Proceedings* 96:35–38.

52 Hyder, P. 2008. "Recycling Revenue from an International Carbon Tax to Fund an International Investment Programme in Sustainable Energy and Poverty Reduction." *Global Environmental Change* 18:521–38; Nordhaus, W.D. 2007. "To Tax or Not to Tax: Alternative Approaches to Slowing Global Warming." *Review of Environmental Economics and Policy* 1:26–44; and Nordhaus, W.D. 2010. "Economic Aspects of Global Warming in a Post-Copenhagen Environment." *Proceedings of the National Academy of Sciences* 107(26):11721–26.

53 Hyder, 2008, *op. cit.*

54 Nordhaus, 2010, *op. cit.*, pp. 11725–26,

55 Information on the IFFIm can be obtained from its website <www.iff-immunisation.org>

56 Addison, T., G. Mavrotas and M. McGillivray. 2005. "Aid, Debt Relief and New Sources of Finance for Meeting the Millennium Development Goals." *Journal of International Affairs* 58:113–27.

57 Moss, T. 2005. "Ten Myths of the International Finance Facility." Working Paper No. 60, Center for Global Development, Washington, DC, May.

58 UNCTAD. 2011. *The Least Developed Countries Report 2011: The Potential Role of South–South Cooperation for Inclusive and Sustainable Development.* UNCTAD, New York.

59 *Innovation With Impact: Financing 21st Century Development.* A Report by Bill Gates to G20 leaders, Cannes Summit, November 2011. <http://www.thegatesnotes.com/Topics/Development/G20-Report-Innovation-with-Impact>

60 See, for example, Addison et al., 2005, *op. cit.*; Clemençon, 2006, *op. cit*; Griffith-Jones, S. 2010. "The Movers and the Makers." *The Broker* 22(Oct./Nov.):15–17; Koch-Weser, M.R.v.B. 2002. "Sustaining Global Environmental Governance: Innovation in Environment and Development Finance." In D. Esty and M. Ivanova, eds. *Global Environmental Governance.* Yale University Press, New Haven, CT, pp. 1–23; and Spahn, P.B. 2010. "A Double Dividend." *The Broker* 22(Oct./Nov.):8–14.

61 Griffith-Jones, 2010, *op. cit.*

62 *Innovation With Impact.* A Report by Bill Gates, *op. cit.*

63 Spahn, 2010, *op. cit.*

64 Addison et al., 2005, *op. cit.*; Brzoska, M. 2004. "Taxation of the Global Arms Trade? An Overview of the Issues." *Kyklos* 57:149–72; and Koch-Weser, 2002, *op. cit.*

65 *Innovation With Impact.* A Report by Bill Gates, *op. cit.*

66 Rodrik, Dani. 2009. "Growth after the Crisis." Commission on Growth and Development Working Paper No. 65. World Bank, Washington, DC.

67 For further discussion of China's green recovery efforts and long-run development plans, see Barbier, 2010, *A Global Green New Deal, op. cit.*

68 For further discussion of South Korea's green recovery efforts and long-run development plans, see Barbier, 2010, *A Global Green New Deal, op. cit.*, and Barbier, E.B. 2010. "A Global Green Recovery, the G20 and International STI Cooperation in Clean Energy." *STI Policy Review* 1(3):1–15.

69 Considine, Timothy J. and Donald F. Larson. 2009. "Substitution and Technological Change under Carbon Cap and Trade: Lessons from Europe." World Bank Policy Research Working Paper No 4957. World Bank, Washington, DC.

70 For further discussion of these and other examples, see Barbier, 2010, *A Global Green New Deal, op. cit.*

71 Cleetus, Rachel, Steven Clemmer and David Friedman. 2009. *Climate 2030: A National Blueprint for a Clean Energy Economy.* Union of Concerned Scientists (UCS), Cambridge, MA.

72 Alix-Garcia, J., A. De Janvry and E. Sadoulet. 2008. "The Role of Deforestation Risk and Calibrated Compensation in Designing Payments for Environmental Services." *Environment and Development Economics* 13:375–94; Barbier, E.B. 2008. "Poverty, Development, and Ecological Services." *International Review of Environmental and Resource Economics* 2(1):1–27; Grieg-Gran, M.-A., I. Porras and S. Wunder. 2005. "How Can Market Mechanisms for Forest Environmental Services Help the Poor? Preliminary Lessons from Latin America." *World Development* 33(9):1511–27; Pagiola, S., A. Arcenas and G. Platais. 2005. "Can Payments for Environmental Services Help Reduce Poverty? An Exploration of the Issues and the Evidence to Date from Latin America." *World Development* 33(2):237–53; Wunder, Sven. 2008. "Payments for Environmental Services and the Poor: Concepts and Preliminary Evidence." *Environment and Development Economics* 13:279–97; and Zilberman, D., L. Lipper and N. McCarthy. 2008. "When Could Payments for Environmental Services Benefit the Poor?" *Environment and Development Economics* 13:255–78.

73 Elbers, C., T. Fujii, P. Lanjouw, B. Özler and W. Yin. 2007. "Poverty Alleviation through Geographic Targeting: How Much Does Disaggregation Help?" *Journal of Development Economics* 83:198–213.

74 Coady, D., M. Grosh and J. Hoddinott. 2004. "Targeting Outcomes Redux." *World Bank Research Observer* 19(1):61–85.

75 UNDP, 2006, *op. cit.*

76 For further discussion see Barbier, 2010, *A Global Green New Deal, op. cit.*, and Barbier, 2010, "A Global Green Recovery, the G20 and International STI Cooperation in Clean Energy," *op. cit.*

77 United Nations Framework Convention on Climate Change (UNFCCC). 2007. *Investment and Financial Flows to Address Climate Change.* UNFCCC, Bonn.

78 High-Level Task Force (HLTF) on the Global Food Crisis. 2008. *Comprehensive Framework for Action.* July. United Nations, New York.

79 Project Catalyst. 2009. *Scaling Up Climate Finance.* Policy Briefing Paper. September. ClimateWorks Foundation, San Francisco, CA.

80 From "London Summit – Leaders' Statement 2 April 2009," *op. cit.*

8 Conclusion

1 Pearce, D.W., A. Markandya and E.B. Barbier. 1989. *Blueprint for a Green Economy*. Earthscan Publications, London, p. xv.
2 UNEP. 2011. *Towards a Green Economy: Pathways to Sustainable Development and Poverty Eradication – A Synthesis for Policymakers*. UNEP, Nairobi. <www.unep. org/greeneconomy>
3 The G20 Seoul Summit Leaders' Declaration, November 11–12, 2010. <http:// www.ilo.org/wcmsp5/groups/public/@dgreports/@dcomm/documents/ statement/wcms_146479.pdf>

INDEX